Local Politics and Nation-States

Studies in International and Comparative Politics

PETER H. MERKL, SERIES EDITOR

Local Politics and Nation-States

Case Studies in Politics and Policy

Ann Schulz

Clio Books

SANTA BARBARA, CALIFORNIA   OXFORD, ENGLAND

Library of Congress Cataloging in Publication Data

Schulz, Ann.
    Local politics and nation states.

    (Studies in international and comparative politics; 12)
    Includes bibliographical references and index.
    1. Local government—Case studies.
I. Title. II. Series.
JS67.S38 320   79-11416
ISBN 0-87436-289-X

American Bibliographical Center—Clio Press
2040 Alameda Padre Serra, Box 4397
Santa Barbara, California 93103

Clio Press, Ltd.
Woodside House, Hinksey Hill
Oxford, OX1 5BE, England

Manufactured in the United States of America

Contents

About the Studies in International and Comparative Politics *Series*

Studies in International and Comparative Politics draws on current political and sociological theories to facilitate analysis and comparison within a broad international spectrum. Titles in this series are diverse in focus and perspective. They range from historical and sociological to fresh analyses of the particular policies and principles under which people form governments. The series is designed to add sophistication and new perspectives to courses in political science and sociology, and to the humanities.

PETER H. MERKL

Foreword

Scholars will welcome this book as a reflection of their resurgent interest in local politics. Government officials and policy-makers worldwide have recognized that local affairs are especially relevant in formulating national policies. It is therefore appropriate to acknowledge the importance of studying local politics within the context of developing nation-states.

People have been interested in self government since before the Greek city-states. Similarly, local communities are known to be the site of truly meaningful political participation. But, the academic community has only recently begun to acknowledge the increasing importance of the complex relationships arising from the interplay of local and national politics in the modern world. In this book Professor Schulz examines the potential for conflict between individuals, groups, and entire societies arising from the underlying motivations of local and national politicians. She also documents the need for increasing vigor at both levels of government.

The attitudes of politicians at each level of government are based upon diverse, often conflicting, concerns, motives, and aspirations. Those engaged in local politics often strive to limit the influence of "outsiders" and their "alien" values, while the members of modernizing national elites argue that local governments perpetuate "traditional" institutions and inhibit development. National governments thus rationalize their penetration into local affairs on the basis of nationalistic referents.

Thus most countries will find it necessary to strike a proper balance between centralization and decentralization—although change may be difficult to implement even when it is necessary and desirable. For example, centralization is a cultural, historical, institutional, and financial fact of life in France and Turkey and the social changes that would result from decentralization are virtually inconceivable. At the other extreme the regionalization of services in countries like the United States will continue to be resisted at the local level despite irrefutable fiscal logic.

Professor Schulz explores these problems by comparing them in developed and developing nations. She identifies several pervasive issues that have strikingly similar characteristics despite the differences of the countries in which they appear. The foundations laid by Professor Schulz in this volume will hopefully lead to a thorough examination of local communities and their political interests. I am sure that the greatly improved theoretical framework which she and other students of local politics are developing will lead to a better understanding and ultimately improve the quality of life throughout the world.

Walter F. Weiker
Professor of Political Science
Rutgers University

Preface

Local government and politics has been the target of reform-minded citizens in the United States for most of the twentieth century. The apparent pervasiveness of local political corruption and the capacity, or incapacity, of local authorities to make policy in a high-technology, interdependent world have undermined the legitimacy of local governments. Local political machines were challenged by demands for nonpartisan elections in the first half-century, and local social and environmental policies were increasingly subject to the influence of state and federal legislation in the second.

The reform of local government and politics has become a preoccupation of major proportions in most contemporary nation-states. In the summer of 1978, the British Labour government, preparing for fall elections, brought out a plan for enlarging the scope of the Greater London Council's authority in response to the replication and confusion of local policy-making agencies outside the council's domain. The publications of the International Union of Local Authorities indicate how widespread is the tendency, observed in the United States and Britain, to revise the structure of local government in response to a wide variety of political ills.

Several comparative descriptions of local government have been published. This book does not attempt to duplicate these, although it treats important, nearly universal trends in local government, like the creation of elected local councils and the tendency to consolidate political and administrative authority in one district-level official. But beyond describing these similarities among formal institutions of local government, my purpose here is to show that the similarities appear because of common political dilemmas encountered by the leaders of nation-states throughout the contemporary world.

How local politicians manage to exercise influence from their subordinate position and how national elites intervene in local politics are central themes. As a student of comparative politics, I am interested in the striking similarity of local government and politics in vastly different national regimes. This study illustrates these commonalities by looking at the ways local politicians deal with the state and vice versa. Chapters include, first, an overview of local politics from the perspective of process, roles, and public policy and, second, case studies illustrating those themes in specific country contexts. The notes for the case studies are intended to help students of comparative and local politics begin research, not to provide a substitute for further research.

The book is dedicated in spirit to local politicians. They may well have the most frustrating job in the world of politics—making the state palatable to their constituents without losing their constituents' support. They usually have little money or status to use in that effort and in supporting their constituents' demands on the state, even when that support may jeopardize their own positions of influence. Observing one such politician who found himself in the middle of these conflicting demands and dilemmas served as a stimulus for this book. He was a big city council president in Iran. He was expected to simultaneously (1) keep national regime elites quiescent by maintaining the semblance of an active city council despite its lack of real power, (2) satisfy the military with the services provided to a new air base, (3) help his family by finding them jobs in the municipality, (4) keep merchants content despite stringent public health laws, and more. His was a vastly complex and political office.

The inclusion of both modern, industrial states and Third World states is intended to emphasize the similar political dynamics of center-local relationships. It took precisely one field trip to a Third World country and the return to our New Hampshire home for me to realize empirically what is now increasingly acknowledged theoretically—that many of the stark contrasts drawn between the two "types" of nation-states would be tempered by looking at how regime leaders deal with challenges to regime stability. Most significant, their strategies often center on managing center-local relationships.

Such a revisionist view of comparative analysis is common among my colleagues in the international development program at Clark University, who seem to excel in fostering provocative discussions of conventional development concepts. Portions of the manuscript were constructively criticized by Cynthia H. Enloe, Sharon Perlman Krefetz, and (outside Clark) by Robert Hudson, Carol Lewis, John Ochsenwald, Helen Tibbitts, Raymond Hopkins, Walter Weiker, and Lloyd W. Garrison. It was typed and retyped by Terry Reynolds, Rene Baril, Grace Peterson, and Pixie Monahan. The erasers and card catalogue were well manned as always by Jim, Jean, Karin, Steve, and Linda. My sincere thanks; final responsibility for the work is, of course, mine.

Local Politics and Nation-States

Local Politics and National Regimes

1 Local politics is one internal dimension of contemporary nation-states. The authority of local politicians, like that of politicians representing ethnic or economic groups, is derived from the nation-state. Local politicians do not enjoy sovereign authority; nation-state representatives do. The local politician's influence is legitimized by the delegation of authority by the nation-state.

National politicians often have more effective power than do local politicians. For example, local governments are notoriously underfinanced, while national treasuries universally underwrite local debts. So much of local power and authority is derived from the nation-state that local politics cannot be usefully separated from that context; local politics is shaped by the state bureaucracy, by national political parties, by extralocal economic processes, and by the class structure of the nation-state as a whole.

Still, the preeminence of the nation-state in the modern world has not supplanted local politics entirely. Instead, nationalism and state-building have revitalized local politics. This seemingly Hegelian evolution of local politics can be seen in many ways. The local political process affects (1) the legitimization of state power, (2) the containment of regime opposition within particular localities, (3) the local politician's influence over the distribution of political rewards within the nation-state, and (4) the implementation of public policy.

Finally, and all too often for their own careers, local politicians serve as scapegoats for the political consequences of policy decisions made at the national level. Because local politicians make public policy at the grass roots, the stability of national regimes often depends upon local politics and local politicians. Local politics both shapes and is shaped by aggregate political forces whose structure and significance transcend any single locality or collection of localities.[1]

The salience of local politics and its importance to the stability and performance of larger political units and to prevailing authority structures predate the modern democratic nation-state. Such a view of local politics was well established by eighteenth-century political theorists. Montesquieu wrote, in *The Spirit of the Laws*, that "it is dependent and subordinate intermediary authorities that form the essence of Monarchy. . . . The fundamental laws governing the Monarchy necessarily presuppose some middle channels through which power flows."[2]

By the nineteenth century, Montesquieu's ideal local commonwealth had become a relic of hereditary privilege. The "historical cult of intermediary bodies" was replaced by local agents of the sovereign, who attempted to legitimize the state with public works and political education. Historically, "there is strong theoretical justification for beginning the analysis of local politics with the national sphere."[3]

LOCAL POLITICS AND REGIME SECURITY

The relationship between state-building and local politics is a vital one. Deliberate attempts to decentralize decision-making processes through formal transfers of authority to local government officials have been more successful where state authority has been accepted. The tension between the Kenyan national regime and the Nairobi City Council evident in the years following independence originated in a lack of consensus over "legally sanctioned and socially sanctioned" political power.[4] In fact, Werlin argues, "decentralization cannot properly take place without centralization. . . ."[5]

In Kenya, the tension resulted in continual confrontations over specific policy issues that were as much related to the contest for power between national and city authorities as they were to the substance of the issues. For example, Nairobi's mayor, Charles Rubia, opposed accepting a United States AID loan offer in 1964 because the terms restricted bidding on the contract to the United States and local firms and left the mayor's office out of the negotiations. Rubia's worst fears about his mayoral prerogatives were confirmed when the nation's finance minister ignored Rubia's opposition.[6]

Local politicians often exercise quasi-legal or illegal power. In the absence of state legitimacy, local politicians provide a critical link between the state and the populace. Although chieftaincies were legally abolished in independent Tanzania, for example, the effective power of chiefs and their subordinate headmen persisted.[7] Many headmen had taken administrative posts and some assumed positions in the governing party, Tanganyika African National Union (TANU). From these positions, the traditional leaders could affect the implementation of national policy.

It would have been too costly, financially and politically, to replace the headmen with new leaders during the early years of the independent regime. So the lack of consensus on national development priorities gave the headmen an opportunity to mediate the conflicting interests of the state bureaucracy, on the one hand, and their local tribal constituents, on the other.

Local politicians fill the breach between state objectives and local interests in more modern settings also. State economic plans in the

Soviet Union often involve fulfilling targets that are only realistic so long as local party and ministry officials cooperate with one another. As a result, the local political process has assumed an importance beyond the limited authority delegated to local officials. The smooth functioning of local politics can make or break a local official's career; implementation of the state plan (Gosplan) also depends upon local politics.

As in the Soviet Union, bureaucratic bargaining in France gives local politicians opportunities to wield power. State bureaucrats seek alliances with local politicians by offering them specific public services that the bureaucrats can, in turn, use to claim a greater share of the national budget for their own ministries.[8] In other situations, the local politician's role has been to protect his constituents from the state bureaucracy. A mayor of Peyranne, in southern France, made it his business not to collect information that would benefit state tax agents.[9]

Local politicians can also provide valuable political feedback to national decision-makers. Public opinion on national policy issues frequently is transmitted through local politicians. One of the functions of city councillors in India, for example, is to articulate public opinion or, on occasion, to form public opinion.[10] Most of the initiative in making policy rests with local bureaucrats who are accountable to the center. Nonetheless, these same bureaucrats rely on the city councillors to work out a consensus among their constituents.

Where consensus appears to be unattainable, opposition parties gain and use local office as a public forum. Beyond that, local offices are not a good base for extending opposition party strength into the national political arena. In fact, local authority diminishes the ability of opposition parties to compete nationally. India's two Communist parties have had that experience in the states of West Bengal and Kerala. The communists participated in governing at the local and state levels but were stymied by vetoes and foot-dragging at the national level in their attempts to implement their redistributive programs. Unable to implement effective programs without support from the center, local leftist officials have appeared to the voters as ineffectual and lacking commitment to social reforms.

Italy's Communist party has been caught in the same vicious circle of isolation and "programmatic sabotage." Italian municipalities—especially those governed by socialists, communists, or coalitions of the two—have experienced deepening fiscal crises. Local Italian authorities owed $36 billion at the end of 1976.[11] Interest on these debts, contracted with private and public lending agencies, effectively prevented leftist officials from expanding the range of public services (schools, day-care centers, etc.) and providing subsidies to them. The municipality of Siena, for example, was in debt for $12 million, and a leftwing community council member confirmed the fiscal squeeze:

"Whatever is done will be an emergency solution, and the quality of services will deteriorate."[12] More recently, Neopolitan Communist officials were forced by the same financial plight to order striking hospital personnel back to work without meeting their demands.[13]

What happened in Italy was that the central government guaranteed local loans and thereby encouraged local authorities to expand their debt. But before the debt could be repaid, the same central government took away much of the local authorities' taxing power.[14]

In France, too, leftist party strength has been contained at the local level. Many predicted that the Communist and Socialist parties' coalition would jointly form the national government in 1978. These forecasts were based upon the coalition's local election victories. Leftist party candidates in the 1977 municipal elections won seats in 33 city councils that formerly had been controlled by the Gaullist-centrist parties. Those successes brought the total number of city governments controlled by the leftist bloc to 163. Politicians on the left and on the right assumed that these local victories were a precursor to leftist gains in the 1978 parliamentary elections. For the center, the most ominous sign was that six centrist government ministers were defeated in the 1977 elections. (French politicians may hold local and national offices concurrently, so these six were running in both sets of elections.)

If the left had gained control of the French Parliament in the 1978 elections, Parliament and the presidency would have been in opposition for the first time in the Fifth Republic. The 1978 elections, however, produced a vote of confidence for the center. Although French voters had used local elections to register their dissatisfaction with the national government, they appeared equally skeptical about the left's ability to govern.

While the Italian and French communists have been distracted from national politics by local financial crises, elsewhere local government has been used to isolate regime opponents even more explicitly. The most striking example has been the white South African regime's policy of granting municipal powers to black townships. Under this policy, Soweto was slated in April 1978 to become a self-governing city. One journalist described the policy as "a spoonful of sweet reasonableness" with which to mask the bitter apartheid regime.[15] The regime's devolution policy was its response to the increasing politicization and economic power of black South Africans. Its use of racial segregation among townships and the devolution of authority to township governments was essentially a "divide and rule" strategy. Such strategies have often been used by "central elites when confronted with ethnic heterogeneity potent enough to jeopardize state authority and operational efficacy."[16] The recurring protests against apartheid by black South Africans in Soweto, for example, indicate that ethnic heterogeneity has indeed become that potent.

State authority can be jeopardized by fundamental conflicts over civil rights, class, and race issues (or all three in combination). Where these fundamental conflicts have existed, local political processes have been very carefully managed by state elites. Divide and rule strategies, like those of South Africa, are perhaps the most extreme form of conflict management involving local politics. Indirect political containment, as in India and Italy, has been far more common and entails fewer political risks, mainly because the means by which opposition forces are blunted are less visible.

Another strategy used by state elites who do not have a popular consensus behind them is direct intervention in local electoral processes. Forms of intervention range from selectively proroguing local elected councils to hand-choosing candidates for local office to campaigning on behalf of candidates acceptable to the national regime.

The prevalence of national intervention in local elections indicates how concerned regime elites can be about local election outcomes. When regime opponents successfully build a base of support in local politics, regime elites deliberately undermine the legitimacy of local elections. One newspaper headline noted: "Brazilians Vote in Local Elections That Won't Affect Regime's Firm Grasp But Will Test Its Popularity."[17] President Geisel controlled the elections so that the outcomes would not affect "the regime's firm grasp." The president's party, the Alliance for National Renewal, campaigned with several advantages. The president monopolized radio and television coverage of the elections. He appeared publicly with local Alliance candidates for a year before the elections. Lastly, the Alliance entered the elections with incumbent mayors in five cities. Incumbents had been appointed earlier by the government on the grounds that "the cities were important to the *national defense* [emphasis added]."

Indonesia held local elections in 1977, concurrent with regional and national elections. The local elections there were manipulated by the ruling Golkar party, the bureaucracy, and the army, together.[18] The Kediri regency of East Java was a stronghold of the Communist party before it was banned. The government candidate for office in Kediri, R. S. Chambali, successfully challenged the opposition, Moslem-based Development Unity party. Chambali's opponents were prevented from competing fully in the campaign because direct criticism of the government was not allowed. According to the *New York Times* report, civil servants were told that they would lose their jobs if they did not get voters to the polls.

LOCAL POLITICS AND POLITICAL PARTICIPATION

The importance of local politics to the stability and legitimacy of national regimes has encouraged national elites to criticize local political processes. National regime elites justify their intervention in local politics by arguing that local officials are irresponsible, local debate is petty, and local politics is elitist. Academic assessments of local politics have been similarly critical. James Fesler, for example, writes that "the doctrinal case for decentralization usually rests on a romantic (and inaccurate) view of both the locality and the region as rural, pastoral societies."[19] Fesler notes that village governments can be conservative, elitist, routinized, or inflexible. Probably "no level of government is less disposed to vote to raise taxes. Yet without increased revenue no advances can be made in education, public health, and other 'local' responsibilities."[20]

Local officials do find it difficult to raise taxes, but that has more to do with their power and authority relative to that of national officials than with any innate conservatism. National regimes enjoy tax powers that are derived from the authority of the nation-state directly, from the police powers of the state, and from its bureaucratic capacity. Local officials have none of this support when they try to raise taxes.

Similarly misleading is the assertion that people are not interested in local politics. Survey data from *The Civic Culture* study, for example, show that voters in the United States, Britain, Germany, Italy, and Mexico feel more competent in local politics.[21] And subsequent studies have found similar patterns, with high turnout in local elections.[22] The disparity between these findings indicates that local political competition and participation varies according to the issues involved in the elections, opposition party strategies, the local political culture, and the national regime's attitude toward intervention in local politics.

When local elections have been staged by regime elites without allowing meaningful competition, voting rates have depended on the elite's willingness to coerce voters into going to the polls. Brazil's recent elections stimulated little interest among voters. Elections were not competitive nor did the regime force voters to the polls.

Similarly, regime-sponsored political parties have tended to produce shallow local organizations with little popular participation. They are typically organizations whose national headquarters are busier than are their local offices or "storefronts."[23]

Political participation is likely to be low if there are no concrete benefits to be received from political activity.[24] One theory of peasant politics seeks to explain how grass-roots apathy develops in rural, agricultural regions where the peasant's major concern is protecting himself against the state, which he cannot control.[25] According to Joel Migdal, what appears to be apathy is the peasant's refusal to participate in a competition that cannot be won. Consequently, state-run political parties often find that they are unable to get strong grass-roots support.

LOCAL ELITES AND REGIME ELITES

Regime elites and local politicians, together, often make use of pork barrel to stimulate local support and participation. In southern Italy, local politics became more competitive when there were national funds available for local distribution. The funds guaranteed influence for the politicians that controlled them. National pork barrel did not lead to a more equal distribution of influence and wealth within the communes; rather, power was used "as a means of enrichment for a rising middle class."[26] Nonetheless, local politics in Italy was invigorated by the availability of rewards that national regime elites were willing to provide through local party leaders to strengthen the local party organizations.

A similar reward system, in which the local party leader plays an important intermediary role, has been used in Mexico to solidify support for the governing party.[27] Mexico's pork barrel system exists side by side with striking inequalities within and among localities in the distribution of income and wealth, and with the hierarchical organization of power within the ruling party. The influence of local politicians over the distribution of rewards within the community guarantees neither effective local control over major policy decisions nor a more equitable distribution of those rewards. To those party loyalists who benefit from the system, however, it provides a measure of economic security, all the more valuable because it is rare.

The pork barrel system illustrates the way in which an interventionist state, with material resources to distribute, interacts with local politics to produce alliances between national elites and local politicians. The prevalence of pork barrel and spoils systems in contemporary nation-states creates a major problem for proponents of decentralization. To many of these proponents, decentralization is desirable because local government is more accessible and enables citizens to participate more effectively in making public policy.[28] Moreover, it appears to be more difficult for a particular elite to dominate ten local decision-making arenas than to dominate one national arena.

But the pork barrel system destroys several of these advantages. In the context of the interventionist state, for example, power is not additive but cumulative. Regime elites who have national resources to distribute can wield influence in all the localities where those resources are distributed. The number of decision-making arenas is only one factor in the distribution of power within the nation-state as a whole.

Decentralization also may simply transfer power to local elites who are so closely identified with national regime elites that decentralization has no practical impact upon policy decisions. These links between local elites and "external" state elites were especially visible in colonial states. For example, many of the Vietnam village elites who were in power before the French took over were willing to meet the demands of the new French rulers.[29] The local elites had personally benefited from their control of local politics under the prior regime. Hence, they could not count on receiving local support even if they did oppose French rule. Instead they sided with the colonial state and kept their power.

The politics of modern nation-states often resembles colonial regimes in this regard. Carlo Levi's description of a southern Italian town pointed to the existence of social and political inequalities that were perpetuated by town elites in cooperation with national politicians.[30] De Tocqueville's enthusiastic claim that "man creates kingdoms and republics but townships seem to spring from the hand of God," clearly had little to do with Eboli.[31] Conversely, the controversial image of local communities as bastions of elitism within reform-minded national regimes is an excessively romantic view of the nation-state that exaggerates the isolation of local politics from the national regime.

In the United States, competition among local groups—businessmen, developers, bankers, and professional city managers—is mitigated by the locality's financial dependence upon outside resources. City governments, particularly, must prove that they are good credit risks. Stability is an important ingredient in risk assessment. That constraint places a high cost on local conflict, and rewards consensus among local elites. Extralocal elites in the private sector have the same impact on local elite support that regime elites do in state-run economies elsewhere.

Power and Local Politics

Describing local politics as an internal dimension of a national regime emphasizes its intermediary role but does not lead to very specific propositions about *local power*. Does it make sense to talk about power in local politics? Local politicians may be more or less influential intermediaries. They may obtain more or less status or wealth as a consequence of their influence. But can what they do be called shaping and sharing power?

The constitutional authority of local politicians is derived. The authoritative allocation of values as a definition of power therefore excludes most local politicians. Whether the national regime is unitary (with authority vested in national officials) or federal, the difference between the authority of national officials and the influence of individual local politicians is vast. In both systems, the nation-state is the source of legitimacy; officials exercise power on its behalf. In both, the local politician's bargaining skills often are his only guarantee of influence.

Local power seldom is legitimized in political doctrine. National regime elites can more often cloak their use and abuse of political power in a framework of legitimacy. The influence of local politicians, when it is visible, appears to be more explicitly political. Hobbes's Leviathan (the nation-state) and Plunkitt's tales of Tammany Hall create very different images.[32] The Leviathan is an awesome creature; Plunkitt's tales are reserved for moments of levity.

Local politicians make decisions based upon realities of national and local politics. In their quest for certainty in assessing local power—the "locust taking a vow to eat a pyramid?"—Ostrowski and Teune write that local *politics* should be distinguished from a local political *system* in which local power is not contingent upon external events.[33] Local politics is effective influence by local politicians, as distinct from the authority of local government officials. Local politics comprises all the exchanges of influence at the local level that involve public decisions, both "intergovernmental" and "extragovernmental" exchanges.[34]

Local influence grows out of the uncertainties of public power at the national level. First, *the structure of national regimes* depends partly upon how compatible the objectives of local and national politicians are and upon the resilience of local power networks to state intervention (chapter two). Second, national *political processes* have local dimensions (chapter three). Political issues often arise first in local politics. Once raised, political issues can be either contained or magnified at the local level. Local networks of influence support or undermine the grass-roots organization of political parties. In other words, local politics makes a difference.

In the Soviet Union (chapter four), *local politicians and bureaucrats* have had important roles to play in creating certainty from the uncertain context of state economic plans. In fact, national policies rarely are administered with certainty in any political system, and hence influential local politicians and state bureaucrats make ready allies.

Third, local power is reflected in the resolution of specific policy issues. *Economic growth and the distribution of public resources* both influence and are influenced by local politics (chapter five). *Redistributive policies* give local politicians additional opportunities to increase their influence (chapter six). By the mid-twentieth century, public welfare and education programs had extended the scope of state power in modern, industrialized states and had begun to affect nonindustrialized states in the same manner. Within these interventionist states, local politics continued to influence the initiation and implementation of specific redistributive policies. In so intervening, local politicians defuse demands for major reforms by distributing public resources strategically among the poor.

What the local politician does know with certainty is that his political environment is one of uncertainty. Diagram 1 illustrates (1) the ways in which regime elites rely upon local politicians to manage popular demands and/or to implement policies and (2) the political control that regime elites have over politics. The local politician's environment is transformed indirectly by substantive national policies; his financial insecurity is legendary; and his power and authority of office afford him little leeway for error.

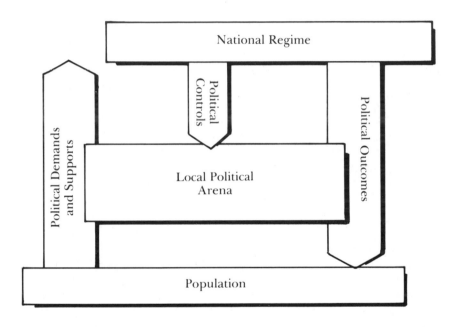

Diagram 1: Local/National Political Interchanges

Similarities in local politics from country to country exist regardless of differences in national regimes and in ways in which local authority is structured. Politicians in such an uncertain environment develop unique ways of acquiring and exercising influence that national regime elites do not share. There are many similarities among local politicians in different countries—in the strategies they pursue to gain influence and in the characteristics of local political processes.

What local politicians share most of all is a strategic perspective. "Genius of place" was coined to refer to the local politician's special understanding of public affairs, fostered by his close relationships with his constituents and by his knowledge of the local environment.[35] But perhaps the genius of place is most centrally a political genius that local politicians need more than others; it is the ability of the local politician to use his local constituency in such a manner as to successfully compete with regime elites for influence within local political arenas. The genius of place, for example, produced stand-in chiefs in place of the legitimate chiefs with whom the British wanted to work in their African colonies. The legitimate chiefs were protected from colonial influence by their local political communities.

While local politics could be defined by its special or unique political strategies, in the chapters to follow local politics refers specifically to the political processes surrounding (1) local governments, (2) local units of the state bureaucracy, and (3) local constituencies of national elective offices. Even within these conventional boundaries, the scope of local politics is very broad. It includes characteristic political processes that have evolved at the local level, local political roles, and public policies at the local level.

We will discuss the relationship between state-building and local politics; local political and bureaucratic roles; and national growth and redistributive policies in a local context. The underlying proposition here is that local politicians have opportunities to gain influence in contemporary nation-states. They often seize these opportunities by opposing national regimes. Communist mayors serve in conservative France, antibusing school boards meet in Boston, black mayors are elected in the southern United States, and "urban-industrial complexes" survive in the Soviet Union's party-state. At the same time, local politicians who have gained influence through opposition contribute to the stability of the regimes they seem to oppose. Regime stability is a question of political doctrine, of police capabilities, of bureaucratic capacity. It also involves the local power broker.

The Political Economy of Local Politics and State-Building

2 Local politics is shaped by the ways in which state and regime elites organize territory, resources, and power. Local politics takes place within national regimes and state bureaucracies. How local power is acquired and used depends upon the ways in which regimes evolve and states are built. And for national elites, in turn, local politics plays an important role in determining state-building strategies.

In communities that are relatively isolated from external markets, for example, local political power usually is held by the same individuals who are economically powerful, and local elites are able to consolidate their rule to a degree that rarely is evident in communities that are more integrated into the national economy. So when national regime elites integrate local markets into the national market system in pursuit of economic growth, they undermine local power structures. Ironically, the power structures that take their place often are less able to organize grass-roots support for the national regime.

These effects are evident in several countries, where rural voters participate in national elections more than do urban voters. Local politicians in the rural areas seem to make the difference; they operate in more remote communities, are more powerful, and get voters to the polls more effectively.[1]

The influence of local politicians can be critical to regime stability. But at the same time, the regime's very dependence upon them creates contradictions. For example, national political conflict may stem from ethnic competition that is locally based. In order to minimize ethnic conflict, regime elites rely heavily on local politicians who are ethnic leaders to solicit support for national policies. But local ethnic politicians cannot blatantly ignore their constituents' interests at the request of national politicians and still be useful intermediaries.

In the face of such opposing demands, local politicians characteristically act behind-the-scenes more than in public. Power has been traditionally defined, in American political science, as the *right* or *authority* to influence public decisions. Political power, according to this definition, belongs to national government officials. This formal definition has limited our understanding of local politics because local politicians operate so informally and much of their influence is not constitutionally authorized.

The de facto power of local government officials often is much greater than their constitutional authority. Political economy is a better concept for understanding this power. There are many ways in which local politicians influence decisions about how material resources within a political system are distributed. And local political competition is similarly influenced by national contests for control over material resources.

The social isolation of a locality also can inhibit the development of political links between local and national politicians. Karl Deutsch, for example, discusses the influence of social communications upon national politics.[2] In a polity where the physical and organizational bases for social communications are absent or undeveloped, national political life may be virtually nonexistent. John Badgley reaches such a conclusion about politics in Burma, where, he argues, it is important to have a local base of power even for national office.[3] At the other extreme, there are some countries in which most local communities have many links with other communities and other regions. In these countries, local political issues typically have extralocal angles.

These differences in the economic and social integration of nation-states are important, but they have been exaggerated. Few localities, either historically or in the contemporary world, have been totally isolated. Commerce and trade took place long before superhighways, railroads, trucks, telecommunications, and credit cards shortened distances. Farmers in remote villages, where there were no automobiles, nonetheless managed to get to town to sell their crops and to borrow money.

Ethiopia, for example, is a country whose provinces probably are as isolated from one another as those of any country in the contemporary world. But local politics and municipal administration in Ethiopia is very much part of national and global politics.[4] In the early 1970s, Ethiopian officials lobbied eight foreign governments for city planning support. As a result of their lobbying effort, West Germany provided a loan for city water systems that was equal in sum to half of the *total* provincial administration budget of the Ethiopian Ministry of Interior. Ethiopia's strategic position on the Horn of Africa affected municipal development at the local level, just as did local bureaucratic politics.

Another limitation of broad social theories of local politics is that environment does not account for all local political outcomes; politics matters.[5] T. J. Keil and C. A. Eckstrom's study of why some U.S. cities were more successful in raising revenues for public projects than were others concluded that environmental variables were not as helpful as political variables.[6] Accordingly, urban sociology is becoming more political, and "the trend towards the study of institutional or structural power and conflict in cities is much more wide-spread than some critics [of urban sociology] care to admit."[7]

Local public policy and the structure of local power clearly are part of the larger spatial and economic environment. Even more significant is the way in which local politics is shaped by the process of state-building. Local politics is strongly affected by how national regime elites pursue security. The ways in which they manage economic activities and organize state bureaucracies and political competition structure local political processes and shape the strategic options of local politicians.

CENTER-PERIPHERY POLITICS

The relationship between national regimes and local politics is one of center and periphery—a concept borrowed from geography.[8] In the case of local politics, *periphery* emphasizes the subordination of local politicians to national regime politics. Geographic location is not all that is important. Local politicians in capital cities are politically peripheral.[9]

The political center and periphery are linked so that the center gets more power out of the relationship than does the periphery. National politicians intervene in local politics and they compete for the same resources that local politicians do. They are in the political game together. In fact, national politicians become more powerful than local politicians because of the links between the two. National treasuries are fuller, and national development plans must be taken more seriously. This is true in part because local politicians help to legitimize national regimes and, at other times, serve as scapegoats for national problems. Local (or peripheral) politicians do not exercise much initiative or acquire much significant power of their own; their power is derived.

Disputes over national and local jurisdictions reflect the political character of national-local relationships. These disputes are not typically arguments about organizational charts. More frequently, they are over substantive policy issues and over access to political resources. A long-term trend toward the centralization of power and authority in the nation-state has left less and less power and authority in the hands of local politicians. In the wake of this increasing centralization, however, doubts have increasingly been expressed about the capacity of national governments. *Deconcentrating* national administration and the more extreme alternative of *decentralizing* political power have been recommended as means to relieve national regimes of the (self-imposed) burdens of centralization.

But politicians rarely give up power voluntarily. Decentralization programs are no exception. Centralization occurs as a result of political decisions, and unless the rationale for those decisions disappears, little decentralization is likely to occur.

Political centralization in contemporary nation-states was encouraged by the twin objectives of economic growth and state security within a given technological environment. When local politics has appeared to be peripheral to these two interests, it has become politically peripheral. Deconcentration and/or decentralization will be avoided if it seems to contradict the interests that national political elites, in particular, and society, in general, have in economic growth and in state security (as they are defined by the national regime). As observed by the Spanish political philosopher Miguel de Unamuno, "neither of a man nor of a people can a change be demanded which breaks the unity and continuity of the State's personality."[10]

BUILDING NATION-STATES

The theory of the state's personality has evolved over several centuries. W. Hardy Wickwar traces the theoretical evolution from the early emphasis on the state's constituent parts, in the seventeenth and eighteenth centuries, to the twentieth century view of unitary states.[11]

Centralization and the unitary nation-state are two aspects of the same phenomenon. Although the former topic has been reserved for discussions of domestic politics, builders of nation-states, when unopposed, have built effectively centralized bureaucracies. So theories of nation-building provide useful suggestions about the process of political centralization. For example, some scholars think that technological change, having brought people physically closer together, indirectly contributed to the unification of nation-states. Others contend that technological change contributed directly to political centralizaton.[12]

Technology had a significant impact on politics when it opened the way for economic growth. Early federations of city-states in Greece were based on the opportunities that they offered for promoting economic interests shared by the members. Representatives of the city-states that were members of the Amphictyonic League were required to take an oath that they would "not cut off streams, destroy cities, nor pillage the property of God."[13] The Amphictyonic League was to preserve resources that were shared.

Later, Europe's vigorous commercial life led to the creation of the Hanseatic League. Eventually, that was replaced by the nation-state. According to Brij Sharma and L. P. Choudry, the commercial classes and the rising industrialists in Germany's feudal principalities found their interests to be so strongly linked that their coalition could support a state bureaucracy. There was no longer room in the new Germany for individual feudal states.

John Herz, on political development, writes that the discovery of gunpowder stimulated the appearance of nation-states in Europe.[14] Gunpowder raised the costs of war significantly. As a result, large armies and state bureaucracies became more valuable.

Both economic and military development brought state bureaucracies. As national regimes imposed their rule over more extensive territories, national integration and state centralization increased; so too did local resistance to national regimes.

The history of railroad construction, for example, is replete with relevant cases of the politics of conquering territory. Railroads permeated many regions far from industrial Europe as early as the first half of the twentieth century. Because railroads increased mobility and control, they became a symbol of the potential for national consolidation under the elites that built them. The race to build the famous Berlin-to-Baghdad railway in 1908 was duplicated in many other places during the succeeding decades. Moving men and materials quickly was the secret of control, and the railroad could do that well.

Less is heard of the territories through which the railroads were laid than of their builders' objectives. Through the mobility and control that they made possible, the localities through which the railroads passed lost much of their autonomy.

A detailed study of railroads and imperial politics in the Ottoman Empire shows that many tribes and villagers were strongly opposed to the development of new railroads and the resulting encroachments of the government in Istanbul on local politics.[15] An early railroad built by Sultan Abdul-Hamid II passed through southern Syria and the Hijaz on its way from Istanbul to Yemen. According to Ochsenwald's account, the sultan was not especially interested in Syria or in the Hijaz. Rather he saw the railroad as a means to get his troops to Yemen to quell a local rebellion.

Historically, the two great religious cities of the Hijaz, Medina and Mecca, had been regarded as valuable prizes by the sultans in Istanbul. But the provinces had little to offer. The railroad sparked a series of revolts in the provinces despite their poverty. Most of the railroad stations had to have barbed wire fences, trenches, earthworks, and garrisons of troops to guard them.

The experience of the Ottoman railroad has been repeated many times since then. The countries that became independent after World War II began their independent histories with less gunpowder, less industry, and fewer superhighways than their leaders thought were needed for consolidating the new nation-states. Since independence, national leaders have tried to change that situation by investing in these. National consolidation is a political "crisis" that confronted the leaders of these newly independent states, and one strategy for achieving consolidation is to consolidate territory.[16]

Building railroads does not always bring local rebellions as it did in the Ottoman Empire. The nature of center-periphery relations depends largely upon whether local politics threatens the security of national regimes.[17] Cultural diversity, particularly when compounded by economic inequalities, often creates conflict between a locality and the dominant national leadership group, for example.[18] The southern border regions of the Soviet Union (Takhzikestan and Kazakhestan), the Berber regions in North Africa, western France, and the southern United States all illustrate the variability of center-periphery relations where there are cultural differences.

In each of these regions, there is conflict between center and periphery, although the conflict is over different issues and of different magnitude. In Morocco, Berber towns typically have close-knit economic and social systems, and local Berber leaders have successfully resisted the imposition of state rule in efforts to preserve this autonomy.[19] In western France, demands for local autonomy, and anti-state sentiments also can be found. But at the same time, local politicians there have been willing, if occasional, allies of state bureaucrats on specific policy issues or to gain access to the national pork barrel.

LOCAL INTERESTS WITHIN NATION-STATES

The interdependence among localities within nations that has been fostered by industrialization, transportation, and sophisticated weapons often has contributed to national integration and to political centralization. Because of the influence of factors like ethnicity, however, the process of state-building has not been completed in any contemporary nation-state. Nor has it occurred uniformly throughout specific states. The state-building process has drawn varied reactions from local politicians. However mobile and interdependent a population became, local authority often had a continuing appeal and local politics a certain vitality.

At the same time, the objectives of national politicians often encourage them to intervene more in some localities than in others. Stein Rokkan attributes variations in center-periphery political relations in Norway to how important were electoral victories in particular localities.[20] Where elections were based upon proportional representation, national politicians had to compete harder, and consequently they actively organized local party branches in those constituencies. The proliferation of party branches in turn stimulated local political competition. The peripheral localities that had not adopted proportional representation had lower turnouts in local elections.

The centralization of power in political parties and in state bureaucracies is limited by the use that politicians make of local interests. The persistence of local interests in the face of centralizing trends is in large measure a result of their political utility. Local politicians appeal to local interests—evoking social and historical images, defending local economic interests and local statutory authority—when such appeals offer them opportunities to increase their influence.

At least five types of interests have been used to support local networks of influence: (1) social identities; (2) a shared, local, political culture; (3) distinct economic activities and interests; (4) the statutory powers of local authorities; and (5) the interests of local political party organizations. These are not mutually exclusive; many social groups with local bases also share political cultures, for example. Similarly, local officials often use the symbols of distinct local political cultures to legitimize their statutory authority.

All types of local interests continue to play vital roles in political competition despite trends toward heightened interdependence, the passing of territoriality, and political centralization. Small-scale entrepreneurs in Peru, for example, interpreted their distinct economic organization as a basis for becoming involved in the competition for local offices.[21] The entrepreneurs had little influence over state economic planning decisions. When the state does initiate local projects, local enterprises are seldom used to implement the projects. Local politics gave these local entrepreneurs their only opportunity to influence public economic policy. They used their local influence to avoid state commercial regulations.

What we have described as local interests rarely are local in the sense that they represent an entire locality or are unique to just one locality. Appeals to local interests or "local initiative" are made even when they favor one group or class in a community. Or they may be used to defuse class conflict at the national level.

In one such example, local initiative was used as a justification for an antipoverty program in the United States. The Community Action Program (CAP) was drawn up in the 1960s by white leaders at the national level "on behalf of" the black (and white) poor. According to the legislation, the local poor were to participate in formulating and implementing local projects.

Many of the black poor, however, were more aware of their class interests than they were interested in local initiative. A 1976 survey of American attitudes toward national, state, and local government, for example, showed that nonwhite Americans felt that it was the federal government that gave them "the most for their money."[22] Indeed, the program stood little chance of being effectively implemented in many states where whites dominated state politics because it did emphasize black political participation.

In conflicts between local and national politicians, local ideologies and symbols, local organizations, and local government institutions are frequently used to advance specific leaders and specific demands. The central issue may be the competition itself, rather than its local ideological or organizational manifestations. The "genius of place" (in which local politicians are reputed to have a natural virtue) is instead the "genius of politicians that use place" to compete in the larger political environment (as discussed in chapter one).

For example, local politicians often find that local ideologies and organizations are helpful in influencing national politicians. Nicholas Hopkins's study of local politics in the Malian town of Kita describes such strategies.[23] He discovered that two distinct ideological systems were prevalent—that of the official party representatives serving in Kita, on the one hand, and that of the Kitans who participated in politics, on the other.

Officials of the ruling party held that the regime's objective was to bring about enlightened social change. Local Kitans, however, were skeptical. The local ideology held that politics, i.e., national politics, was "dirty" and the politicians would never willingly and accurately inform their constituents about public policy.

The local ideology was useful to Kitan politicians at the local level. They could use it to provide themselves with some leverage over national politicians and party officials. As a result, national party officials had to be careful about appearing too arrogant.

Local political associations in Kita were formed on the basis of tactical advantage and around the political fortunes of particular politicians. The leaders of these factions would try to mobilize public opinion behind themselves by disassociating themselves from specific policies of the national regime. So town meetings and ward-level elections often raised national policy issues, and national politicians often found it useful to intervene in local, factional politics.

THE STRUCTURE OF LOCAL POLITICS

The interest of national politicians in intervening in local politics may come from their concern about economic conflict. The outcome of contests to influence economic policy in turn affects the organization of politics at the local level.

One analysis of Syrian politics, for example, emphasizes the significance of the "agro-city" in explaining the diffuseness of Syria's national politics.[24] The Syrian agro-city existed as a marketing center for a regionally based agricultural economy. Little population mobility existed outside the environs of the agro-city, although there was considerable mobility within it.

Because the regional economy and society were relatively self-contained, Syrian politicians entered into national politics from a regional agro-city base. Once in national politics, the politician used whatever political resources were available at the national level to consolidate his position in the agro-city, but most of his political calculations revolved around regional organizations and interests. Consequently, political competition within the agro-city regions was greater than that among the regions. What mattered most to politicians was their regional influence.

Serious economic disparities existed within the regions. In Latakia, for example, land was unevenly distributed and the Alawis, a religious minority, tended to have the smallest holdings. They were economically insecure and had little leverage over the Sunni merchants who bought their crops at harvest. Many Alawi farmers, living at the margin of subsistence, turned to the cities in the hope of finding jobs.

By the 1960s, Syria had become more urbanized and industrialized. Along with these changes came a change in the agro-city basis of politics. The Alawis rose to occupy controlling positions in the national Ba'th party. They began to use that position to destroy the larger landowners' local influence, through local units of the Ba'th party. Local politics became more organized in the process.

In contrast to Syrian cities, those in industrialized countries were a source of political influence for the less advantaged, while regional structures were an avenue for the perpetuation of economic advantage. In that context, local government and local political organizations became less, rather than more, influential.

Central cities played a vital role in national economic life, but the class tensions that developed along with urbanization threatened political stability. One writer traces the development of national police in Europe to the need to keep order in the cities during the industrial revolution—a time when wages were low and food prices high.[25] Class tensions took a different form when many of the wealthy fled the cities for the suburbs, leaving the cities with insufficient resources to support schools, housing, and health services.

One view of urbanization in the United States distinguishes three periods—mercantile, industrial, and metropolitan.[26] The last period characterizes the post-Depression years. The increasing concentration of industrial activity and the efforts to maintain high levels of consumption through appropriate public policies encouraged the migration of the poor to the cities and the wealthy to the suburbs.

This has led to a "modern" regional political system—that of the metropolis; it has been a selective regionalization of politics. Metropolitan authorities have taken over public services, while the social services—specific to the poor—have more often remained within the jurisdiction of the central city authorities. Metropolitan agencies have been established for transportation, power and electricity, water and sewage, and metropolitan land use planning.

These metropolitan authorities operate with few political controls. Robert Wood, head of the Metropolitan Boston Transit Authority from 1966 to 1969, writes that independent metropolitan authorities provide leadership that is "unequipped with institutions and unbridled by legal stricture." According to Wood, the (past) "system of corrupt bosses and unbridled private interests [is thereby transformed] to one of huge bureaucracies and unbridled public administration."[27]

Local party organizations in the United States have not been able to adapt to the shift of power to metropolitan authorities. So metropolitan bureaucracies increasingly have taken the place of local political machines.

From the two examples of regional politics, we see that population mobility and economic interdependence have not initiated irreversible processes of political centralization. Centralization has occurred selectively. In industrial cities, the political impact of mobility typically has been on the extended metropolitan system. But even there, metropolitan authority has not extended to all areas of public policy. In the United States, for example, suburban authorities have vigorously defended their local jurisdiction over schools and housing (see chapter six). In that case, race and class conflict prevented metropolitan consolidation.

THE STRUCTURE OF LOCAL GOVERNMENT—PREFECTS AND MAYORS

Political and industrial revolutions have shaped the structures of local government as well as the distribution of local power. Napoleon responded to the challenge of developing an industrial nation-state in France by creating a centralized system of territorial government under the Ministry of Interior and its district *prefectures*. In Britain, by contrast, many government functions were left within the authority of local councils.

The political opportunities that industrialization presented to the national elites of the two countries were different. French communities were affected deeply by the revolution. Political authority at the local level was virtually destroyed, while the threat of factionalism and instability continued.[28] The prefecture system was strengthened to reestablish local authority and political order. In contrast, transformations in the British economy during that period were guided by the landed gentry, whose control over the local borough power structures went virtually unchallenged.[29]

Systems of local government in many contemporary nation-states did not develop gradually under local regimes but were imposed by colonial rulers. Even outside the colonial system, most countries have adopted either British, French, or Soviet local government systems as models.[30] So the basic characteristics of these three systems provide a guide to local government everywhere.

British local government consists of layers of elected councils whose work is carried out by committees. There are no intermediate-level representatives of the central government. In the Soviet Union, on the other hand, all local government agencies are part of the nation-state bureaucracy, in one manner or another. The boards and committees of the local councils (soviets), for example, are subject to the authority of the boards and committees at the next higher level.

In the majority of countries throughout the world, center-periphery relations are organized in prefectural systems similar to that of France. The central government's authority extends through the prefects to their districts, which are often of limited size. The central authority comes close to the grass roots.

One of the attractions of the prefectural system for many regimes is its emphasis on political order. Prefects, or their equivalents, have general rather than technical governing responsibilities. The prefect represents more than a collection of specific policies. As an official under the interior ministry, the prefect is the embodiment or representative of the "core" of the state as opposed to its "service" sector (i.e., the specialized ministries).[31] The prefect's office is political. In essence, the prefect is the regional authority responsible for political stability.[32] As such, his potential influence is substantial.

Within any local government system, however, much of the influence of local officials is informal. Whether a prefect develops his potential influence depends in part upon how he works with other officials in his immediate surroundings.[33] The prefect, to be influential, must elicit cooperation from the district officials of the specialized ministries. This is not easy because these officials typically must be responsive to their superiors within their own ministries if they are to advance professionally. Mayors of cities within the prefectures also have their own distinct constituencies and may not always be susceptible to the prefects' attempts to create alliances with them. Finally, the prefects' contacts with the interior ministry are channeled through provincial governors.

In sum, prefects operate in the midst of a network of formal and informal ministry and local government relationships. This network can enhance the prefects' potential influence and, at the same time, makes the exercise of that influence more complicated. British councils are formally part of a more decentralized system. But their prerogatives are limited by restrictive national legislation and by national officials' oversight of their activities. Both systems, in practice, leave substantial power with national officials. Both, too, leave room for much political maneuvering at the local level.

SUMMARY—LOCAL POLITICS AND STATE-BUILDING

The roles that local politicians and officials play within the nation-state depend upon what kind of political relationship they have with national regime elites. Local politicians have used local interests to build political support in opposition to national regimes. Others have acted as intermediaries between national regimes and their local constituents.

The extension of political control by national regime elites through the physical, economic, and social integration of the nation-state has a significant impact on local politics. Center-periphery relations have affected the ways in which local politicians develop local issues, how competitive local politics is, and how stable are local power structures.

One significant factor in determining how center-periphery relations are structured is the position of specific localities in the national economic system. Another is the salience of class issues and the relationship of class issues to regime security. The institutions of local government and the structure of local power reflect the outcomes of political contests over such issues.

Mexico—A Case Study of Local Politics in a Corporate State

Mexico's national politicians, like national elites elsewhere, have placed a high priority upon gaining control over local politics and politicians. The "revolutionary coalition," as the national politicians are known, has devised several strategies for centralizing politics that are as unique to Mexico as they are similar in their intent to consolidate the coalition's power. Mexico's politics has been affected by the length and intensity of its revolution, the structure of its agricultural sector, and its subsequent drive toward industrialization.

The institutional structures and political strategies that define center-periphery relationships were created by the coalition within the larger context of Mexico's evolving political economy. As a result, local politics and local politicians in Mexico are affected by the state-building experience differently from their counterparts elsewhere. In addition, local politicians in Mexico can use different political strategies to maximize their own influence locally, regionally, and nationally.

The Mexican revolutionary period was protracted. Although the republican constitution was promulgated in 1917, revolutionary conflict lasted, effectively, from 1910 until the late 1920s. At the outset, small landholders and peasants joined the revolution in opposition to the absolutist regime of Porfirio Diaz and to the large agricultural corporations [haciendas] associated with it. Peasants armed themselves and fought alongside the legendary Madero, Zapata, and Viela. Others fled from the countryside to the relative safety of the cities, only to return home after the fighting was over.

From the more than twenty years of revolution and migration, Mexican peasants acquired an unusually strong involvement in politics beyond the village. In 1930, 74 percent of Mexico's population lived in small, widely dispersed towns. But that was no indication of the political involvement or isolation of those Mexicans. The political experi-

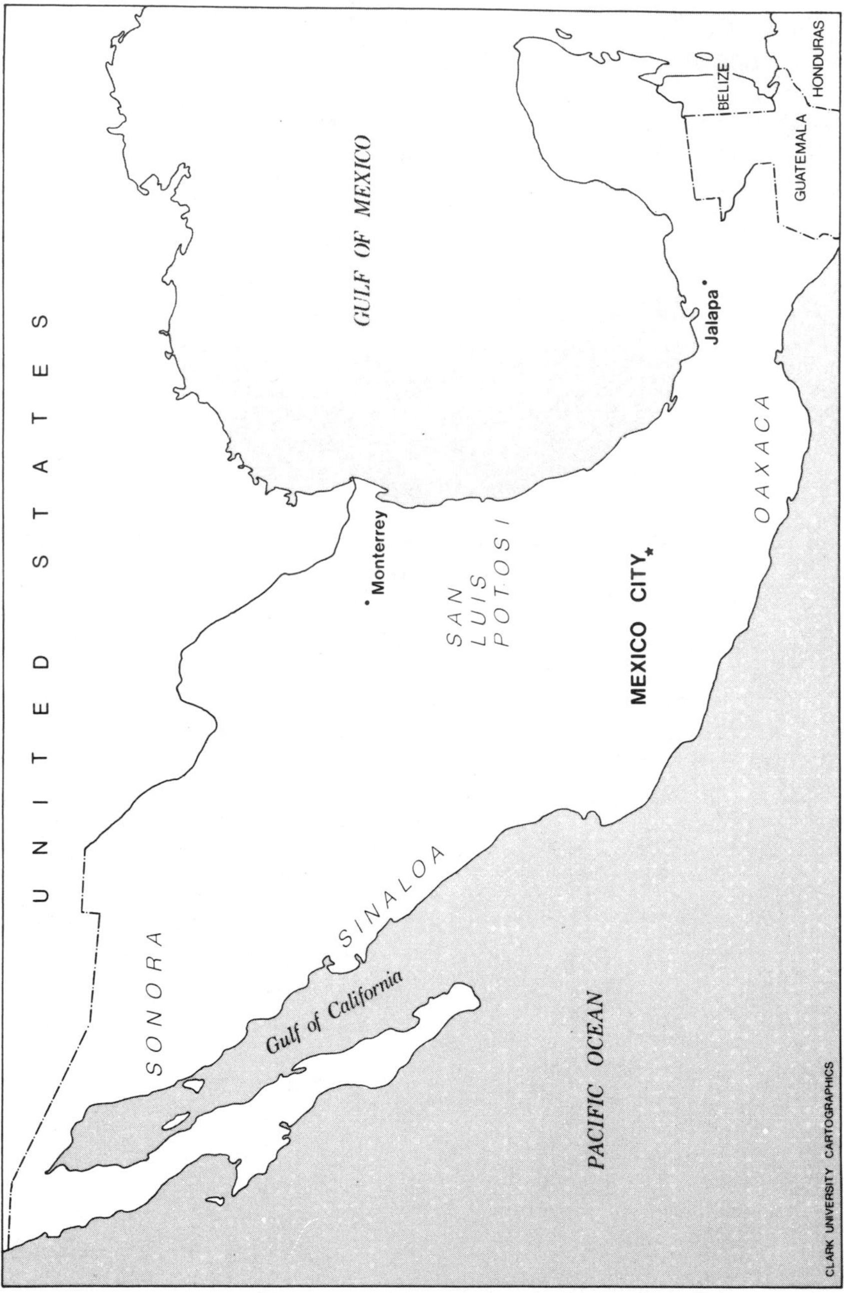
UNITED STATES
GULF OF MEXICO
BELIZE
HONDURAS
GUATEMALA
Jalapa
OAXACA
Monterrey
SAN LUIS POTOSI
MEXICO CITY
SINALOA
SONORA
Gulf of California
PACIFIC OCEAN
CLARK UNIVERSITY CARTOGRAPHICS

ences of the peasants who participated in the revolution made them a factor to be contended with by the postrevolution leadership.

In some cases, the politicized peasants were used by the national leadership in quite radical ways. When President Cárdenas took office in 1934, he organized armed peasants to challenge the revolutionary "generals," or *caudillos*, who continued to resist the imposition of national authority from their regional strongholds.

But that tactic also could be turned against the president. When Cárdenas began to implement land redistribution, some landowners were able to resist by arming peasants who were loyal to them. One of these generals was Saturnino Cedillo of San Luis Potosi, a state in central Mexico. When President Cárdenas took office, Cedillo still commanded his own army of 15,000 peasants and several planes, and was reaping the profits from extensive agricultural holdings.[34] Cedillo redistributed land within his region to solidify his position among the peasants. But he left the land that belonged to himself and to his friends intact. The success of Cedillo limited the power of national politicians who had to balance the power of the large landowners and the *caudillos* against that of the numerically preponderant peasants. Cedillo himself eventually became a staunch ally of President Cárdenas and even served for a time as his minister of agriculture.

Because the Mexican peasants were politicized to a relatively large degree, the ruling revolutionary coalition had to extend its control to the rural areas as well as the rapidly growing cities. This was accomplished by creating a peasant organization, tying it to the ruling party, and distributing development funds through government agencies.

Rural development and land redistribution programs in Mexico have not been particularly revolutionary, but they have been continuous and substantial.[35] They have brought agricultural credits and federal land improvement projects to the countryside along with government party leaders. The potential for political reciprocity—credit for votes—has been sufficient in most cases to sustain the ruling party's rural support. In fact, the ruling party has had stronger rural support than urban.

These patterns of political economy are the local dimension of Mexican corporate politics. Corporatism in politics means a highly structured competition for power, with bargaining among organizations rather than groups or individuals.[36] In Mexican corporatist politics the dividing line between what is public and what is private is vague; corporate politics links the two. What is particularly significant in the Mexican case is the extent to which the corporation extends down to the grass roots. Mexican corporate politics is the substantive framework through which local political processes are tied horizontally to those of other localities. It is also the framework through which local political processes are linked to the state, regional, and national decision-making centers. These links are cemented by clientelism and cooptation.

THE POLITICAL CORPORATION IN THE COUNTRYSIDE

Political life is much more organized in Mexico than in many countries, and the contrast is particularly strong in the rural sector. Two of the national farmers' organizations (the National Confederation of Peasants and the Mexican Confederation of Workers) are affiliated with the ruling party, the Party of the Institutionalized Revolution (PRI). A third, the National Confederation of Workers and Peasants, is affiliated with the Socialist party. These organizations are official, direct links between national party leaders and individual farmers. The federations are one avenue through which farmers' interests are transmitted to state and national officials. At the same time, they offer extralocal politicians the opportunity to channel peasants' demands into areas that will not challenge the regime. Finally, because the opportunity for limited competition between the federations exists, local politicians can advance their own careers by using these farmers' organizations.

Despite this tactical flexibility, local opposition groups within and outside of the ruling party do not directly affect the structure of policy alternatives at the center. The several organizations provide a vehicle for local political competition and local elite "circulation." But local leaders must limit their criticism of PRI leaders, who control agricultural credit.

This contained political competition is most characteristic of *ejidos,* or communal farms; there the stakes of local politics are relatively limited. The system has been far less effective where land has not been redistributed; in these areas, the political stakes of local conflict are high and extend well beyond the local arena.

Redistributive issues are highly salient in rural local politics, although the issues are different in different regions. Land redistribution was first carried out in Mexico in those states with poorer land, where profitable commercial farming was less entrenched. In areas like the profitable sugar-producing lands of the north, structural change in agriculture has proceeded much more slowly. As a result, the many landless farm workers in those regions have little stake in either the existing system of production or its politics. At the same time, the cash crops these workers help produce are a valuable source of foreign exchange, and therefore land redistribution is considered potentially as damaging to the immediate interests of national governmental elites as to the landowners.

Consequently, in those regions the circulation of local elites is not sufficient to resolve conflicts or to allay potential conflicts. In 1976, for example, President Echeverría Alvarez (1970–1976) announced the expropriation of 200,000 acres of rich farmlands in two states, Sonora and Sinaloa, just eleven days before he was to end his term of office. Just as some farm workers had predicted, when Echeverría left office, the promised redistribution collapsed. But in many areas, there was a reaction by farm workers who had anticipated acquiring land; they mobilized and occupied the land. In Sinaloa, army and police units had to be called out to evict the workers.[37] Local leaders of the PRI's National Confederation of Peasants appeared to desert the workers in the face of the army's intervention. Spokesmen for the squatters complained that they were entirely on their own.

The experience indicates the delicate balance between the federation leaders and their landless constituents, as well as the continuing influence of landowning farmers on Mexican politics. The question that confronted the national politicians is whether the same political structures and strategies that are used in reformed *ejido* areas can prevent political conflict in the unreformed areas. The peasant sector of the ruling party apparently cannot contain the farm laborers' demands for land redistribution with the same cooptive strategies that it used in the *ejidos*. Where local politics is so polarized, local politicians can be only marginally effective as intermediaries.

Another kind of politics of scarcity exists in the *ejidos*. In the *ejido* system, land is owned in common. That is, *ejido* land cannot be transferred by individuals. If a peasant wishes to relinquish his holding, he must do so through the communal organization. But in practice *ejido* lands are farmed in much the same manner as are private farms—in small plots, not communally. Accordingly, *ejido* politics varies from community to community, depending in large part upon how much opportunity for growth there is; some of the lands that have been redistributed and incorporated into *ejidos* are more productive than others. Poor *ejidos* exist in the same regions as more prosperous ones. Yet the politics of the poorer *ejidos* resemble those of the large private farms more than they do the prosperous *ejidos*. They have developed their own politics of scarcity.

A political anthropologist, Manuel L. Carlos, has characterized the poor *ejidos* as *ejidos organizados*.[38] The *ejidos organizados* have "fused" political structures. Conflict is subdued. Fewer farmers involve themselves in politics. At the same time, fewer community development projects are initiated in these *ejidos,* and less of their land has been improved.

Many of the differences between the *ejidos organizados* and the more advantaged *ejidos dividios* stem from their historical positions in the agricultural production system. *Ejidos organizados* tended to be farther from cities. Consequently, they were more removed from the broader network of the national economy, even before land distribution was implemented. Some of the *ejido* lands were formerly part of grain-producing *haciendas;* others were marginal Indian-owned lands that had been farmed communally.[39]

By contrast, the *ejidos dividos* are former sugar cane *haciendas.* They have long been producing for external markets, and they are located closer to marketing outlets. In general, these lands had more resources invested in them before redistribution than did the others.

Where redistributive issues are highly salient, open conflict carries with it the potential for irreversible and fundamental political change. The farmers' organizations have not mobilized the *ejidos organizados* because of the difficulty of limiting issues to representation and leadership competition. Fewer politicians from the *ejidos organizados* participate in the national farmer organizations. Politics tends to be conducted through informal, personal networks. Characteristically, the politics of scarcity in the *ejidos organizados* emphasizes less visible political processes because the costs of open conflict are high for all concerned. By containing disputes within the *ejido,* local leaders help prevent issues from being transmitted to the state and national levels.[40]

Local farmers' organizations are more successful when they can attract agricultural credits. While the federal *ejido* bank (BANDIJAL) provides credit to farmers on noncommercial terms, commercial criteria do influence bank decisions, since the bank's losses can be minimized by investing in the most productive *ejidos.* Because fewer resources are available for investing in the less-productive *ejidos,* there are also fewer incentives for the ruling party to organize them. Political organizations create expectations of reciprocity. Farmers are reluctant to make commitments to these organizations if there are no gains to be enjoyed as a result. As local party representatives, *ejido* leaders can often influence decisions regarding who will get agricultural credit. When local *ejido* leaders cannot produce agricultural credits, it is difficult for them to build strong bases of power. The way in which the national regime has structured the political game in the poorer *ejidos* has limited the stakes and competition. Regime elites know this; so the *ejidos organizados* are left alone. Hence, these *ejidos* remain marginal— geographically, economically, and politically.

CORPORATE POLITICS AND URBAN WARD HEELERS

Urban local politics operates in much the same way as rural politics. Local politicians are intermediaries between their constituents and both the ruling party and bureaucratic officials at higher levels. This intermediate role has several dimensions. First, local officials of the ruling party are subordinate to state-level directive committees.[41]

For example, the local municipal committees of the ruling party do not play a major role in selecting nominees for mayor, although they do select candidates for the six other municipal council seats. Much of the party's power is centralized in the National Executive Committee. This committee can remove party officials at lower levels and can convene state party assemblies to legitimize the committee's decisions. When conflicts that could develop into major challenges to the party hierarchy arise at the local level, party assemblies are used to protect that hierarchy. In one case, a local candidate for secretary-general of the National Executive Committee was rejected as the party's nominee by the state nominating committee. The local candidate tried to reverse the decision by bringing his popular support to their attention. The state committee responded by calling a state party assembly that it could dominate to legitimize its decision.[42]

Second, neither mayor nor council has much power. The power of local institutions is diffused by the cross-cutting organization of the party into functional groups. Organizations for national party workers, farmers, and white-collar and professional people extend down to the local level. Politicians, especially in the cities, compete with each other through these functional organizations.

Within the locally diffuse and nationally centralized structure of authority, local politicians are sometimes able to construct areas of marginal influence for themselves. Urban *caciques* or ward heelers, for example, can often influence the appointment of local party and bureaucratic officials. However, they have much less influence in state capitals, where the governor dominates local politics.[43] In addition, while *caciques* cannot influence general policy directions, they can intervene in specific decisions that affect their own constituents directly— decisions about landownership, business licenses, taxes, etc.

The *cacique*'s area of power is limited to reconciling specific conflicts. Because the *cacique*'s role often is informal—chiefly one of intervening on behalf of relatively powerless constituents—his power often is wielded in an arbitrary manner. Consequently, the *cacique*'s clients often appeal to influential politicians at higher levels for protection from his arbitrary power.

The *cacique* system has not been easily challenged, in large part because of its usefulness to politicians at higher levels. At one point, President Echeverría disassociated himself from the *cacique* system and called for its abolition. The president's position did not bring about any radical changes. However, it did permit him to reap the political advantages of both aligning with the opponents of *caciquismo* and making further action against *caciquismo* appear unnecessary.

Because *caciquismo* is an unofficial and informal system of influence, it cannot be abolished by presidential fiat. Furthermore, for the lower-ranking party politicians and government officials, *caciquismo* continues to be useful.[44] Strong *caciques* can successfully mediate local political conflicts. So as long as the *cacique* system is functioning smoothly at the local level, national leaders can continue to advocate democratizing the party without having to actually implement any of their proposals.

The *cacique* system is informal; formal local government officials have virtually no power—either through their offices or through their control of municipal financial resources. Mexican local governments are probably the financially poorest of all those described in our ten case studies. Municipality revenue is what is left over after the federal and state governments "preempt" their portions of the tax sources available.[45] In 1960, what was left over was less than 3 percent of all public revenues.[46] Padgett calculated an all-Mexico average municipal income of $22,000 per year. For poor states, such as Oaxaca, the average income was about $1,166 per year. Most municipal revenues were earned jointly with the state; commercial, residential property tax, and licensing fees are shared by the states and their subordinate municipalities on a percentage basis. Despite such miniscule budgets, state authorities must approve the budgets before the money can be spent by local officials.

Municipalities have been prevented from collecting taxes, so they cannot afford to provide urban public services. That function has been assumed by state and federal authorities. Consequently, municipal officials in Mexico have unusually limited governing roles.

In addition, while the formal powers of state authorities vary from state to state, the effective distribution of power in all permits state authorities to dismiss municipal officials at will. And the state governors in turn are selected by the president of the republic.

The chain of control over municipal affairs quite often leads directly to Mexico City. The caveat "quite often" is important because not every issue is carried to the president before it is resolved. The more conflicts that a governor is able to resolve on his own, without referring to his supervisors, the more valuable he is to the president. In contrast, very few issues are within the capacity of municipal officials to decide.

State governors can also dominate local *caciques*. In the city of Jalapa, a local *cacique* system has not developed because the state governor is powerful and willing to extend his influence to local power networks without turning over portions of that influence to local bosses.[47] He has been assisted by the state leaders of the ruling party, who have allocated city council seats so that disadvantaged groups receive a share of the seats. This token representation of various city constituencies on the council helps to dissuade local politicians from opposing the governor.

THE LOCAL POLITICAL ECONOMY OF CORPORATE POLITICS

Where the *cacique*'s role as an intermediary with the poor has been assumed by others, *caciquismo* has been weakened. But the *cacique* system is somewhat more deep-rooted than its specific political functions suggest. *Caciques* perform their ward heeling activities within the larger economic context. This larger context is another aspect of the corporate party regime. The *cacique* is able to wield limited, yet arbitrary, power because he operates in marginal communities. Communities where the *cacique* system flourishes are typically both economically and politically marginal; wealthy communities generally do not have *caciques*. The major economic activities carried out within the marginal communities are usually controlled by outsiders. The *cacique*'s constituents have little to offer him in the way of support. As a result, the *cacique*'s position is not likely to be challenged by local competitors.

Industrial managers influence both economic activities and social life in marginal communities. A survey of several squatter settlements on the outskirts of Mexico City found little indigenous industrial activity within the settlements.[48] Most of the profitable businesses were owned by outsiders, who took their profits out of the community with them. These nonlocal firms also hired nonlocal laborers. Leisure activities, arranged by the employers for the migrant laborers, emphasized the ties of the migrant laborers with their hometowns, not with their place of employment. For example, local priests were not used in religious functions; instead, priests were from the migrant workers' towns of origin.

The structure of the ruling party also effectively splits unorganized migrants from members of unions (which the party supports and from which party leaders elicit support for themselves).[49] Workers' federations that are affiliated with the ruling party also are used by local leaders to advance themselves in public office. The recruitment of labor leaders into local offices is managed by leaders higher in the party or by officials in the Ministry of Labor. The workers' federations are structured in much the same way as the farmers' organizations. They are highly centralized and join with other sectors in the party's state and national executive committees.

The labor federations usually are docile organizations—better for promoting individual interests than group demands. Although government-sponsored unions are regarded by American employers in Mexico as far less docile than are employer-sponsored unions, the PRI unions have been closely linked to the party.[50] On the other hand, industrialists in Mexico's "second" city, Monterrey, at one point threatened to support opposition party candidates through an informal coalition called the Monterrey Group.[51] The tactical flexibility of the industrialists limits the extent to which the government can mobilize its unions in economic conflicts.

Since the ruling party's national regime wants to avoid taking sides in industrial conflicts, it has created "decentralized agencies" to undertake particular economic development activities. These agencies have begun to play a major role in implementing national policy; they spend more and have more employees than do the regular ministries and departments of the government. They include agencies that run federal enterprises, public service agencies, and banks.[52]

The decentralized agencies are politically misnamed because in reality they are not decentralized. They are run by boards of directors that include ministers and department heads from various ministries and other government agencies—essentially the interlocking directorate of the "national corporate regime." The semiautonomous status of the agencies enables the government to influence economic policy in a less visible manner than it can by intervening directly in labor-management relations.

Despite the predominantly centralized nature of the Mexican economy, local politics is still important to small business. In general, the more resources one controls, the less likely it is that local politicians will be useful in protecting one's interests. The state government becomes the court of first resort for the industrialist. Small businessmen, on the other hand, participate in local organizations—the Chamber of Commerce or the PRI.[53]

Labor unions also have access to the local party and the bureaucracy. But even at that level their influence is curbed by members' dependence upon the government for employment.

Local politics is politics for the weak. Still, the limited leverage that the less powerful acquire through local *caciques,* city councils, and the various party organizations has been sufficient to stimulate demands for greater local autonomy and decentralization. In 1959, the National Congress of Municipal Governors advocated at least minimal control for the municipalities over their own officials.[54] Six years later, the ruling party experimented briefly with direct primaries for some local offices. But few leaders have both the incentive and the influence to sustain the demands for increased local autonomy—demands that would amount to a radical change in the structure of corporate politics as it has evolved in Mexico.

Summary—The Party, Stability, and the Corporation

The ecology of power in Mexican local politics can be summed up thus: who you are and where you live determines what you get from politics and how you get it. Local politicians assume disproportionate importance in determining what you get if you are relatively poor or if you live in a rural area. Local political influence characteristically provides specific, material rewards—not influence over public policy. Overall, public policy directions are set by the national corporate elite and implemented through the highly centralized corporate political organizations.

Mexico's revolutionary period—with the centrifugal influence of its *caudillos* and local *caciques*—set the stage for the evolving corporate structure. Preservation of the corporate structure and its political arm, the PRI, has been the central objective of the governing "revolutionary coalition."

Support for the corporate system has come from diverse quarters. Among the many Mexicans who have discussed the desirability of more political decentralization, one journalist has argued that "there ought to be a change toward more municipal autonomy . . . but it ought to come slowly, not with one blow or *golpe*, not through a revolt. . . ."[55]

Even many of the less-advantaged citizens are defensive about political stability. When serious conflict has occurred, the less advantaged often have lost the most. At the same time, during periods of stability, large numbers of the disadvantaged received some attention from the ruling party and bureaucratic officials.

The party has been a central vehicle for transmitting specific demands from the local level to higher authorities. Competition within the ruling party and between it and other parties has been tolerated so long as it has been contained. In the late 1920s and 1930s, and again in the 1970s, revolts against established government authorities have spread from one locality to another. As a result of this experience, the Mexican elite has inherited a wariness of "pocket" theories of political opposition. Local politics—whether it means controlled opposition, *cacique* rule, or competition within the party—is integral to regime security.

The evolution of Mexican local politics has been profoundly affected by the revolutionary coalition's corporatist strategies. The corporatism of the ruling regime has made it easier for the ruling party to control local politics through a unique state structure and the informal influence of local politicians.

Turkey—A Case Study of Local Politics in a Party State

What is now the heartland of Turkey was more than a century ago the hinterland of the Ottoman Empire. Political undercurrents in Damascus (Syria) once reached the sultan's ear more rapidly than did news of local politics in many Turkish towns. The cosmopolitan empire sprawled south across the Fertile Crescent onto the Arabian Peninsula and north into the Balkans. Although the Ottoman bureaucracy was staffed largely by Moslem Turks, the top-level posts were reserved for non-Moslems selected by the sultan.

With the final disintegration of the Ottoman Empire in the first years of the twentieth century, the idea of Turkish nationalism gained popularity. Then, with the need to defend what remained of Turkish territory after World War I, a more organized form of Turkish nationalism materialized.

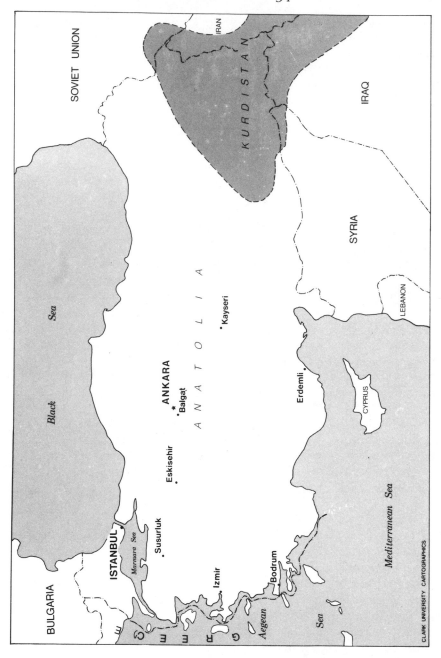

The organization of Turkish *national* politics gave a salicency to *local* politics that was unusual for a regime developing under the aegis of a single party. The Turkish nationalist revolution was short, in contrast to Mexico's. As a result, the emergent republican regime was based upon a less structured revolutionary coalition.[56] Between the two world wars, more emphasis was placed upon laying the physical groundwork for national development than upon a lasting political structure permeating the countryside. Post–World War II Turkish politics, then, can be characterized by the resulting competition between a politically shallow republican center and the local politicial opposition—a competition occurring under the rubric of a multiparty regime during this later period.

The Old Periphery

Turkey was, and still remains in many ways, a country of villages—spread out across roughly a thousand miles, from the Mediterranean in the West to Iran in the East. According to the census of 1970, 60 percent of the Turkish population lives in villages, with these villages spread out rather evenly throughout the country.

This village structure was important in the early days of the republic. Roads and other means of communication were more limited, and village agriculture was tied to the national market economy to a lesser extent than now. Villages in Turkey offered both a challenge and an opportunity to the founders of the First Turkish Republic (1919–1924). Their reaction was to piece together from the scattered grass-roots Defense of Rights organizations (formed during the war) an alternative to the remnants of the Ottoman regime in Istanbul.

Economic life during the Ottoman period was centered in the western cities of Istanbul and Izmir.[57] Under the regime of President Mustafa Kamal Ataturk (1924–1938), the capital of Turkey was moved to Ankara, and as a result, the Anatolian plateau around it grew in importance. Ataturk's strategy for consolidating his power to defeat the remnants of the Ottoman sultanate was to bring together the disparate and relatively independent regional and local leaders.

Ataturk continued this process of integration during the 1930s by building up *central* Turkey's industrial base. His political strategy of using public resources to draw in outlying regions had an important impact on the ultimate pattern of industrial development in Turkey. The provincial distribution of state industries is now far more equal than is the distribution of private industrial establishments.[58]

For many years after the republic was founded, the political character of Ataturk's regime was influenced by its local organizational base. of the twentieth century, the idea of Turkish nationalism gained popularity. Then, with the need to defend what remained of Turkish

Ataturk's Republican People's party (RPP) was a coalition of national bureaucrats and traditional local notables—especially in the eastern, more isolated, provinces. At the time that Ataturk founded the RPP, the diffuse social and economic character of the country encouraged such organizational diffuseness. The RPP helped to paper over existing cleavages between urban modernizers and rural elites that might have otherwise made their political cooperation impossible.

Apparently Ataturk was reluctant to undermine already existing local power networks and thereby create, what seemed to him, unnecessary political conflict. His successors were equally conservative. A warning went out from the RPP headquarters in 1946 stating: "Do not go into the provincial towns and villages to gather support. Our national unity will be undermined."[59]

The confederate structure of the party—local power bases combined at the apex—was a pragmatic approach to political organization during that early period. But it had rather long-lasting consequences, indirectly limiting the policy options available to the RPP leadership. The diffuseness hindered reform. The local notables that made up the provincial base of the RPP were politically influential, so many of the social and economic reforms that the republican regime legislated were not actually implemented in the provinces.[60]

Toward the end of the 1960s, with Turkey under a military stewardship that began in 1961, this loose coalition within the RPP began to break down. The ruling group moved toward the left in response to radical movements at the national level. In 1966, many of the local notables left the party, protesting its leftward turn and forming the Reliance party (RP). Their action undermined still further what was by then a minority status for the RPP in the parliament. It was not until the national parliamentary elections of 1977 that the new reformist stance paid off. In that year the urban vote was large enough to give the RPP a plurality again.

The RPP's organization was first tested after World War II. At that time Ataturk's successor, Ismet Inönü, committed himself and the RPP to open competition with other political parties for national and local offices. By 1950 the Democratic party overtook the RPP and replaced it as the majority party in the parliament. While the RPP was preoccupied with politics in the capital, the Democratic party had given major attention to organizing the periphery. It had effectively organized voters, particularly in Turkey's medium-sized towns. As a result, when Turkey's first open and competitive national election was held in 1950, the RPP lost.[61] In 1961, Turkey's military leaders outlawed party organizations beneath the provincial level, but by that time, the conservative opposition already had a strong base of support.

The organization that the RPP had relied upon in the countryside seemed more deeply rooted than it actually was. Some villages switched completely over from the Republican party's column to that of the

Democratic party. "Single-party villages" were those whose voters supported one party nearly unanimously in one election, and another, equally unanimously, in the next election. Village notables were very effective in mobilizing voters, but they had competitors who capitalized on the Democratic party's presence. When the contending elites came along to challenge the local establishment, they too could take a high proportion of the voters with them.

As well as personal factions, local party competition began to acquire an ideological dimension. Party affiliations developed broader meaning for their members than the personal alliances from which they grew. Family or faction might have been the original basis for an individual's party identification, but eventually the parties' national positions engaged more of their members' attention. The Democratic party came to represent antibureaucratic sentiments and the desire to slow down the pace of modernization.

At first, though, the issues were more of power than policy, and they could easily assume local or national proportions. Voters gave their support to the DP candidates as much to turn the "ins" out of office as to support any radical shifts in policy. The Democratic party put forward successful candidates for both local and national offices. In at least some towns, local issues were the central issues, and the DP was ready to respond with appropriate local candidates. The voters' initial interest in changing local leaders contributed to the victory of DP candidates for national office.[62]

For many years after assuming power, Ataturk's republican regime had "dealt" with the fundamental issues of center-periphery politics by avoiding them. The regime did attempt to make the center and periphery closer economically and socially — a strategy that was easier in the days when the periphery was geographically more peripheral. But the costs of ignoring grass-roots organization were brought home to the regime even before the Reliance party broke away in 1966. The electoral defeats that the regime suffered during the 1950s were a dramatic reminder of those potential costs.

THE NEW PERIPHERY

Center-periphery relations have changed in several ways since the beginning of the First Republic. Physically, the territory is more integrated. Turkey's rail network is the most extensive in the Middle East. Roads also have improved, particularly since the 1950s. Official government survey figures show three-fourths of Turkey's villages lying within two hours travel of a district center and within four hours of a provincial capital.[63] As a result of these and other changes, people in Turkey live closer to one another now, and their lives have been affected accordingly.

Not all of the changes have been positive from the standpoint of the villager. Physical distance can contribute to social distance. But when physical distance decreases, social distance does not always disappear with it. "Once the village was a social foothill to the distant urban peaks, proud in its semi-autonomy. . . ." Now it is the "peripheral lower slopes."[64]

By bringing village, town, and capital closer, local social patterns merged with those of the broader society. The result has been a deterioration in the relative status of rural dwellers. The emerging social stratification system is not more rigid, nor does it necessarily involve wider gaps among classes. But it is different from the old. People are respected for different reasons, and they compare their status with much broader groups (i.e., Anatolians or Turks, rather than fellow villagers). For some, the process of social integration has meant upward mobility; for others, it has meant losing a secure position in the local social hierarchy.

Daniel Lerner traced this process of social integration in the Turkish village of Balgat over the 1950 to 1959 period.[65] His "parable of the [upwardly mobile] grocer and the chief," whose traditional assets—family and age—were no longer valuable, could be applied to many other Turkish towns and villages.

Social change occurs selectively. The chief Lerner describes did not shut out the world beyond the village; he had a radio and sent his sons away to school. Rather, he simply was not prepared, by his training or his interests, to take full advantage of the new opportunities that modernization brought.

One consequence of the integration of village life with city life has been that people have "voted with their feet" to leave the countryside.[66] The growth of towns and of the towns' accessibility have encouraged migration from rural Turkey. Most migrants have seen this as a way to escape from poverty; others leave behind the social disadvantages of the "peripheral lower slopes." The Turkish society that has emerged from these developments is more urbanized and highlights urban values.

It was this changing countryside that the DP successfully mobilized, by correctly assessing its political mood. The Turkish bureaucrat still chastised farmers for not paying their taxes, much like the landlords and tax farmers who preceded him. The resultant tension between farmer and bureaucrat helped the Democratic party bring out voters against the long-standing RPP regime.

Before national politics became openly competitive, local notables and headmen had occasionally acted as buffers between villagers and the tax collectors and gendarmes.[67] The opposition party offered this same potential to voters.

The Democratic party's grass-roots organizers brought in votes and recruited a new set of leaders into national and local office. They were not radical leaders; rather they were politicians who drew their influence more from their communities than from the bureaucracy or the military.[68]

An analysis of post-1950 election data shows that urban migrants also voted against the RPP, despite the fact that the RPP's modernization policies might be seen as conforming with the migrants long-term interests.[69] One explanation for this vote relates to the traditional religious values of migrants. The Democratic party and its successor, the Justice party, supported religious values in the face of the RPP's secularizing programs.

A second explanation is the migrants' upward mobility. They had improved their economic position by moving to the city, and this newly acquired status encouraged them to vote for the "party of entrepreneurs" rather than for the "party of bureaucrats." Later, after many years outside government, the opposition was able to control public funds and to distribute them to its supporters in the private sector as the RPP had to the bureaucracy before it. In this respect, the migrants were part of the periphery that voted to protect its position against the bureaucratic center of the RPP.[70]

The ascendancy of politicians with local roots can be seen in the backgrounds of deputies in Turkey's parliament, the Grand National Assembly. Through successive parliamentary elections in 1946, 1950, and 1954, there were increases in the number of deputies who were born in the constituency that they represented. By 1954, 71 percent of the Grand National Assembly members were local "sons" and 73 percent of the deputies in that year were in the professions or in business (i.e., they were not the usual bureaucrats).[71] The deputies who entered parliament from business often had prior experience in elective local government as well; their political career patterns were the most "local" of all. Finally, the profiles of deputies also pointed to "the rising power of provincial Anatolia," growing out of the way in which Ataturk had constructed his regime. The physical foundation for the Turkish nation to which Ataturk contributed eventually helped the defensive periphery defeat his party of the center.

An event during Ataturk's presidency presaged this outcome. In 1930 a short-lived opposition party—the Free party—contested Turkey's first real local elections with a platform that criticized the national government's railroad-building program.[72] Prime Minister Inönü justified the massive program on the basis of the contribution that it would make to Turkish national security. It was the first campaign—of many—to raise center-periphery questions.

LOCAL POLITICIANS AND NATIONAL DEVELOPMENT

In that same 1930 speech, Prime Minister Inönü first used the term *etatism*. Under Turkish law and according to the Ataturk-Inönü doctrine of etatism, the central government was to be responsible for maintaining internal security, for promoting economic development, and for major education and health programs. Local authorities were to have jurisdiction over public health regulations, land use, and maintenance of public facilities—such as water and sewerage.

Under such a distribution of public functions, the potential impact of the central government's programs on any one locality was great. Etatism was regarded by its supporters as a strategy for rapid development. But its detractors saw it as yet another move to consolidate the bureaucracy's domination of the periphery.

Local government expenditures in Turkey have been low relative to those of other European countries. This has meant that a poor locality's best opportunity to attract outside public investment was through the leverage its leaders wielded in the capital, Ankara. A town's or city's ability to attract private industry by providing an infrastructure and a skilled work force depended upon its access to the national treasury. For the cities outside the more developed Istanbul-Izmir "industrial axis," partisan politics offers an opportunity to compete for public investment resources.

When and how central governments exercise control over local governments depend upon the political issues raised by the localities and upon the capital's access to the localities. Migration into the cities, the visibility of urban poverty, and the importance of municipal party organizations all encouraged the extension of central control to city politics. This control was both more intense and more extensive than it was in the villages.[73]

Budgetary controls over municipalities rested in the hands of the district governor or prefect (*kaymakam*), in the first instance. But he, in turn, sent his estimates of public expenditures on to Ankara, which was the ultimate source of the major portion of municipal revenues. In the city of Erdemli, for example, Szyliowicz found that 67 percent of municipality revenue came from the central government.[74]

The share that any one city received from the central revenues designated for local governments depended legally upon population, not politics. However, central contributions to local coffers could be enlarged through strategic political maneuvering. Erdemli's Democratic mayor and councillors convinced their party's national leaders that they should control the centrally financed Alata River dam and thereby boost municipal revenues by selling water to neighboring villages. Alternatively, the Ministry of Interior maintained the Special Municipality Fund, from which it could make low-interest loans to a city or town.[75]

During the decade that it controlled the national government, the Democratic party reciprocated for the support it received from the smaller towns and cities by increasing disbursements from the public treasury for provincial projects.[76] The expansion of provincial projects, however, contributed to the inflationary period that Turkey experienced at the end of the 1950s, and the Democratic party leadership was severely criticized for its lack of restraint.[77]

Not all towns that had supported the Democrats were equally rewarded. Democrats in Bodrum, a remote town on Turkey's western coast, were unable to get funds for rebuilding major roads into the town. They tried several approaches to convince national Democrats that they expected such help—including resigning from the city and the party councils.[78] Visiting national politicians, among them the prime minister himself, were unmoved. Local voters blamed local party leaders rather than national officials for the failure; the prime minister "had so much on his mind," and "he was kind enough to visit Bodrum." Consequently, the chief victims of the national party leaders' failure to dip into the pork barrel were local politicians—not the national party leaders themselves.

The importance of central government resources to local politicians also weakened partisan alliances among local politicians. Factions appeared within local political party organizations that reflected personal followings and local issues. Such factions tended to persist regardless of the attempts by national party leaders to negotiate these differences. In one case, a Justice party candidate for mayor in the city of Eskisehir was expelled from the party by its national leadership. He was elected anyway, but along with a city council from the opposing faction—a faction that remained loyal to the national leaders.

Local politicians in the cities were particularly aware of their dependence upon outside revenues. With growing populations and small tax bases, mayors and other city officials became increasingly hard pressed to make ends meet. Turkish municipal authority extended beyond the usual street cleaning and sanitation responsibilities to health and social services. As a result of the urban financial crunch, the mayor of Erdemli, interviewed by Joseph Szyliowicz, complained:

> They [the constituents] are fully aware of what they want and what they need, and they come and complain to me all the time. They do not realize that the municipality is poor and that we are doing our best.[79]

National grants-in-aid helped to fill in deficits in the short run. But the grants were not reliable as a basis for long-range planning and municipal development. The grants-in-aid system of local finance was most useful politically—both to the national politicians who allocated those revenues and to the local politicians who could acquire them.

National control of local purse strings did not prevent competition for office at the local level. The split between Eskisehir's mayor and council was exceptional in Turkish politics. The national pork barreling that characterized the Democrats' rule during the 1950s in some cases seemed to encourage local political competition. For example, aside from those in a few "safe" constituencies, "local" deputies in the Grand

National Assembly fared little better at reelection time than did those who were serving constituencies other than those where they were born.[80] Strong political links between national and local politicians— links that benefited both—increased local political competition more than did national domination or local autonomy.

Links between national and local party leaders were firmest when the same party was in control at both levels. For example, the Democratic party was in office in the town of Susurluk in northwest Turkey until the 1960 military coup. After the coup, the national military regime installed a new mayor—an army colonel who made himself quite unpopular with many local groups by his high-handed methods of governing.[81] Later, the town elected a Justice party council whose members' backgrounds were more representative of the town's population, and the country elected a Justice party parliament. The continuous intervention of national politics and party politicians in local politics kept town politics compatible with national politics, whether through electoral or bureaucratic methods.

In the town of Bodrum the same principle applied: "Locals think of local politics in terms of national politics."[82] But communications between local and national party leaders have broken down. In the mid-1960s, the national RPP announced the new left-of-center program that caused considerable stir among local residents. Local RPP leaders had no more information than did their constituents on which to react to the announcement. When explanations were finally forthcoming, the RPP chairman said: "Now I am more able to explain this left-of-center thing to the voters."

REGIONS, MINORITIES, AND POLITICS

Regional ethnic politics also emphasizes the local politician's role in regime security. Regional minority issues make center-periphery politics more critical. During the Ottoman Empire, Armenian and Greek minorities were active in public affairs and accounted for much of the commerce and industry of the empire. After World War I, most of the populations of both groups had left Turkey or had been killed. The one relatively large and politically salient minority group remaining in Turkey was the Kurds, mostly located in the eastern region of Turkey. Throughout the republic's history, Kurdish demands for political autonomy were countered by the imposition of central, military control over the region. Also, the government attempted to coopt Kurdish leaders into national politics.

The physical isolation of the Kurdish region from the rest of Turkey has contributed to its distinct political identity. Most of the Kurdish-speaking population lives in rural areas in the eastern and southeastern regions of the country. "Few roads lead to Kurdistan," and many of the roads through the Kurdish regions are not usable during the winter months.

Over the years, many Kurds have criticized the government's record of economic development in terms of regional and ethnic issues. Under Ataturk's presidency, public investment in the Kurdish region was neglected in favor of the central Ankara region.[83] Industrial employment opportunities in the Kurdish region continued to lag far behind the rest of the country.

In the early 1960s the military government instructed the State Planning Organization to "accelerate the development of 'backward' regions."[84] However, the incremental increases in funds that the planning organizations diverted to the Kurdish region did not prevent the more significant outward flow of manpower and capital resources to more-advanced areas.

By the mid-1970s, the Kurdish region still bore many of the marks of an impoverished society. Its male literacy rate in 1965 was 41 percent, in contrast to 64 percent for the country as a whole. And the number of physicians for each inhabitant was one-third as great as the number for the country as a whole.[85]

Turkish nationalism has provided political reinforcement for the Kurdish region's economic marginality. Two Kurdish revolts early in the republic's life (1925, 1930) paved the way for a "de facto military occupation of the region" and for continuous attempts by the national leadership to de-Kurdify it by discouraging Kurdish ethnic politicians and by removing the Kurdish language from the public school curriculum.[86]

Many Kurdish elites, in the face of these social and political constraints, have accommodated themselves to the national regime by denying their Kurdish ancestry.[87] The RPP's "local notable" approach to party organization also was applied to Kurdistan. They hoped to coopt Kurdish leaders into the RPP in return for protecting the notables' local influence. The strategy worked and the eastern region of Turkey continues to be a single-party area.

The relative absence of competitive local politics in Kurdish Turkey is a function of ethnicity and economics. When ethnic minority politics are involved, the potential for mutual political benefit is lessened. The underdevelopment of minority regions heightens the salience of, and places greater strains on, center-periphery relations. The smaller range of tolerance lessens the number of opportunities for local politicians to serve as brokers. Local political competition is less common, while individual politicians enjoy more influence.

SUMMARY—THE PERIPHERY, NATIONAL DEVELOPMENT, AND LOCAL POLITICS

Turkish local politics has offered considerably more room for accumulating power and influence at the local level and within the political system as a whole than has local politics in many other countries. Turkey's "unfinished revolution"[88] left a decisive imbalance in rural and regional power and encouraged national politicians during the early years to use a geographically balanced development strategy as a nation-building device. At the same time, the absence of a functionally based revolutionary coalition, like that seen in the sections of Mexico's ruling party, afforded local politicians opportunities to construct local bases of power.

Local politics reflects, affects, and builds upon the structure of national political regimes. In Turkey, local political life has been particularly active when national politics has been openly competitive. Conversely, local political life was not very active during the early period of strong RPP control, when the first republican regime was preoccupied with forging a workable ruling coalition at the top. Local politics at that time was often dominated by traditional elites.

If the Democrats gained a reputation as the pork barrel party, the RPP had itself constructed the pork barrel. Ataturk's initial commitment to the positive state and to national development structured the later competition among localities for state financial resources.

While integrating the periphery economically and socially, the national regime also created the basis for revitalized local politics in Turkey. The First Republic established political linkages between localities and the center of a disintegrating empire. By the 1940s, when the Democratic party was organizing in localities for the national elections, the linkages were there to be built upon. "To organize effectively in 40,000 villages had not been an easy task. It could not have been accomplished with horse and donkey transport."[89] At the same time, closer links between localities and the downgrading of the periphery to a "lower slope" gave opposition parties—first the Democratic party and then the RPP—the stimulus to develop stronger local organizations.

Grass-Roots Politics

3 All grass roots are different. How politicians behave is affected by political party competition, local mythologies within the political culture, economic transformations occurring within regions, and the legal-institutional framework that exists. Yet despite these differences, local politics everywhere is the in-between politics of mediation. Local politics is quite simply the issues that local politicians deal with and the strategies they pursue in competing for power.

The informal rules of the game produce variations in local politics within a single nation. National authority may be regarded as binding in some localities; rarely is it so regarded in all localities. In the New England region of the United States, for example, the same formal authority structure applies to town governments throughout each state. Yet within these states and even within particular regions in the states, vast differences among town governments and town politics exist. The city of Rochester, New Hampshire, is run by a long-term, iron-handed mayor. The mayor has been able to do little to improve the local economy, badly depressed since its textile mills moved south. But his constituents have responded to his repeated pledges to keep taxes low. By contrast, in nearby Portsmouth, partisan competition for city office is vigorous and debate is relatively open. Portsmouth's population has been growing rapidly, it is prosperous, and the level of public services is high.

Where local politics stops and national politics begins is difficult to determine. The legal authority of national institutions and that of local institutions usually are separate and distinct. But, politically, policy is made and unmade in a more fluid way. Issues—such as environmental pollution—are raised in local politics that are national in scope. Conversely, local politicians turn to national elites for allies in local conflicts. Local politics is an arena with legal boundaries but one with political limits that can only be strategically defined. The web of power that distinguishes local from state and national politics is defined by political competition—(1) the politicians who participate in the fray, (2) the issues that arise, and (3) the strategies employed to acquire influence. Strategies developed by political actors define the jurisdictional scope of local and national governments as much as do formal allocations of authority.

LOCAL POLITICIANS

Political competition at the local level comes as much from the interaction of national and local politicians as it does from predominantly local conflict. Local politicians often are caught in the middle, between national politicians and their constituents. For example, it is upon the skills of the local politicians that resolving conflicts between national policies and local interests depends. Local politicians share this intermediate position, and the flexibility it permits them in defining their roles.

There are almost as many different kinds of local politicians as there are positions for them to fill. Mexico's *cacique* (a local political boss) brings entrepreneurial skills to his job and perhaps the reputation of gallant ancestors—but usually not electoral victories. The lineage subchief of West Africa tries to live up to his distinguished family name and chooses his advisors on the basis of their wisdom and age. In India, city councillors look forward to eventually moving into national offices through their alliances with state politicians; if they can build enough support in a political party, they are likely to succeed.

The Mexican *cacique*'s way of politics is informal. The activities in which he engages, his political strategies, and the standards by which his leadership abilities are evaluated are not specified in any authoritative document. In fact, the *cacique*'s position often is hereditary partly because the necessary skills can be learned best by observation rather than formal training. On the other hand, the *commandant de cercle* (mayor) in Mali occupies an office that carries with it formal authority; its occupant has very specific tasks.[1]

We can make sense of such an assortment of offices and roles by categorizing local politicians on the basis of whether their roles are formally defined and whether their offices are elective or appointive.[2] In nearly every country, local politicians can be found who fit these different categories. And in every country, local politicians define their roles in many different ways.

The Malian *commandant,* for example, is an important figure in the local party organization even though his job description does not include party activities. Other local politicians in practice define their roles more narrowly than is called for legally. For example, municipal decision-makers often complain that, in the face of steadily rising demands for expanded public services, they are unable to use their legal authority to the fullest extent because of the severe constraints those demands place upon local financial resources.

The distinction between the skills and performance of politicians who are accustomed to electoral politics and those who are not can be deceptively slight. This is particularly true in the developing countries where elective offices are comparatively new and corresponding political roles are still vaguely defined.

Many traditional politicians readily adapt themselves to elections because their influence has always involved a measure of popular consent. Local politics encourages this kind of flexibility because local constituencies are smaller, politics is more personal. Historically, Mexican *caciques* were not elected. But modern *caciques* often seek the legitimacy of elected office and have proved themselves adept at secular political organization and tactical maneuver.

Similarly, in the course of Iran's constitutional movement at the turn of the twentieth century, local councils (*anjomans*) were formed and run by coalitions of religious and business leaders. One such renowned Iranian nationalist and clergyman, Seyyed Hossein Taqizadeh, showed his "modern" political skills through his highly successful career as an orator, writer, parliamentarian, and faction leader. Even in contemporary politics the Iranian clergy plays political roles in the parishes similar to that of the urban ward heelers in American politics.

In addition to describing local politicians' roles as traditional or modern, or formal or informal, we can describe them as mediating roles. Local politicians have unique concerns as middlemen. At the core of the local politician's role is a strategic choice. Grass-roots politicians must choose between accommodating or opposing national politics.

During the Cultural Revolution in China, for example, local factions each claimed to have the most valid interpretation of Chairman Mao Tse-tung's ideas. Eventually, this factionalism thwarted the implementation of central government policies so severely that ending it became an overriding objective for the national regime. The cleavages had divided administrative units and levels of government. Consequently, those local politicians who served as mediators in such cross-cutting conflicts had to have influence that spanned the formal boundaries of office. Within that context, those local politicians who could pull various factions together were highly praised. Shanghai, for example, was singled out "as a national model of success in creating alliances of both old and new cadres."[3]

From the perspective of national elites, the most valuable attribute which local leaders can possess is an ability to support the national regime by creating alliances among local influentials. Local administrators have been compared to team captains "that cooperatively seek to influence public outcomes."[4] Such a description applies equally to local politicians in elective offices.

Local politicians use various strategies in their roles as mediators between the grass roots and the nation. Where political, social, and economic power are merged at the local level, conflict management becomes a question of *protecting the local elite structure* against extralocal intervention. Where more local competition prevails, local politicians seize more opportunities to serve actively as *spokesmen for specific local interests* within extralocal political arenas. Where both approaches fail, as they sometimes do, local politicians become arms of the national regime—regardless of how much formal authority their offices possess.

ISSUES IN LOCAL POLITICS

Local politicians build their influence by developing local and extralocal alliances. Local alliances tend to be based on personal favors or personal relationships. Sometimes politicians use public issues to develop local support, but that usually occurs when they are interested in going on to national office or trying to help political allies at the national level. The issues that preoccupy local officeholders are either "grievance issues," or issues around which people within a locality can be rallied against nonlocals or outsiders. The most consistent complaint of local officeholders is that constituents themselves tend to raise specific demands on an individual basis (grievances) but rarely make general policy recommendations. Cleaning specific streets and putting in particular sewers often takes priority over promoting a general policy on streets and sewers that takes in the entire locality. General policy issues arise more often in conjunction with competition between local and extralocal groups.

Local and extralocal politics are woven together within the calculus of specific decisions. Some issues seem by nature solely local in content—such as decisions about which streets to pave. Others become local because the politicians who raise them benefit from defining them as local. National politicians may seek to contain debate on issues by emphasizing their particularistic qualities. Or local politicians will try to expand their influence by emphasizing the need for their services as middlemen. For example, the local politician might argue that a particular national issue is also a local issue and, hence, that there is a need for a local mediator to resolve it.

Localizing issues involves relating them to the underlying local interests outlined in chapter two—cultural, political, historical, economic, and authoritative. The political alliances that are formed in the process can be predominantly local or a mixture of local and national—depending upon the coalition of interests involved.

Environmental control has this kind of an elusive identity. Japanese voters, in response to worsening environmental pollution, have raised home rule demands and emphasized the local aspects of the issue. In

Iran, similar environmental concerns have been raised as questions about planning priorities at the national level.

Environmentalists in Japan, like those in Iran, view rapid and uncontrolled industrialization as the cause of their pollution problems. Japanese environmentalists saw the political problem as being related to the decisions made during the 1950s and 1960s by the ruling Liberal Democratic party. But they chose to bring political pressure to bear at the local level for reasons of strategy; their concerns overlapped with those of leftist parties' members, who were opposing the Liberal Democratic regime and winning local offices.

Japanese opposition party candidates had been only moderately successful in national elections when campaigning on foreign policy issues. But they were elected to local offices in increasing numbers on the basis of environmental platforms.[5] At the same time, Japan's antipollution movement produced a new ideology of community action through citizens movements and consultation between citizens and officeholders. In the end, both specific local electoral outcomes and local political processes were affected by what originally was a national issue.

Certain political issues like pollution, when raised in one locality, have immediate repercussions beyond the locality itself. Such local issues are expandable extralocally by virtue of their policy impacts and their consequent political potential. Expandable issues involve interests that are found in more than one locality and that therefore have the potential for being broadly mobilized. These interests arise from shared situations that are turned into political issues in one locality after another until they either become national issues or are resolved. The process of issue expansion is hastened or retarded by rapid communications among localities but ultimately depends upon the ability of local politicians to perceive the advantages of developing the local dimensions of extralocal issues.

For example, the prices that agricultural products command are a matter of common interest among French farmers. Farmers' groups have been organized from time to time, both to influence the central government's agricultural price policies and to solicit votes for specific political parties. Yet these French farmers' organizations have consistently failed to build effective links among localities that historically tended to hold one another in mutual suspicion (see chapter five).

Other issues are more localized by nature. They revolve around controversies over specific problems unique to a locality. Controversies over which streets will be paved within a locality are often decided more by competition among residents than they are by relations between local residents and outsiders. While transportation does have an extralocal dimension, where to pave streets usually does not affect national policy to the same extent as do attempts to organize French farmers or Japanese environmentalists.

In sum, issue expansion among levels and localities is a complex process, but a few guidelines do apply. First, there is a *policy impact,* a factor often highlighted in the public administration literature. Second, the *similarity of particular conditions* from locality to locality can encourage collaboration among local politicians and administrators (e.g., mayors' conferences on municipal fiscal problems). Third, local issues are expanded when the process offers local politicians *opportunities to obtain extralocal allies* or when it offers national politicians a means to shift the focus of conflict over an issue to an arena which they can more readily dominate. In the Japanese case, national Liberal Democratic politicians turned the local platforms of leftist parties (which advocated *minimal security*—a combination of welfare and environment) into a Liberal Democratic national plank favoring devolution of authority for welfare programs to city government. If successful, such a maneuver could relieve the Liberal Democratic party of responsibility for welfare problems, thereby preventing them from affecting national elections, but leaving them to plague the leftist mayors.

POLITICAL STRATEGIES AND LOCAL POLITICS

Local politics is especially salient in competitive party regimes. Partisan electoral strategies heighten the significance of local politics both through pork barrel politics and through party opposition strategies. In competitive political systems where national leaders are elected from local territorial constituencies, every election is to some degree a local election. Candidates appeal to voters by agreeing to promote local interests. During election campaigns, the overlap between national and local issues becomes especially evident, although it persists in a more subtle form between elections.

For example, local politicians can support ruling parties and thereby bring national resources to their constituents. "Climbing on the bandwagon" is a maxim that local politicians apply to national politics, just as faction leaders do to intraparty politics. Officeholders who represent localities at the national level can help their constituencies gain access to national resources and influence by supporting the party in power. Voters in the Malaysian village of Rusila supported the United Malays National Organization because that party participated in the ruling alliance. While the alliance controlled the national government, voters thought that the Malays National Organization's candidates would be better able to bring public works funds to the village.[6]

In Malaysia, and elsewhere, an important stimulus for local politicians to support national ruling groups, whether they are parties or factions, is the potential for attracting national resources to the locality. The national pork barrel is a universal foundation upon which national-local political links are established. Influence flows in both directions in such exchange relationships. Local politicians are able to deliver material benefits to their constituents, and national elites can acquire political allies at the local level who can marshall votes, intervene in the policy implementation process, and interpret their objectives to local constituencies.

Local politicians, by their example, also can contribute to the legitimacy of the political rules of the game. This function is particularly valuable to political regimes whose rule has not been legitimized over time. For example, in the years prior to the 1972 imposition of martial law in the Philippines, local politicians were instrumental in implementing regime objectives. By 1972, however, these local politicians had become less supportive of the national regime and of the political process that supported it. A study of local politicians' attitudes during this period showed that these politicians had become increasingly disillusioned with the rigged elections and strong-arm tactics of national elites, which they were expected to support.[7] Without this local support, President Marcos had no possibility of ruling without resort to coercion.

In such an extreme situation, the national pork barrel probably cannot create enough influence to maintain supportive national-local linkages. In fact, where there is strong partisan opposition to national elites, the local political arena often is the focal point for opposition strategies in which much more is at stake than incremental decisions about the distribution of public resources. Chae-Jin Lee's and Young Whan Kihl's studies of Korean politics, which examined the relationship between the distribution of central government resources and urban political opposition to the ruling Democratic Republic party, found no significant correlation between the two.[8] Pork barrel is used more successfully to *reaffirm* supportive relationships than to try to influence opposition groups.

In openly competitive political systems, local and extralocal politics frequently merge as a result of competition among organized political parties. Local offices provide opposition parties with opportunities to gain a foothold in national politics without risking too many resources. Opposition party leaders also find the less visible local political arena to be a more secure setting—an arena in which opposition politics can be played with less risk of suppression. The Italian Communist party, for example, has adopted this strategy, as has the Indian Communist party.

Similarly, new groups that are trying to advance *within* parties sometimes try first to enter local office or to control local party machinery. This pattern has been followed by such diverse groups as the McGovern Democrats in the United States prior to the 1972 party convention and various rural elites in India who, after migrating to the cities, wanted to move into urban political life through the Congress party.

How useful local politics is as an entry point to national office in competitive political systems depends upon the structure of political competition at the national level. Table 1 illustrates the differences. Local politics tends to be more competitive in a national dominant-party system, where incremental (local) gains in power are marginally more valuable to the minority party than they are to opposition parties in a more pluralistic national setting.

Table 1: Variations in Party Competition

Type Elections	Dominant-Party System	Two or Three Party Balanced System
Local	Vigorous Opposition	Irregular Opposition
National	Opposition in Isolated Areas	Vigorous Opposition

Political parties operate differently in local politics than they do in national political competition. Many writers have noted the presence of nonpartisan political traditions within local political arenas.[9] The nonpartisan quality of local politics makes it more difficult for political opposition groups to organize grass-roots support.

Three factors contribute to the nonpartisanship of local politics. First, within small political units any political cleavage appears to be potentially more threatening.[10] Second, local politics is often viewed as a management issue—one responsive to administrative solutions but not amenable to competitive political solutions.[11] Third, many local administrators and their allies in business build their own influence by condemning the evils of politics and politicians.[12]

That local politics is more than a management issue is apparent in the way that it is used by political opponents of national ruling elites. Even insurrectionist groups with national objectives often try to proceed from well-entrenched local positions, despite the fact that their objectives lie beyond capturing specific local offices. Because their strategies are so similar, the different objectives of insurrectionists (or separatists) as compared to merely competitive groups can be hard to discern.

The Nigerian regime, even after the Biafran separatist war, has continued to face severe regional conflict. In order to reduce regional cleavages during the first decade after the Biafran war, the four political regions existing before the war were transformed into twelve states and their governments staffed by appointees of the national regime. The military regime has provided the basis for an alliance between those who favor a return to constitutional rule, those who support a revitalization of regional and local government, and advocates of social reform. Local politics is part of a broad challenge to the national regime.

As the Nigerian example indicates, nonelectoral strategies also bring local politics into the national arena. In order to reduce opposition by strengthening their control over local politics, national politicians in many countries have tried to change the ground rules of local politics, either indirectly by regulating local institutions or directly by creating new institutions. For example, land reform has been followed in many countries by the creation of new public institutions in the rural areas affected by the reforms. National bureaucratic elites organize local support through government-managed cooperative societies and through local branches of government political parties.

This directed political change is reminiscent of the policies of the former colonial rulers of many countries. British, French, and United States colonial policies all assumed that nationalists' demands for independence could be outflanked by creating institutions of local government and by opening participation in politics at the local level.[13] Some of the local government structures created by the colonial powers still exist in the independent states.

These imported local government systems still influence local politics. Political institutions that were created by newly independent regimes under a strategy of "subordinate participation" have continued to be less powerful than have both older indigenous local institutions and imported ones. It takes time for political institutions to develop significant roles.[14]

The frequent reform or restructuring of local governing institutions by national politicians contributes to the insecurity of local office-holders as well as to the fragility of the institutions themselves. Consequently, many local politicians try to move up to higher positions and make unusual efforts to avoid assuming political responsibility.

The mobility and insecurity of local politicians in the short run complemented the interests of national elites whose power is threatened by the development of autonomous local power centers. Accordingly, national elites have abolished local institutions outright when they appeared to serve as foundations for local power centers.

Such national intervention is officially justified by the financial insolvency of local institutions, the destructiveness of local factionalism, and/or various national emergencies. In rural localities political intervention is frequently justified by the argument that rural politics is antidemocratic and therefore in need of reform. In this connection, rural voters have been characterized as rigid and uninformed, and rural politics as patron based and elitist. By contrast, city politics is variously portrayed as more competitive, less stagnant, and more complex than rural politics.[15]

Such a polarized view of urban and rural politics is not warranted, however, according to evidence available from a broad spectrum of rural areas. Detailed analyses of election turnouts dispel the once-accepted notion that local politics universally stimulates less voter participation than does national. Rural voting turnout can be just as high as turnout in urban areas.[16] In fact, voting patterns in Japanese elections show that rural Japanese participate more than do urban voters in both local and national politics.[17] Local elections do bring out rural voters. In contrast, the ballots of urban voters are not sufficiently effective in influencing policy to keep turnout consistently high.

On the other hand, rural voters appear to vote out of habit as much as from their positive assessments of what each vote can accomplish. Rural turnouts depend upon the existence of political cultures in which local influentials support voting—not because of their commitment to democratic norms but because votes can legitimize the influentials' positions. By introducing new governing institutions in rural areas, national regimes create additional avenues for extralocal influence to enter the local political arena and challenge traditional elites. Although these changes may make local politics more competitive, they also may indirectly cause rural voting turnouts to decline over time.

Urban local politics appears to be affected by extralocal influences more frequently and more regularly than rural politics. More competition for local office is one consequence of that impact. In France, for example, urban political contests draw more contestants than do rural.[18] Together, the cities' lower voter turnouts and higher number of contestants for office suggest an interpretation of urban/rural contrasts other than that which associates urbanization with democratization. Urban power configurations are less stable. Potential officeholders are able to find extralocal support to challenge incumbents. In other words, the power that is exercised by the urban officeholders is more contingent.

Table 2 illustrates the ways in which politicians reach across jurisdictional boundaries, building upon the contingency of local power. The success of the strategies depends upon the alignment of political forces at the national and local levels. Because rural voters turn out in larger numbers for local and national elections, for example, conservative national regimes often can rely upon rural support. But this outcome is contingent upon the local political culture and the local influentials who get out the vote. National strategies that undermine those local influentials may also undermine the basis for rural mobilization.

Table 2: Political Strategies and Localizing Issues

Type Strategy	National Politicians	Local Politicians
Long Term	Directed political change—creating new institutions or changing the rules of the game.	"Capturing" local offices for opposing national elites. Demanding regionalization of national institutions.
Short Term	Offering specific "rewards" to localities—pork barreling	Making extralocal alliances around specific issues and/or favors

Such strategic calculations have nonpolitical dimensions too. As the case studies of India and Japan that follow show, a realistic model of grass-roots politics also would place these strategies within the context of socioeconomic processes. Grass-roots politics is a three dimensional pattern of local and extralocal linkages in which politicians' strategies influence and are influenced by socioeconomic processes. The case studies focus on the political issues and actors against that background.

SUMMARY—THE MEDIATING INFLUENCE OF LOCAL POLITICS

Local politics is the court of *first* resort—the first layer of conflict and compromise in a political system. It involves a wide range of issues—from personal favors to the implementation of major policies. Local leaders seldom have as much authority as do national leaders. And they rarely control the instruments of violence—the police and the military. As mediating or in-between politics, the possibility and the incentive for buck-passing present themselves here as nowhere else.

Nonetheless, the local politician's role is critical. Individual politicians can develop positions of considerable influence as intermediaries. Many of them exhibit a Tammany Hall knack for seizing available opportunities. While the discussion of political strategies in this chapter relates primarily to competitive political systems, the analysis of issues and actors applies to noncompetitive systems too. The political repertoire of local politicians does not depend upon electoral strategies alone. Pork barrel politics, the creation of new local institutions, and the regionalization of national politics are universal means of using local politics in the competition for influence.

Japan—A Case Study in Progressive Parties and Local Politics

Japanese local politics attracted an unusual amount of attention during the mid-1970s. Most of the publicity was a result of the election of increasing numbers of "progressive" local governments—governments supported by coalitions of Japan's Socialist, Communist, and Komeita parties. Observers speculated about what this progressive trend at the local level meant. There was particular interest in what would be the political future of the Liberal Democrats, who had dominated Japanese politics since 1955 and even earlier under other party names.

Of almost equal interest to students of Japanese politics was the unusually high rate of participation in local elections.[19] Local elections had brought as much as 90 percent of the voters to the polls. The Japanese experience contradicted the then widespread assumption that local political contests could not attract voters to the polls. In Japan's relatively centralized political system, voters did indeed turn out in response to appeals from local political candidates.

This case study focuses upon the trend of electing progressive local governments—how it occurred and the extent to which these elections represented a permanent shift in Japanese politics. Answering that question leads us to fundamental attributes of local politics—some characteristically Japanese and others shared by many political systems.

Japanese politics is unique in the way that the local political contests are structured. Japanese municipal and prefectural offices are elective. Yet, the Japanese governmental system as a whole is unitary, not federal. Consequently, local election outcomes are tied to national political processes to an unusual extent.

At a more general level, these national links mean that local politics in Japan is similar to that in other competitive political systems. National issues arise in local elections. Conversely, national politicians respond to issues that arise first in local politics.

Opposition parties use voters' interest in local politics to coalesce grass-roots support. As a result, local politicians in Japan find themselves embroiled in conflicts over extralocal issues the outcomes of which they cannot effectively control through local government. They also take advantage of the opportunities that the national political arena affords them for building support locally. Particularly in Japan's rural areas, local politicians also can benefit from the traditions of local participation and political obligation that contributed to stable political support systems.

Local politics in Japan is sufficiently distinct from national politics to be regarded as a significant means of political expression. At the same time, *local* Japanese politics mirrors two models that have been derived from *national* politics—"Japan, Inc.," and factionalism.[20]

Japan, Inc., refers to an interlocking directorate of ruling politicians and top industrialists that forms the national governing coalition in Japan. A similar coalition of political and economic interests has been visible at the local level as well. Industrial growth objectives and industrialists themselves have influenced local political competition.

In local elections progressive parties have capitalized on the maleffects of industrialization and economic growth, particularly the problems of environmental pollution, to draw votes away from the ruling Liberal Democratic party (LDP). Factionalism prevails in local politics as it does at the national level; the fortunes of the LDP and of the several parties that have opposed the LDP give form to local political competition. Factionalism within the LDP and the factions among the opposition parties create a particularly fluid electoral politics at the municipal and prefectural levels.

PARTY POLITICS AND LOCAL POLITICS

Contemporary Japanese local politics has been strongly influenced by the fact that the Liberal Democratic party has been in power since World War II. Local political competition in Japan has come largely from leftist opposition to entrenched LDP elites and opposition to the social and environmental effects of industrialization. The LDP has presided over Japan's postwar economic recovery. But it has been an economic recovery accompanied by the movement of industries out from the cities and by urban congestion and pollution. Japan's prime ministers have governed, albeit uneasily at times, with the backing of an industrial establishment that had been effectively intertwined with government since well before the war.

Factions have dominated intraparty politics in LDP. Party cohesion, when it has been achieved, has been an outcome of overlapping interests among individual party leaders—primarily parliamentary representatives. During elections, the LDP has been a collection of personal factions from the national governing body (the Diet), rather than a unified machine or a collection of local, prefectural, and national officials. Several candidates for parliamentary posts have run simultaneously under the LDP banner in multimember Diet constituencies, for example. That has exacerbated the instability of electoral alignments.

The LDP's factionalism exists within a centralized party structure. Decisions about party nominations have been made by national party leaders, so local politicians have had little incentive to work on the party's grass-roots organization. The party's candidates have been more dependent upon national patrons than upon local support. For many years, running on the coattails of the central government's performance was the most successful strategy for a new candidate.

By the 1970s, this had ceased to be true in many constituencies. By 1974, opposition mayors had been elected in more than two hundred Japanese cities.[21] Opposition governors had been elected in the prefectures of Tokyo, Osaka, Kyoto, Soitam, and Okinawa. Observers began to speculate about what the local opposition victories augured for national electoral trends. Could the opposition parties capitalize upon their local victories in national elections and effectively challenge the LDP at the highest level? Or were local elections an entirely separate phenomenon, with voters responding to different issues and with different coalition patterns appearing at that level?[22]

National LDP politicians had proven themselves able to protect their power before. In the 1950s, the Japanese Socialist party had offered a serious threat to the LDP leadership. But the socialist challenge was curbed by the LDP's economic record and by the close-knit elite structures of Japan, Inc.

The succeeding two decades of power increased the liabilities of the LDP sufficiently that they could be challenged once again—this time by parties with effective grass-roots organizations that had acquired control of local offices. Since little was known about Japan's grass-roots politics and party organizations, particularly in terms of their links with national elites, the progressive parties' electoral victories came as a surprise. Yasumasa Kuroda, a student of Japanese politics (whose field research was carried out in 1963, before the swing toward progressive local authorities), found the LDP firmly entrenched in the locality he studied—Reedtown.[23] According to Kuroda, national pork barrel would keep local voters in line and, more notably, could be used to induce local political leaders to remain with the LDP. Kuroda found that although only 43 percent of the general public reported a preference for the LDP, 95 percent of the "top leadership" in the town chose the LDP.[24] Kuroda attributes this rather remarkable cleavage between the LDP leadership and the voters of Reedtown to the effects of holding local office in a highly centralized polity; local officials have too little power to make themselves distinct from national party leaders.

In retrospect, the Reedtown case can be interpreted as an example of a highly unstable alignment of local party supporters. The Japanese Communist party had been building strength over the post–World War II period. By the 1970s, the Communist party had become a major opposition party at the local level, whereas in the past the Japanese Communist party and the Japanese Socialist party had competed and split the progressive vote. Over a period of twenty-four years, for example, election statistics for Kyoto show that the Japanese Communist party and the LDP consistently backed different candidates. In later years, the Japanese Socialist party joined forces with the LDP.[25]

The serious commitment of the Japanese Communist party to electoral politics has been partly responsible for the growing numbers of opposition local governments. Traditionally, candidates for local office in Japan have run as independents, and partisanship at the local level has been criticized as detrimental to the spirit of the collectivity. The more recent polarization of voting between the LDP and the Japanese Communist party indicates a new type of local political competition.

Nonetheless, at the national level the LDP has been able to retain narrow control of the cabinet. Disputes within the opposition parties sapped their strength, often by pitting national and local leaders against one another. In the 1974 Kyoto gubernatorial elections, the Japanese Socialist party incumbent very nearly lost his office as a result of a split between his party's national leadership and the local Kyoto branch of the party. Local Socialist party politicians were anxious to support a new candidate in preference to the governor, Ninagawa Torazo, who had been in office since 1950. Local Socialist party leaders thought Ninagawa's candidacy would contradict the long-standing disapproval by socialists of "gerontocratic rule."

Ohashi Kazutaka, the local party's choice, was expelled from the party by the national leadership. But he continued the race for governor and acquired the support of the LDP along the way. For the first time, the LDP did not run a candidate of its own.

The progressive coalition that had voted Ninagawa into office in previous elections had split, and as a result, the LDP could influence the elections despite its minority position. Ninagawa won in 1974, as he had in the six previous elections, but his majority was far slimmer than it had been before. Between the years 1970 and 1974, his margin declined from 140,000 to 4,500.[26]

National leaders in the LDP had decided to pursue a more flexible strategy, distinguishing between local elections—which they felt could be lost—and national contests—which were more critical. In not fielding a candidate for the governorship, the LDP leaders could play a balancing role in the local elections. At the same time, the party could run its own candidate in national elections, where it had the advantage of being the ruling party. That strategy seemed to work. In the same year (1974), the LDP candidate won the Kyoto prefecture by-elections for the Diet. The LDP's Diet vote was higher than was the socialist governor's—winning by a margin of 31,000 votes. By contrast, the Japanese Socialist party candidate for parliament was the weakest vote-getter.

As long as the LDP maintained political control at the national level, its leaders could develop other kinds of strategies for influencing local elections too—gerrymandering was one. Gerrymandering alters the boundaries of voting districts. It enables politicians essentially to choose their constituencies. The LDP manipulated city boundaries to the party's advantage by strategic metropolitan consolidation maneuvers.

Metropolitan consolidation often is advocated as a means to improve public services and to expand the city's tax base. In Japan's case, the LDP has also benefited politically in municipal elections by incorporating conservative suburban and village voters into the city's rolls. Kariya, a city near Osaka, was consolidated in this manner. As a result of gerrymandering, the LDP was able to continue its control over Kariya local politics throughout most of the 1960s—despite industrial development in the city and growing numbers of working-class voters.[27]

Kariya's candidates from the progressive parties relied upon local union organizations for support. Kariya had a large labor base that could be mobilized; 62 percent of the city's employed were in secondary occupations in 1969 (i.e., mining, construction, and manufactures). Kariya was the center of Toyota's automobile manufacturing enterprises, and affiliated industries had also located there over the years. Union leaders in the city participated in a local labor council, and at least one council leader reached the prefectural assembly.

According to Gary Allinson's political history of Kariya, progressive candidates for national offices did receive a relatively united vote from some parts of Kariya. Still the union vote was less united than it might have been. Local progressive candidates were not successful prior to 1967, and much of their success after that could be attributed to the fact that Kariya's industrial leaders lost interest in city politics.[28]

Cleavages among progressive union voters at the local level were encouraged by the structure of the unions nationally and by the orientation of Japanese firms toward their employees. First, the local unions were affiliated with different national "centers" or federations. Such vertical links emphasized the factional, personalistic tendencies of Japanese politics. They made it more difficult to move union political goals beyond the more personal successes of progressive local politicians. Second, Japanese industrial leaders have unusually comprehensive employee policies. Workers' living accommodations and social activities are usually provided by the firm for which they work. As a consequence, employers' political opinions are weighted more heavily by their employees.

For a number of reasons, then, the potential for the mobilization of labor by progressive parties is limited. "Throwing the (LDP) rascals out" can be more easily accomplished at the local level. Voters distinguish between local and national elections, using local elections to register protests against ruling LDP elites, while using national elections to ensure a more conservative, stability-oriented approach. Both the organization of the progressives' union constituency and the LDP's opportunities to structure elections to their own advantage further contribute to this insular character of Japanese local politics.

ISSUES IN LOCAL ELECTIONS

In addition to the LDP's long tenure in power, a second possible explanation for the turn to the left in Japanese local elections is the way in which specific issues were developed and used by local politicians. Concurrently with the LDP's emphasis upon regional development and the creation of conservative metropolitan constituencies, LDP leaders tried to stimulate party activism at the grass roots to counter opposition party strength at that level. Earlier, during the 1950s, the challenge had been at the national level, spearheaded by the socialists. By the mid-1960s, both the ruling party and the opposition had turned toward local political strategies. The specific political issues over which the LDP and the opposition were competing were national—national in origin and, ultimately, national in effect. Still they provided a basis for successfully challenging the LDP at the local level.

Tokyo's Metropolitan Assembly elections in 1973, for example, raised issues related to the performance of the LDP cabinet, not specifically local questions. A poll taken prior to the election showed voters thought that the most serious problems facing Tokyo were inflation (27 percent), housing shortages (21 percent), environment (16 percent), and the welfare of the aged and handicapped (13 percent).[29] These problems all related to policies within the scope of the national LDP government's authority, but it was the local LDP that lost seats in that election.

In response to the local defeats, a coalition of younger LDP Dietmen pressed for a less conservative image. Fukuda, the leading contender for then Prime Minister Tanaka's office, publicized his stand in favor of a redistribution of national wealth, a halt to inflation, and a stabilization of economic growth.[30]

At the same time that the LDP was absorbing opposition demands, some of the opposition parties were falling into line with one another on extralocal issues. Leaders of Komeita, a "clean government" party derived from one sect of Buddhism, decided to support the abrogation of Japan's security treaty with the United States. In 1973, Komeita gained only one seat in the Tokyo elections, although they expected more. Its leaders had hoped that by bringing their foreign policy stance into line with that of the other opposition parties, specifically the Japanese Communist party and Japanese Socialist party, they would benefit in future local elections.

Japanese local political campaigns raised a host of local and personal issues, as well as serving as a vehicle for opposing national policies.

Japanese politics, in fact, characteristically has been personal and not issue based. The success of candidates has often depended upon their honesty, their ability to deliver material benefits to their constituents, and other similar attributes.

In reality, however, personal and issue-based politics are not distinct categories but spill over into one another. In Reedtown, personal conflicts between the mayor and an erstwhile deputy mayor grew into an issue conflict over a school unification plan. Similarly, streets, economic development, and educaton were mentioned by Reedtown's population and its leaders as the most important issues "facing the town." Voters did not distinguish between issues amenable to control or influence by local officials and those requiring national involvement. Instead, local issues appear to have been viewed as *any* that clearly *affected* the voters.

Pollution, for example, has been a major issue in local elections, despite the fact that national action was needed to combat it. One reason for its local political salience was that it clearly affected some localities more than others. Some localities, in other words, seemed to be bearing more than their share of the costs of Japan's prosperity. Any policy outcome that makes a locality unique (a uniquely dangerous effluent from a town's factories, a uniquely high level of unemployment, etc.) is likely to result in national policies becoming local political issues.

Political capacity, as contrasted with the effects of various issues, has been another basis for raising policy issues at the local or national levels. Even though the local political arena has been a relevant site for raising environmental issues in terms of effect, local politicians do not have the political capacity to confront solutions to these issues in a serious manner. For example, mayors found themselves boxed in; "they . . . could not carry out what they promised their supporters."[31] As a result, environmental pollution remained important locally, with local opposition officeholders still unable to translate local concerns into national support.

Other issues were even less readily transferred from local to national elections. Foreign policy issues, for example, drew the most conservative positions from voters and ultimately benefited ruling centrist parties like the LDP. Sections of Tokyo that were thought to be shifting toward a progressive vote because of their opposition to nearby United States and Japanese Self-Defense Force bases still voted for LDP Metropolitan Assembly candidates.[32] The LDP retaliated against the opposition move to bring foreign policy into the campaign by vigorously attacking communists and communism. That appeared to dull the antimilitarist vote.

Another complicating factor that reduced the relationship between local and national issues was the component of voting that was not issue related. Many voters in Reedtown (half of those asked) mentioned no issues as being important for the town. Nonetheless, they voted. Some voters appear to go to the polls from a sense of obligation, without clearly relating their votes to issues.

The importance of issues was greater than the voters' comments implied, however. Even though many votes were not issue related, the policies that officials pursued suggested that politicians did interpret some issues along partisan lines. For example, the budget appropriations for the city of Kariya reflected the progressive electoral trends. During Kariya's rapid industrial growth, when business and conservative political interests were most closely allied and the LDP controlled local offices, much of the city government's revenue went toward the construction of industrial infrastructure—roads, electric lines, and housing. Later, under a more progressive city government, public expenditures brought more broadly shared urban services, like parks and roads throughout the city rather than just near the Toyota plant.

Local political processes in general, and electoral strategies in particular, contribute to the containment of opposition issues within the local political arena. LDP politicians have been most concerned with containing those opposition demands that interfere with the economic growth and security objectives of central ruling elites—that is, interference with the stability of the national regime. The central bureaucracy has supported the LDP leadership in these concerns through its control of bureaucrats serving at the local level and through its control of budgetary allocations.

LOCAL GOVERNMENT AND INSTRUMENTS OF CENTRAL CONTROL

The centralization of Japanese politics and administration, which was regarded as so helpful to the establishment of LDP power, had much to do with its eventual defeats at the local polls and its ability to maintain control over the national government at the same time. The ability of national elites to influence local politics by manipulating the allocation of public resources, for example, was a result of both the way in which authority was allocated among the three levels of government in Japan and the record of economic growth during the postwar period.[33] In the context of Japan's promising economic prospects, centralization of its politics meant that the political benefits of economic growth went to the national ruling party. In order to reap the rewards of this growth, however, the LDP leadership had to guide and direct it. The state administrative process was one means by which this could be accomplished; the state bureaucracy was as willing a partner in the postwar economic machine as it had been in earlier periods.

Japan has a unitary structure of local government, but it is unitary government with a popular twist. Beneath the national level are forty-six prefectures whose governors and unicameral assemblies are popularly elected. The Japanese local government system, as restructured by United States advisors during occupation, emphasizes the formal accountability of subnational authorities. Nonetheless, most of the functions of the prefectural authorities still are delegated by the national government. The number of such delegated functions began to increase after the occupation was over. But some, such as authority over police and education, have since reverted to the national level. The functions of Japanese local authorities are similar to those of local authorities in other countries—managing water, gas, and electricity supplies, collecting garbage, regulating markets, and managing schools. Perhaps the more unusual characteristic of local authority in Japan is its transformation since the war.

Because the 1945 structure was imposed from outside (i.e., by the United States), the postwar period has been a period of adaptation—a period during which the governing structure was made more appropriate to Japan. The central government, for example, has encouraged small towns to consolidate into larger metropolitan units. In addition, a plan was drafted by the central Autonomy Ministry to create federations of prefectures. The LDP bureaucracy's hope was to consolidate the prefectural system by making the governor's office appointive.[34] The political significance of this proposal was clear; no longer could governorships be captured by leftist opposition candidates.

Opposition governors have not behaved in office as differently from their LDP counterparts as one might imagine from the attention that reorganizing the prefectural system has received. Public office helps to determine the roles that public officials play, regardless of their party affiliation. Japan's progressive governors were encouraged to define their authority conservatively. The prefectural governor's major role has been to exercise political control over his district as a contribution to the stability of the larger system. Governors have fulfilled that political role regardless of party; they have accepted the definition of the office imposed by state doctrine. Japanese mayors, on the other hand, have exercised more diffused social control over their urban constituents.[35]

Yet official roles do change, sometimes without any explicit change in the authority of the office or in the party politics of its occupant. Pork barrel politics typically makes the roles of the prefect and mayor more significant, and this has been the case in Japan. The approach of the LDP central leadership to growth and stability was to spread the benefits of growth around sufficiently to help the party develop a broad electoral base. One means of accomplishing this regionalization of growth was to use national resources to help local authorities to attract industry.[36] Incentives in the form of national grants-in-aid were

matched by local initiatives to grant tax exemptions and other induce-
ments to industries seeking to relocate.

Both local officials and parliamentary representatives began performing the role of middleman for their localities—lobbying central
politicians and administrators for public revenues and for direct intervention with industrial leaders. In this manner, prefecture and city
officials became more explicitly political than they had been before.
Their contacts with central elites made the pork barrel system work and
gave local politicians influence. The traditional community leader became more specialized and more accountable for the costs and benefits
of growth and urban transformation. If national policies lost political
ground locally, so did the local politicians associated with them.

Cities that industrialized either very little or very late have tended to
have stronger political defenses against industrial elites. Moreover,
their officials have tended to be skeptical of the LDP's growth policies.
This negative response to industrial growth counterbalanced the nor-
mally conservative socioeconomic profiles of such cities. Kyoto, for
example, has a basically commercial, traditional economy with little
large industry. The city's small businessmen have been less favorable to
Japan's industrial growth under the LDP leadership than have the
country's industrial elites. Consequently, for many years Kyoto voted
in progressive local governments.

Other towns, like Kariya, are "has been" company towns. Their
industries moved out or expanded into cleaner, greener pastures.
Concurrently, LDP strength declined. When Toyota expanded into the
towns neighboring Kariya, progressive party candidates in Kariya
began to receive higher votes, and Toyota officials took a less active part
in city politics.

SUMMARY—THE LOCAL POLITICS OF PROTEST

"Natural" progressive or "natural" conservative constituencies in
Japanese local politics are difficult to identify without knowing the
effects of economic change upon particular local groups and of the
organization of the public sector on local economic change. Local
elections and the structure of local politics are influenced by the political economy of party competition.

The short-run strategies used by party leaders to influence election
outcomes have only short-run effects upon voting behavior. For example, Liberal Democratic politicians cannot rely completely upon national pork barrel politics to ensure solid majorities for their local
candidates in every city. National grants-in-aid to particular localities
rarely change the basic structure of the local economy. Cities that have
not been part of Japan's industrial "miracle" either have not been as

receptive to the LDP's pork barrel incentives or have not been offered those incentives. Pork barrel influence seems to be extended more effectively to party supporters than to local opposition party leaders.

Despite the limitations of influencing electoral outcomes by manipulating the distribution of public resources, the progressives' local successes did not necessarily indicate future progressive victories in national politics. The issues raised by the progressives in local elections often have been potentially national in scope, but voters have not translated them into national candidate preferences. Other issues have remained local because of their limited and temporary character.

The LDP's long-term strategies—gerrymandering voting districts that overrepresent rural voters and the proposed abolition of elected prefectural officials who now are increasingly progressive—remained in the background while the progressives' local influence grew. But by the mid-1970s, the fact that progressives had become encumbered with local authority began to dampen their ability to criticize the LDP's record. With the progressives in city hall, they were also in positions to be held at least partly accountable to the voters for the quality of urban life, an issue most had campaigned on earlier. LDP leaders could afford to adopt flexible local tactics—including supporting occasional progressive candidates—while mustering their strength for national contests. Local politics remained divided while the LDP ruled.

Japanese party politics has been relatively unorganized at the constituency level. Local factionalism has helped to insulate the LDP party at the center from local opposition challenges. Opposition voting patterns suggest that the Japanese Communist party may be becoming an opposition force of consequence. Local opposition organizations, however, still cannot support candidates for any office who do not have strong personal followings.

"Japan, Inc." and "factional Japan" summarize the dilemmas of local opposition politics. Local politics in Japan has been the court of first resort for progressive parties and for antigrowth environmental groups. Local politics may also be the court of last resort for both.

India—A Case Study in the Politics of Scarcity at the Local Level

For most Indians, local politics means village politics, and village politics is the politics of the land. Four-fifths of India's population lives in rural villages. They are governed at the local level by a complex structure of public and semipublic institutions. The structure is an amalgam of Indian and British tradition and contemporary theories about community development. Within this institutional framework, politics and power revolve around family, class, caste, party, and personality. Competition for public offices, and for the economic resources which officeholders allocate, takes place both during and between elections and in open debate and private counsel. Indian rural affairs, contrary

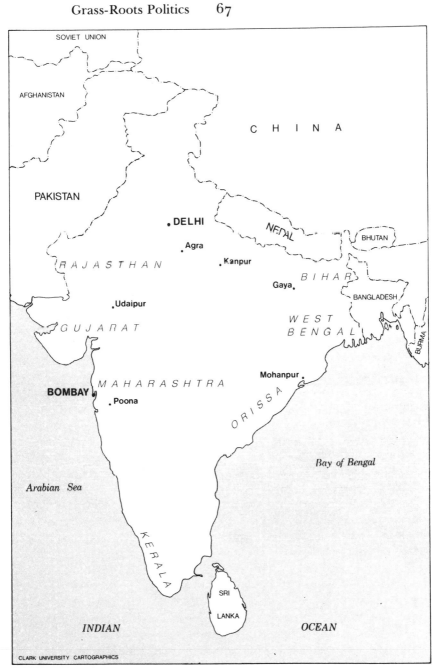

SOVIET UNION

AFGHANISTAN

C H I N A

PAKISTAN

•DELHI

•Agra

•Kanpur

R A J A S T H A N

NEPAL

BHUTAN

B I H A R

Gaya•

BANGLADESH

•Udaipur

W E S T
B E N G A L

G U J A R A T

BURMA

MAHARASHTRA

Mohanpur•

BOMBAY

•Poona

O R I S S A

Bay of Bengal

Arabian Sea

K
E
R
A
L
A

SRI

LANKA

INDIAN

OCEAN

CLARK UNIVERSITY CARTOGRAPHICS

to their image of simplicity and isolation, require politicians to operate within a complex network of influences that extends from the *village* cooperatives to the chief minister of the *state,* and even beyond to the *national* bureaucracy in New Delhi.

Because land is a vital asset, landownership historically has had a strong influence on village politics. Also historically, rural leaders have had wide influence, legitimized by extralocal political regimes—even when localities appeared to be relatively autonomous.

In the cities, as well as the villages, economic issues play a major role in local politics. Consequently, many characteristics of local politics also are shaped by what Myron Weiner has called India's "politics of scarcity."[37] Local government and party politics in independent India (1948–1977) contributed to the stability of the national regime. India's politics of scarcity has meant that grass-roots politics, while openly competitive, has been kept isolated as much as possible by the national regime so that redistributive issues raised there will not spread to national politics. In so far as that strategy has been successful, grass-roots democracy has been a valuable safety valve.

The Indian countryside is a mixture of farms, shops, and small industries. It is not exclusively agricultural, nor is it insulated from national politics and development policies. Decisions at the national level to emphasize public investment in industry, for example, reduce the amount of resources available for agriculture. In addition, the location of factories and processing plants affects local economies— changing employment opportunities, land values, and social inequalities.

Economic change has affected village political life directly. As village economies became more diverse, local political conflict became more complex. New cleavages developed within the population as factory owners competed with farmers for land and water. Land consolidation reduced tenant farmers to farm laborers. The laborers' political identities became those of socioeconomic class rather than traditional patron-client factions.[38]

Since independence, land reform programs have begun to equalize farmers' landholdings and have provided a legal framework for some former tenants to buy the land they farmed. Still, implementation of reforms is slow, and many farm workers are without land rights and without real employment security.[39]

Nonetheless, political competition has not significantly improved the weak position of the landless and has kept benefits flowing to those farmers well endowed with both land and capital. Local elites have been valuable political allies for national politicians, who themselves have been reluctant to undermine the elites' power by implementing economic reforms. Local institutions of popular government exist side by side with a continuing local politics of privilege.

In the past, local elites were landowners whose influence was a result of their local economic power and was legitimized by extralocal authority. For example, in the west Indian state of Maharashtra, land grants were made to individuals as payment for government service all through recent centuries.[40] The land grantees (*vatandars*) enjoyed tax-free occupancy of the land, which in many cases became a hereditary right. *Vatan* lands were sometimes purchased outright, in shares or in whole. One eighteenth-century deed, for example, stipulated a half-share in a land grant—this one made in exchange for collecting taxes and keeping order in a village.

Vatandars were very powerful in the villages because, in addition to collecting taxes and rents, they often allocated land. Although tax-free land grants and most of the associated duties have been abolished, many officeholders in Maharashtran villages are former *vatandars*.[41]

As the *vatandar* example shows, political power and economic privilege overlapped. Land tenancy laws favored larger and wealthier landholders—tax laws did also. Capital improvements of land to increase agricultural production did not affect the owner's tax assessments (which in some parts of India did not increase for periods of as long as thirty years). Legal requirements that land rents be paid in cash (not in kind or crops) forced tenant farmers and small landholders to participate in the cash economy. Although legal disadvantages have been abolished, small landholders and tenant farmers still are at a decided disadvantage in obtaining credit, in making farm improvements, and in influencing community decisions about crop production.

CONTEMPORARY LOCAL POLITICS IN RURAL INDIA

Credit and farming decisions are made within an institutional structure that is formally democratic. India's political system is federal. Indian villages within the states are at the base of a three-tiered system of local elective and administrative offices—the *panchayati raj*. The larger number of elective offices within the *panchayat* system provides ambitious vote-seekers with virtually an embarrassment of riches. Popular councils exist at all three levels—the village, the county (or block), and the district. The officers of the cooperative societies are also elected.

State governments have the authority to determine how rural subordinate councils are organized, just as they control the structure of municipal governments. This means that slight variations exist from state to state.

In the state of Maharashtra, a typical example, rural council members are both directly and indirectly elected. The village councillors are directly elected by all enfranchised citizens, who vote by wards. The size of the council depends upon the size of the village's population. Beyond the village, members of county and district councils are selected either (1) by a combination of direct election and indirect cooptation from other public organizations or (2) by agencies with specific functions, like the cooperatives. Block councils (*panchayati samiti*) include chairmen of cooperative societies within the block and district, and village councillors.[42] Finally, district-level popular councils (*zilla parishads*) include district cooperative society chairmen, elected members, and block council chairmen.

In addition to the popular councils and cooperatives, local politics in India involves political parties, trade unions, and voluntary associations. Most politicians have had experience in several of these organizations. These contacts can produce useful alliances with politicians from other villages.[43]

The formal connections among local political organizations often cause officeholders' domains to merge. One cooperative society, for example, can acquire voting membership in another and can send representatives to local popular councils. Cooperative society boards are chosen by only those members who have paid entrance fees. The cooperative leadership is a restrictive, interlocking group.

The diffusion of local power also is reduced by political alliances and networks of influence among officials in popular institutions. These alliances are fostered by political party interests. In one Maharashtra village council election, the district Congress party committee assured a particular candidate that he could be elected without opposition (*bin virodh*). This committee was made up of a trade union president, a member of the board of directors of a sugar factory (from a *vatandar* family), and a cooperative society officer. The candidate who was so favored went on to higher elective office and became the Congress district committee secretary.

The formal structure of Indian local government, the *panchayati raj*, also contributes to insulating local politics from severe partisan or issue conflict.[44] The *panchayati raj*, established in 1959, probably has received more international attention than any other system of local government and is regarded as a remarkably strong initiative toward decentralization for a newly independent and poor country. It is a unique blend of tradition and modern forms of local self-government, and a blend of carefully specified duties at each level.

Within the system, the district was given a major role in allocating government resources to the blocks within it.[45] Because control of the purse is at that level, the presidency of the district is a valuable "plum." Congress strategies focus on capturing that office and staying out of village factional politics. Professional politicians usually enter politics at the district level.

The district president's allocation of government resources gives him influence in local politics, but his influence has limits. Within the nationwide *panchayat* system, considerable variation in district-local relations exists; local politicians respond to external influence differently. For example, local politicians in a town in Orissa state turned down external grants-in-aid in order to preserve their autonomy.[46] The town, Mohanpur, was close to larger population centers and, in other respects too, quite integrated into the state's political system. But the local elites were still defensive of their influence. In addition to refusing certain forms of outside aid, they selected council members through the traditional town council rather than through elections.

The large number of elective offices does not mean that grass-roots politics is synonymous with grass-roots democracy. It is not. In Maharashtra, as elsewhere in India, cooperative, trade union, and political party leaders tend to be coopted from above rather than directly selected by each organization's membership at large. It is risky for a politician to appeal directly to voters without first being accepted by other politicians.

Much of the elite structure of Maharashtran rural politics revolves around bread-and-butter issues. As suggested by earlier examples, these issues are often resolved in favor of existing elites. Because economic issues are so important, popular councils have less power than do the cooperative societies, where voting members also are paying members. The opportunity to participate in cooperative politics is significant because cooperative societies are at the center of a network that controls agricultural credit, marketing arrangements, the employment of farm workers, harvesting schedules, and the operation of village retail stores.

The distribution of power within cooperatives and popular councils tends to mirror the distribution of agricultural wealth. Loans are granted to applicants with the largest farms, that is, to those who seem to be the best credit risks. Decisions made at the state and national levels sometimes contribute to rural inequality.[47] For example, farmer cooperatives are not subsidized enough to be helpful to poor farmers.

Outside the cooperatives, other aspects of grass-roots politics also indicate that wealth is an important basis for political influence. Particularly in north-central India, private farms and farm marketing organizations can be large enough to carry their owners into political networks. Paul Brass describes Congress party politics in a sugar-producing region of Uttar Pradesh as dominated by the larger growers and by the cane workers' unions.[48] Such a combination of party supporters is difficult to sustain, however, given that the major issues at the district level are both agricultural *prices* and agricultural *wages*. As a result, the Congress party organization had to rely partly upon a system of patron-client relations within the cane worker unions, which blurred the substantive issues, and partly upon tightening its control over district government. If they controlled district offices, Congress leaders could engage in a variety of maneuvers, like accusing mill owners of tax delinquencies, in order to gain support for the party.

The traditional economic power of landowners, and employers in general, still influences local voters. Village council elections in India show the effects of economic relationships upon politics. They indicate that lower classes are reluctant to vote against local landowners with whom they have had traditional peasant-retainer relationships.[49] The landowners, in turn, are often able to preserve their holdings through their positions on local councils.

Even the Communist party of India has apparently not made major efforts to bring the rural poor into its local organization.[50] In fact, in the Orissa town of Mohanpur mentioned above, the Communist party candidate for the state legislative assembly was a Brahmin (high caste). The local party made no attempt to recruit untouchables.

Local elections are not cut-and-dried affairs, though. Competition among factions is common. Competition has been so vigorous, in fact, that in one village the traditional Shramdan week, during which villagers donate their labor for a common public project, became a time for political maneuvering, not for community endeavors. Each faction had its own project and used the project as a vote-getting gimmick.

Factional competition has made intercaste alliances useful. Beyond the general powerlessness of the untouchables, India's caste system has provided a surprisingly flexible basis for contemporary political associations.[51] Despite the formal rigidity of caste designations, the large number and geographic diversity of castes has made it possible for individuals to change castes for political reasons. Recruiting members of lower castes also has been a symbolically valuable tactic for the major parties.

Intervention by district party leaders, seeking to broaden the base of a party's support, ensured the nomination of lower-caste candidates to local offices. On the other hand, the election of lower-caste village officials has rarely given them effective power over village affairs. The underlying reality is that power within village institutions is unevenly distributed.

PARTY POLITICS AND CITY GOVERNMENT

As a result of the political and economic limitations on Indian rural development, many of the rural poor have migrated to the cities. As a consequence, rural politics has had an impact well beyond the village. It is generally agreed by Indian social planners that even a modest redistribution of wealth to the rural poor would help stem urban migration.

Urban migration is politically important in at least two ways. First, national politicians fear that the urban poor can be more readily mobilized by radical politicians than they could as rural poor. Second, growing numbers of the poor further tax already strained urban public services.

By and large, rapid urbanization in India has been avoided. India has had one of the lowest rates of urbanization among Third World countries—less than 4 percent each year.[52] No one is quite certain why this has happened, although many have cited cultural values. Despite rural poverty and the very real political conflicts that accompany that poverty, village life in India has been idealized and hence is thought to discourage migration.[53] Much of this positive image of rural life, especially among the politically aware, is a reaction to India's experience as a British colony. Cities were seen as the locus of British control over India. Urban governments were meant to ensure the smooth functioning of the empire, with public subsidies from local taxes when necessary.[54]

Urban politics during the colonial period were full of nationalist debates. These debates eventually began to take priority over administering colonial public service. Many nationalist politicians were schooled in municipal office, including the late Prime Minister Jawaharlal Nehru. Nehru explained in his autobiography: "It so happened that year [1920] that leading Congressmen all over the country became presidents of municipalities."[55] And that experience in local government led to a strong commitment to elective local politics.

Together, the urban nationalist movement, efforts to prevent urban growth, and the village mystique caused urban and rural local political issues to merge. The links between urban and rural politics are political only; urban government is not part of the *panchayati* system. Urban local government is patterned after the British municipal corporation, which was exported to India and to Britain's other colonies. The first municipal corporation in India was established by the Bombay Municipal Act in 1888. According to this system, elected councillors serve alongside the municipality's chief executive officer and standing committees composed of both councillors and administrators. The chief executive officer is a member of the national Indian Administrative Service. As such he is subject to appointment by the government of the state in which the municipality is located and subject to transfer by the Administrative Service.

The chief executive officer is the key executive. There is an office of mayor, filled by election from among the corporation councillors. But the mayor's office tends to be more prestigious than powerful.

City residents vote for their councillors in wards, which are either multi- or single-member constituencies. Because residential segregation is confined to relatively small areas (areas smaller than in American cities, for example), some of the wards are quite heterogeneous in their caste composition.

The heterogeneity of wards accounts for the complicated ethnic arithmetic that Indian political parties use in urban elections. Socially diverse groups have been brought together in electoral alliances among the smaller parties and through decisions within the larger Congress party about candidates and issues. Urban Congress party membership has typically spanned caste and ethnic status, and its candidates for local office reflect the party leader's attempt to similarly balance the slate offered to the voters.

Local politics has been a safety valve for potential caste conflict. It is less common to find members of lower castes at upper levels of the Congress party leadership. Party membership offers opportunities for leaders of "the discontented castes" to participate in urban politics without radically changing the caste patterns of the party hierarchy.[56]

This balancing means that urban politics has been an amalgam of ethnic, class, and factional alliances. As a result, negotiations over nominations for city councils are extremely complicated. For example, leaders of the Jan Sangh party in Agra, who identify themselves with Hindu nationalism, have formed alliances for city council elections with Moslem parties.[57]

The ethnic arithmetic of Congress and other major parties often has countered the influence of specifically ethnic parties. For example, the Congress party during the mid-1960s nominated candidates from various ethnic communities for the Poona (Maharashtra) city council in response to the Marathan ethnic appeal of the Samuykta Maharashtra Samiti (SMS), a single-issue coalition. This coalition originally was formed to campaign for a separate Maharashtran state (established in 1966) but it competed in city and state elections as well. During that period, local Congress leaders had to contend with the national party's commitment to a bilingual, non-Marathan state. The local leaders opposed the national position and won, giving themselves a more secure position in state politics. In response to the Congress stance, the SMS appealed for support from local Gujaratis, residents of Poona who had migrated there from Gujarat state.

As these examples show, local politicians lean toward multiethnic appeals because safe electoral majorities usually depend on them. Marathan separatism gained political saliency with Poona's population growth and its development as an industrial center. According to the coalition statements, the Marathans' share in the economic benefits of development was a major political issue that, nonetheless, could not be resolved without support from outside the Marathan community. When Marathan dominance of state politics later appeared to have become a distinct possibility, non-Marathan voters returned to the Congress party.

In addition to ethnic and class conflicts, urban growth brings political cleavages that become the basis for partisan strategies. Urban growth exacerbates urban-rural conflicts. Accordingly, political parties often couch their appeals in terms of sectional interest. Urban politicians in both Agra and Poona felt "dwarfed" by their respective hinterlands.

The Congress party, ruling from independence until 1977, has been stronger in rural areas. As a result, Congress politicians have welcomed recommendations from city planners to extend metropolitan boundaries into adjacent rural areas. Metropolitan planning, consequently, has generated substantial conflict between Congress and those parties whose bargaining strength was affected.

In the cities, Congress' main competitors have been the Communist and Jan Sangh parties—part of the coalition ruling India in 1978. In the face of this competition, Congress leaders have been particularly concerned about division within the party. They knew that intraparty factionalism could severely hinder the performance of Congress city officials and hurt the party at the polls. Higher Congress party officials, therefore, intervened in urban factional disputes more than in rural conflicts. Higher officials also kept close watch over the performance of local Congress officials. Local officials were passed over for higher positions or denied access to party funds as a result of ineptness and factionalism. In one example, the Kanpur Development Board failed to complete a housing program for city workers. The late Prime Minister Nehru came to the city on tour and, discovering the incomplete program, suggested that the president of the board "be hanged."[58]

Congress leaders have used more than verbal threats to influence urban politics. For example, they have created special purpose metropolitan agencies whose members were appointed by Congress government officials at higher levels. The agencies exercised significant power over municipal affairs and afforded the Congress party opportunities to outflank opposition city officials. The city of Udaipur's Improvement Trust, for example, had a strong majority of Congress members even though the Jan Sangh party frequently dominated the elective municipal council.[59]

Congress leaders also have rejected proposals to give urban areas representation in district councils because such representation would provide opposition parties with an opening to the countryside.[60] Government leaders at the state level also have used their authority over local elections for partisan advantage. In 1967, the Congress government in Uttar Pradesh postponed municipal elections until after the scheduled general elections because its leaders thought they needed the time to mend factional disputes.

The municipality of Gaya was prorogued from 1955 until 1972 by the Congress-led Bihar state government. It was prorogued on the grounds of financial insolvency, but Gaya's insolvency only increased during its prorogation—in fact by thirty-four times. R. C. Prasad argues that the real motive of the predominantly rural state politicians for supersession was to gain power for the rural elites who were moving into city politics.[61]

Pork barrel politics was still another of the political strategies used by the Congress party to protect its organization. The public sector's role in the Indian economy is substantial, and the Congress party controlled the purse strings at the national level. Consequently, Congress leaders were in a position to offer significant rewards to loyal supporters. Conversely, if a village or town were to elect members of opposition parties, it could find that roads, dispensaries, and fertilizers were no longer available to it. For example, one survey of Rajasthan state legislators showed that districts with Congress party legislators received development funds and welfare allocations; districts with legislators representing opposition parties did not.[62]

In India, as in Japan, however, the pork barrel has not guaranteed local influence to the party ruling at the center. Jan Sangh candidates have enjoyed a nearly continuous plurality in Lucknow's municipal council, for example, despite the Congress candidates' access to state and national resources.[63]

ISSUES IN LOCAL POLITICS

Party considerations often involve local politicians in extralocal issues. Although Bombay is the capital of Maharashtra state, Bombay city councillors voted on a resolution to censor certain actions of the Communist-led Kerala state government.[64] The resolution did not involve Maharashtra, but it did involve the tactics of the Bombay council members' political parties. In fact, the resolution was regarded as so important that the Praja-Socialist party members on the council voted under an imposed whip.

Requiring local councillors to support a party position on foreign policy questions may seem far afield of their position as local representatives of local constituents, but the constituents of Bombay councillors have expressed more interest in issues like China's occupation of Tibet than in municipal issues like transportation and taxes. At the other extreme are the individual grievances that constituents take to their municipal councillors. Constituency "casework" usually involves complaints about housing and accounts for a major share of the contacts between councillors and their constituents. Local politics in the city is usually played pragmatically, according to a mixture of ward heeling, partisan alliance, and ethnic community interests. This was quite compatible with temporary, personal alliances among experienced politicians.

In some states and localities, economic issues have arisen in more direct ways. First, control of local elective offices has been a stepping stone to higher office for members of radical opposition parties, especially in the states of West Bengal and Kerala, where the Communist party is strong. This tactic has been used often enough, in fact, to put an end to the idea that Indians always vote ethnically or according to personalities. Indians "vote their pocketbooks" too, and that shows up in local elections. Voting patterns suggest that it is the uneven distribution of land within these states that accounts for much radical politics.[65]

Partisan conflict and economic conflict often overlap to such an extent that it becomes difficult to distinguish them. In Maharashtra, even the unionization of the two sugar factories was partisan. The All-India Trade Union Congress, in which the Communist party is active, organized the Shriram Cooperative Sugar Factory. The Congress party's Indian Trade Union Congress subsumed the other sugar workers' union, which controls the (privately owned) Phaltan Sugar Works.[66] Consequently, local labor disputes became enmeshed in statewide party conflicts through the two trade unions. The party-union alliances had the effect of merging economic and partisan interests. At the same time, the weblike political network dulled polarized confrontations because politicians were responsive to several different local constituencies. The same process that tied local politics to state arenas also papered over class conflicts and blunted moves toward a major redistribution of wealth.

Continuing failure to resolve fundamental redistributive issues played a role in bringing about the 1975 "Emergency" which abridged opposition rights. Yet, even with the declaration of the "Emergency" the de facto detente between the national Congress party and the Communist party of India remained intact. The new Congress leaders adopted a rural development stance championed earlier by the communists. Under strong pressure from the national Congress leadership, the redistribution of agricultural land was reportedly speeded up in many states. Several of these states had just previously come under president's rule, with the ministerial governments elected by the respective legislative assemblies being prorogued. At the same time, state government officials were encouraged to oversee the activities of lower officials, including village headmen who were responsible for the distribution of food rations. What remained to be seen was whether, in the long run, local politics could resume its role of insulating the national regime from class conflict.

Summary—Local Factions and Regime Stability

During the nearly three decades that elapsed between India's independence and the early 1970s, grass-roots politics was the politics of office-seeking and favor-seeking. Beneath the surface of competitive local politics stood the basic structure of status and wealth within which that competition took place.

The competitiveness and pragmatism of local politics in India temporized more than resolved the pressing issues of economic and social inequalities. Government at the grass roots has been partly a non-partisan, personalized politics of grievances. Political party leaders at the district, state, and national levels have tried to remain removed from the quagmire of local factional in-fighting.

Nonetheless, local contests continue to be fought, and governments to be formed and dissolved, on the basis of partisan considerations. Local politicians aspire to higher office and invite alliances with politicians at higher levels. Local politicians, conversely, are the foundation of partisan electoral organizations. India's vigorous grass-roots politicking has broadened the scope of political debate and has carried policy issues from the villages to the states and eventually to New Delhi.

The potential influence of local politics upon elections and policy outcomes at higher levels has encouraged extralocal politicians to devise both institutional and pork barrel strategies to maintain control over local political competition. In India, the district has become the locus of local-national and local-state relations. It is at that level that local and functional interests are merged into the party structure. It is also at that level that the "politicians of scarcity" try to insulate political competition from the issues of scarcity.

Bureaucrats and Politicians

4 Local politics is a brokerage for national regimes, and bureaucrats, like politicians, are the brokers. Local issues become national issues through partisan and bureaucratic interests that transcend local boundaries. Similarly, local bureaucrats and politicians often create alliances across administrative-political boundaries. National bureaucrats serving at the local level often have sufficient power to establish political alliances outside their own organizations. Local politicians find their political activities curbed by the intervention of officials at higher levels; they implement policy more than make it.

The roles that local officials play are not exclusively political or administrative. Studies of local officials' attitudes have shown that officials who are elected tend to view their jobs as political, while appointed officials tend to think in terms of administrative roles.[1] But when one looks at what those officials actually do in their positions, the distinction becomes blurred. In fact, administrators (or bureaucrats) often act like politicians and politicians like bureaucrats. One study found city councillors in Lucknow, India, to be "administratively oriented," with limited decision-making power. Another simply classified Chilean city councillors as "administrative officials" and Ministry of Interior employees as "political."

The relationships between bureaucrats and politicians at the grass roots raise fundamental questions about the two roles. Why do bureaucrats at the local level behave like politicians and politicians like bureaucrats? Is it the local political context that encourages the two to reverse their roles? Or is it conceptual rigidity superseding political realities?

The unique context of local politics certainly is important. Role reversals occur most often where the bureaucrats are extralocal and the politicians are *local*. Bureaucrats serving at the local level, even though not directly employed by national ministries, usually are part of a national civil service system, which ties such bureaucrats directly to the national political regime and turns them into politicians in their own right.

What the civil service bureaucrat does or does not do at the local level is determined by the role he plays for the national regime. K. J. Davey described the Unified Local Government Service in East Africa. The great virtue of the Government Service, he wrote, was that the "transferability and the invariable posting of Chief Officers away from home districts have helped to protect them against local pressures."[2] The bureaucrat's consequent insecurity and his awareness of his political role in maintaining regime stability encourage him to reach out for political allies wherever he can find them.

In making these alliances, bureaucrats are behaving like politicians, as are their politician allies. The politician's role is defined, developed, and protected by power, which he often creates in unstructured or informal ways. The alliances that politicians form are not circumscribed by hierarchical considerations in the same way as those of the ideal-typical bureaucrat. Both local bureaucrats and politicians participate actively in networks of influence that go beyond the authoritative relationships of the elective offices they fill.

In Kenya, for example, county councillors allied themselves with party leaders at the center—especially the Kenyan African Nation Union backbenchers in Parliament. These alliances protected the councils against Parliament's attacks on their authority and the reestablishment of the colonial provincial bureaucracy.[3] While the councillors and the backbenchers stood against the further consolidation of the dominant party leadership through the politicization of regional bureaucrats, they received considerable local support. Local councillors did not collectively determine public policy in their localities. But they were able to affect party policy through skillful bargaining and by forming coalitions with politicians at the other levels in the political system. Precisely because local politicians do "play politics," national regime elites often view them as a threat to the cohesiveness of their regimes.

The images of the political bureaucrat and the bureaucratic politician are both valid. Local bureaucrats do behave in political ways, and local politicians are often left out of significant policy decisions. But the images leave a significant part of the background out of focus: how these local officials are interacting with national or extralocal policymakers and how this interaction influences the roles that they adopt. As the above two East African examples show, both bureaucrat and politician are operating in a milieu formed in large measure by national priorities that, ironically, can throw the local bureaucrat and the politician into one another's arms.

THE INTERVENTIONIST STATE AND ADMINISTRATIVE EFFICIENCY

Insulating the bureaucrat from local political pressures has been justified, as in the East African case, by administrative impartiality and efficiency. But that is a political, not scientific, justification put forth by interventionist regimes. The growth of bureaucratic power in the interventionist state is that of the national bureaucracy; administrative efficiency is the vision of the national administrator. At the local level, administrative efficiency often becomes the bureaucrat's justification for increasing his own influence at the expense of the local politician.

Bureaucrats behave like politicians because they are interested in acquiring, and have opportunities to acquire, power. When, for example, local bureaucrats take over the functions of local councils, the only certain result is that the bureaucrat's power increases and the local councillor's diminishes. Whether or not the result of the bureaucrat's influence is a more efficient distribution of public resources depends upon the values associated with the public policy process. Most policy decisions involve a complex mix of values—such as community participation, economic development, and national political integration. It is difficult, if not impossible, to compare the contribution of competing decision-making structures to efficiency. More often the question of efficiency is raised as a post hoc rationale for the existence of political bureaucracies—not as an evaluation of their performance.

The geographic scope of decision-making structures (whether public or private, political or administrative) is commonly linked to the question of efficiency. The optimum area for a public agency to administer from the standpoint of technical policy requirements—as with transport or food systems—is likely to be larger than the typical size of local governmental units. Consequently, national administrative reforms often have overstepped local governmental units and have created agencies with different jurisdictions.

Restructuring jurisdictions often overemphasizes efficiency at the expense of political competition. Administrative solutions to policy implementation have popular appeal because of their apparent simplicity. By redrawing administrative boundaries, national bureaucracies can protect their own domains from the encroachment of local government officials, while avoiding a political uproar—at least in the short run. In the long run, efficiency is not simply a question of size. It is also political; it depends upon exercising control over the policy process. The bureaucrat whose extended domain has cut into that of local government officials and local politicians often gives up useful allies.

In many Third World countries, agricultural cooperatives encompass these conflicts within one organization because they are typically both popular organizations and part of national bureaucracies. As such, they provide many examples of political bureaucracies. First, cooperative organizations include both elective and appointive officials. Second, cooperatives typically are required both to encourage the participation of farmers in making agricultural policy and to improve the production and distribution of agricultural products. Their emphasis upon participation characteristically falls aside, and the cooperatives function as part of the agricultural bureaucracy.

The experience of one cooperative movement illustrates the tenuous relationship between efficiency and bureaucratic intervention. Senegal's cooperatives were governed during the 1960s by elected boards that in turn elected the cooperative's president.[4] Above the individual cooperative units, several national agencies shared such responsibilities as technical assistance, revenue gathering, the procurement and marketing of produce, and selling machinery, seeds, and fertilizer. During the early years of Senegal's independence, licensed private agents also were permitted to arrange with the cooperatives to market their produce.

After nearly a decade of experience with the cooperative system, the Senegalese government hired an Italian consulting firm to investigate a growing "peasant malaise." It was felt that this malaise was preventing the cooperatives from increasing the participation of farmers or increasing farm output.

A major recommendation of the consulting firm was to enlarge the jurisdiction of the basic cooperative unit. The purpose of this change was to bring the management of the cooperatives under the closer control of local ministry bureaucrats.

The cooperatives' problems were more complicated than the consultant's solution suggested. Among the many issues that influenced the performance of the cooperatives and contributed to the "peasant malaise" were (1) disagreements between producers and the central government about pricing and product—i.e., matters of material incentives; (2) disputes over which central agency would control specific areas of agricultural development; and (3) problems resulting from the diffusion of financial responsibility within the cooperative structure, encouraging indebtedness to, and decreasing investment in, the cooperatives.

The cooperatives' financial losses could be sustained by national grants. The second issue, bureaucratic jurisdiction, is more entrenched. *Interventionist* government shifts power from elected officials to appointed officials. It also contributes to a proliferation of agencies at the local level. As a result, bureaucrats at the local level are competing for control of public policy with one another as often as with local politicians. The constant restructuring of local bureaucracies that very different types of regimes engage in is an attempt to curb the influence of the political bureaucrat.

POLITICAL POLICE

Another aspect of the milieu within which local bureaucrats and politicians function is the high priority assigned by national regimes to maintaining internal security. Except for the United States and Great Britain, authority over local police is rarely invested in local governments. But police activities have an effect upon local politics.[5] Still, watching the police has been left largely to the lawyers, while students of local politics have turned to street repair and zoning regulations.

Police are involved in local politics on a day-to-day basis. While they are the most visible on city streets, they often are most influential in rural settings, where they may be the only official representatives of the central government. In that situation, the role of the police is broad—from controlling banditry to adjudicating civic and criminal disputes to participating in civic action projects. In fact, police officials sometimes are so thoroughly enmeshed in the local political scene that they are regarded as an integral part of local officialdom by the populace. How they perform these varied functions is important, therefore, and their style and tactics become a very relevant part of the local political milieu.

In the Iranian countryside, for example, the gendarmerie irons out personal disputes and conflicts between neighboring villages. In minor local disputes the gendarme is a valued and influential outside arbiter. Land reform and subsequent changes in village government bolstered the authority of the gendarme relative to that of the traditional headmen. His position in the national regime, however, limits his independence in major conflicts—such as those arising over land redistribution or internal security. The gendarmerie is maintained to keep internal order; their local arbitrating activities are secondary. In 1978, civil violence in Iran brought the gendarmerie into the streets in support of the monarchy against the dissidents. The gendarme's position was no longer that of the neutral arbiter.

One student of the police in Western Europe argued that the police were nationalized in order (1) to avoid duplication of efforts and confusion of responsibility and (2) to seize opportunities for better training and equipment programs.[6] Regime security overshadows such administrative niceties. In the United States, when the National Guard was called upon at Kent State, the issue was not training or confused administrative lines. Avoiding the administrative confusion and the duplication of training programs had little to do with Kenyan President Kenyatta's decision to add a predominantly Kikuyu riot control force to the police establishment.[7]

Police provide internal security for political regimes, not neutral states. Regime elites rarely will be willing to rely upon local forces. In Kenya, where political loyalty is so crucial, most of the police were not Kikuyu. In the case of Iran, the local police had neither the numbers, nor the training, nor the loyalty for the task.

INSECURITY AND POLITICAL BUREAUCRATS

When national governments intervene in social and economic processes and when they seek to preserve internal order, the balance of power between legislative and bureaucratic institutions clearly tilts toward the latter.[8] Furthermore, interventionist government and internal order both depend upon a particular type of local bureaucrat to ensure a smoothly functioning system. The ideal local bureaucrat is able to influence local groups while at the same time remaining largely free from their influence. He is to be political without being powerful in his own right.

This constraint forces local bureaucrats to develop distinctive political strategies. Bureaucrats and politicians at the local level relate to one another differently than do national bureaucrats and politicians. If the bureaucrat serving at the local level is political, it is not because "his" ministry is especially powerful. Rather it is usually because, having been denied sufficient resources by his superiors, he must seek his own sources of support in the "wilderness" of local politics.

Conflict between local politicians and bureaucrats sometimes does arise because the two have different constituencies. Local elective officials have to wage public campaigns and end up in office with at least a symbolic mandate. In contrast, bureaucrats are expected to be responsive to their superiors in the administrative hierarchy and to process seemingly endless piles of paperwork. Despite the fact that bureaucrats at the local level will be working with politicians whose objectives frequently are different from their own, they rarely are prepared for political conflict. Their training prepares them to handle formal bureaucratic procedures rather than to deal with the political situations they confront.

The local bureaucrat has few attractive alternatives in this situation. If he passes local conflicts along to his superiors, he is adding to their work and is not likely to be rewarded for his efforts. If, on the other hand, he successfully prevents problems from arising, he may be criticized for behaving as a "politician" and usurping the authority of local elective officials. In some countries, the bureaucrat finds himself in an even more ambiguous position, that of having been recruited through a centralized administrative service into a local government post.

Consequently, many bureaucrats do not like to serve at the local level. This is particularly true of bureaucrats who have received advanced training in public administration and "priced themselves out of the local market," where salaries and status are low.[9] Bureaucrats who try to move up to higher office from local posts can find themselves in a political vacuum—they lack sufficient resources to perform well enough to be rewarded with promotions. The combination of ambition and powerlessness encourages bureaucrats and politicians at the local level to seek mutual support, rather than to compete continually with one another.

Bureaucrats who do not develop informal contacts with local politicians and opinion leaders are at a distinct disadvantage. The successful political bureaucrat creates his own constituency within the community or district that he serves. The bureaucrat's authority comes from above, but his ability to use it effectively depends upon practical skills. A disillusioned Bloc Development Officer in Mysore, India, complained that when he opposed the interests of district politicians, his bureaucratic superiors deserted him.[10] His only alternative to being totally isolated was to make certain that he did not become involved in any conflict that he could not win on the basis of *his own local* power base. The most satisfied development officers in Mysore were those who worked along with local politicians and adapted their tactics to the needs of those politicians.

Political bureaucrats, then, are more a product of their own political positions within national regimes than of depoliticized local environments. This point is demonstrated by the range of townspeople whom John Badgley found to be politically influential in Burma during the early 1960s:

> Businessmen and their buyers [in villages] who may converse or correspond daily. *Many ex-insurgent leaders sustain themselves as traders while maintaining political contacts with village headmen* [emphasis added].

> Vehicle drivers and boat captains who carry freight, mail, and rumors. . . .

> Heads of important town monasteries and Buddhist colleges who are frequently consulted by village leaders and whose opinions are sought in most public issues.[11]

These people were not elective officeholders, since elected district councils were disbanded by the military regime that took office in 1962. Despite this, they were clearly part-time politicians. They wielded influence and had contacts that local bureaucrats wanted to share for their own security. The police and military officials, who acquired considerable "field experience" during the communist insurgency of the 1950s and had a generally bad reputation among villagers, were bureaucrats particularly in need of political support.

Where one or several political parties exist, the political party often is the link between local bureaucrats, as well as between local politicians. In Senegal, a single-party state after 1968, the Union Progressiste Senegalaise was a *localized political* machine—a machine because it specialized in patronage rather than ideology and localized because it operated most effectively at that level. Local party leaders were able to penetrate the central bureaucracy at the local level and provide administrative jobs and favors for supporters.[12]

Cooperation among local party politicians and bureaucrats can go beyond the patronage and special favors that can keep regimes running smoothly. It often takes a political crisis to make clear the dividing line between acceptable and unacceptable coalitions. In the early

1960s, for example, Prime Minister Houphuet-Boigny of the Ivory Coast dismissed scores of local officials who were implicated in a plot to oust him. Appointed prefects and local party officials went out together.[13] The prime minister's supporters were then in a quandry. They did not know whether to rely upon the bureaucracy or the party. Consequently, they vacillated, and successive bureaucratic reorganizations followed repeated party reorganizations. This series of developments culminated in increased coercive control, with neither local politicians nor local bureaucrats allowed much freedom for maneuver.

ROLE PERCEPTIONS AND POLITICAL BUREAUCRATS

In some countries, local politicians and bureaucrats have followed similar career paths, a fact that contributes to the overlap of their roles. The politician-turned-bureaucrat carries his past experiences into his new post but finds it difficult to fit into a hierarchy, especially since he still may have a political constituency. This situation is particularly common in former colonies where preindependence politicians moved into bureaucratic posts and in countries without local civil service regulations. Indonesian local bureaucrats, for example, were both convinced that they should play active decision-making roles and that politics was a legitimate process.[14] They viewed administrative and political roles as compatible and even interchangeable. Those views were encouraged by pressure from the political party leaders, who wanted local spoils used for building party machines and for supporting alliances with bureaucrats.

Expanding urban government created the same kind of situation in the United States, with the "good government" movement at the beginning of the twentieth century. As the role of city government expanded, bureaucrats were able to stake out their claims for control of the policy process, thanks to "good government" pressures. This led to nonpartisan municipal elections and to the establishment of local civil service systems that maximized bureaucratic control over hiring local officials.

Competition among local bureaucrats and politicians is most apparent following periods of rapid change in the environment, like urbanization, or in the national regime, independence. However, cooperation between bureaucrats and politicians is more usual and generally characterizes the relationships between the two. A classic example of this point is city councillors and city managers in the San Francisco Bay Area, who saw their roles as conceptually distinct but behaved as though their roles were very compatible.[15] The typical city manager thought city managers should be strong leaders. But the councillors adamantly insisted that the manager be subservient to the directives of the council. The city managers were pleased with their control of budget preparation and their access to outside expert opinion on policy matters. Councillors wanted an accounting from the manager for specific policy decisions. Each group espoused an ideal image of its role—the active, professional manager, on the one hand, and the alert, watchdog council, on the other. However, the city manager was careful not to bring controversial policies to the council— where he could either be defeated or lose the advantage of his nonpartisan, professional image. The city manager, like the councillors, operated within a milieu that curtailed his freedom of action. The influence of both the manager and the council was limited in terms of the range of policies they could promote and by their dependence upon one another. By cooperating with one another, they could avoid showdowns that made one or the other office "look bad." Of course, for a variety of reasons, they sometimes chose confrontation.

The city councils rarely voted down budgets or even made substantial changes in them. City managers rarely proposed public expenditures that represented radical departures from previous budgets; few managers were innovators. One manager, for example, described a proposal, in which he was actively involved, to purchase land for the city from the Southern Pacific Railway. This land was to be turned into parking lots and then resold at a profit. The proposal would not alter town development or challenge the interests of the railroad or downtown merchants. The manager was making incremental decisions that would have a short-run effect upon town finances and, at the same time, would not raise any major power conflicts.

REFORMING THE BUREAUCRATS

Attempts to balance "efficiency" and "participation," or the local bureaucrat's power and that of the elected official, may simply be making local bureaucrats more accountable to the national regimes they serve. Reforms designed to increase participation by making bureaucracy more accountable to local constituencies simultaneously serve the interests of regime elites by making the bureaucracy more accessible to them.

In effect, some forms of decentralization actually take power *away* from local leaders in order to put it in the hands of persons who can be controlled more easily from the top. For example, the interests of French bureaucrats at the local level (notably the departmental prefects) often have been more compatible with those of political leaders than they have with those of regime elites.[16] This was of particular concern to the regime where the national ruling party, Union des Démocrates pour la Ve République (UDR) did not control local elective offices. In those localities, it was opposition party leaders who had access to the prefects rather than the UDR.

Despite the tendency of bureaucrats at the local level to create informal alliances among themselves and with politicians, many moves to formally coordinate local policy-making have been resisted because of competitive pressures. When the UDR sought to "decentralize" and "rationalize" French administration by creating regional councils, the main resistance came from the local politicians whose informal alliances would be undermined. National bureaucrats were less hostile, since they were to participate in the regional agencies. Many other countries have a formal administrative framework for regional coordination, but their political fortunes wax and wane.

Getting specialized ministries to subordinate their field activities to a single regional agency is as difficult as convincing national ministry officials to abide by the priorities of national planning agencies. The stronger the regime's commitment to the specialized programs, the stronger the specialized ministries become, and the greater the influence of field administrators.

In the early 1960s, Egypt's Ministry of Local Administration was authorized to select a proportion of the members of local councils.[17] Later, however, these appointed members were replaced by local representatives of the individual ministries. The councils' superiors, the provincial governors, were themselves subject to the effects of bureaucratic competition; they were made to report both to the Ministry of Interior and to the Ministry of Local Administration.

In some countries, such as the United States, almost no formal machinery exists to coordinate bureaucratic policy at the local level. But curiously enough, when remedial action is taken to "repoliticize" local politics, the preferred solution is *not* to tamper directly with the bureaucracy. More often it is to create new grass-roots popular bodies or to refurbish the old ones. Such a solution, however, does nothing to bridge the "authority" gap between the politicians and bureaucrats; instead, it usually widens the gap.

Chile's Juntas de Vecinos (neighborhood committees) were one example of this grass-roots tactic for strengthening regime control.[18] The *juntas* were authorized in 1965 as urban neighborhood groups that were to integrate city dwellers into national life. At the same time, they bypassed the existing municipal institutions.

The Chilean reform floundered, in the first instance, as a result of partisan opposition. Hostility toward the *juntas* centered upon the fact that the *juntas* were to be joined under the umbrella of the Consejeria de la Promocion Popular by the ruling Christian Democratic party. Opposition party leaders viewed the committees as a maneuver by the Christian Democrats to make their own party more powerful, rather than to democratize local politics.

Had the *juntas* been successful, they could have given the Christian Democratic party a broader base of support and strengthened its urban organization. This might have been desirable in a period when many Chileans did not participate in political organizations. On the other hand, neighborhood citizen groups did not strengthen the effectiveness of their local councillors, the municipal *regidors,* vis-à-vis either the central ministries, which dealt with urban development, or the governors, who still were much more powerful. The reforms were proposed in the context of the much longer-run trend in which the governor's office was acquiring new powers and the Ministry of Interior bureaucrats were increasingly involved in municipal politics. In order to shift the balance of power toward local politicians, it would have been necessary to consolidate their interests, rather than making them more diffuse by creating new institutions.

One approach to managing political bureaucrats has been to legalize bureaucratic politics. As when legalizing other social vices, one faces up to the existence of the "vice" and brings it out into the open where it can be confronted directly. This option has been tried in such diverse settings as the East African states and the People's Republic of China. The East African "legalization" consisted of placing party officials in supervisory positions and combining party and bureaucratic functions in one position.

Only single-party regimes have tried this solution. Where significant opposition parties exist, ruling party-bureaucracy alliances are less formal.

A form of legalization used by many types of regimes in recent years has been to mix elective representatives and local bureaucrats. Mixed local commissions presumably depoliticize local politics by bringing all the politicians together—both bureaucrats and elected officials— where they must confront one another in an open setting. The arrangement also helps national regime elites keep aware of any political deals made at the local level.

SUMMARY—NATIONAL REGIMES AND THEIR LOCAL BUREAUCRATS

The tendency of national bureaucrats serving at the local level has been to take on political roles. This depends on the bureaucrat's ability to create or participate in networks of influence outside his own administrative hierarchy and to use that influence to advance his own career.

The political role of local bureaucrats cannot be "legislated away," although that has been tried by national regime elites who would like to harness these political energies. The political bureaucrat is an indirect outgrowth of the internal dynamics of national regimes. The bureaucrat serving at the local level is an arm of the interventionist state and of regime security. The political conditions thus imposed upon the bureaucrat's activities encourage him to respond in like manner— politically. Alliances with other bureaucrats and politicians at the local level often help local bureaucrats gain personal security vis-à-vis the regime.

To the extent that local alliances and bureaucratic politics reconcile conflicting interests at the local level, they contribute directly to regime stability. In the Soviet Union, these alliances help local officials to meet their economic planning targets. In Iran, they may legitimize the gendarmerie and thus promote regime security.

Still, national regime elites try to control such alliances. They regularly disrupt local networks of influence by reorganizing bureaucratic and political offices. While that makes good political sense for insecure regimes, if tried too often it encourages bureaucrats to behave even more politically than before.

Tanzania—A Case Study in the Bureaucratization of Party Politics

Tanzania presents an extraordinarily important case for the study of local politics. Several factors account for this. Tanzanian politicians have undertaken very ambitious social changes in an effort to transform the colonial heritage into a socialist decentralized state. And the structure of the Tanzanian regime—with its strong president (Julius Nyerere) and mass party, Tanganyika African National Union (TANU)—seems to be a remarkably stable one. The party and presidency serve not only as the focus of Tanzanian politics but also as a successful paradigm for party-state regimes throughout Africa. Although there is considerable disagreement over the success and relevance of the Tanzanian model, it remains a focal point for the discussion of alternatives for political change and development in the contemporary world.

After independence in 1961, the presidential-party regime slowly evolved, defining its current form and program in the Arusha Declaration of 1967. What distinguished the emergent regime was its avowed dedication to rural development, self-reliance, and party tutelage.

To assess the party's political strength and the success of its programs, one must necessarily follow the party into the villages. Tanzania is among the least urbanized countries in the world. Ninety-three percent of the twelve million Tanzanians live in rural areas. Before 1967, rural settlement patterns were rather like those of the United States; farmers' homes and fields were spread out, with few real village centers.

These living patterns were reflected in social organization. In preindependent mainland Tanzania, authority in most tribes was decentralized, and many people's overriding identification was with their subtribal clans. Zanzibar was largely a caste society, dominated by Arabs until 1964. From the coastal towns permeated with Islamic and Swahili culture to its broad inland valleys, Tanzanian society is diffuse, diverse, and, like most societies, resilient to change.

Nearly a hundred years of colonial occupation on the mainland, first by Germany (1890–1922) and then by Britain (1922–1961), instilled in the Tanzanian culture strong distrust of government. Native chiefs appointed by the British administered British colonial laws in their own tribal areas. No single pattern, direct or indirect rule, prevailed, but everywhere foreign authority was resented. Gradually, after World War I, Africans and eventually traditional leaders joined the nationalist movement on behalf of independence. Their organizations reached beyond tribal boundaries and into the towns.

By 1954, as the drive to independence began, TANU leaders both attacked existing authority and hoped eventually to overcome the accumulated skepticism of their constituents. After independence, they increased their efforts to assimilate or replace the various tribal or special interest-based nationalist associations and to use the TANU organization to mobilize the populace on behalf of development goals.

The British introduced land alienation policies where private land-ownership replaced communal ownership, often by confiscation or fiat. This caused much of the rural opposition to colonial rule. Agrarian politics during that time showed that farmers would join political associations that extended beyond their own villages if their interests could be pursued in that way. Opposition to costly cattle dips, for instance, was a means of recruiting members for TANU in the 1950s.

What remained for the TANU leaders to accomplish after independence was mainly the task of reconciliation. The new independent government needed to reconcile agriculture and rural development policies with the interests of the farmers. This was difficult to do, however. New production techniques disrupted established and valued practices; public resources were scarce; and choices had to be made for spending scarce resources.

After some false starts with capital-intensive projects, the party decided to build a system of *ujamma* villages. (*Ujamma* is Swahili for familyhood and a synonym for socialism.) As a way to build socialism and rural development, this effort captured the imaginations of many observers, from World Bank officials to Chinese diplomats. It promised to be one way in which scarce resources could be utilized to accomplish large-scale change. Priority was given by the government to the *ujamma* villages. Farmers were resettled into them, and the villages were treated as model development units. Not surprisingly, the approach was popular in some regions and resisted in others—resistance occurred particularly in the most prosperous farming areas.[19]

For the remainder of the population, the regional administrative structure has served as a channel for determining which claims would be made successfully upon the government and which would be postponed. *Ujamma* villages, of course, were accorded special consideration in the receipt of funds from national and regional development programs. When problems arose in the regional administrative system, the structure itself was reorganized, but the basic premises for making decisions remained the same—consolidating the presidential-party regime.

PARTY AND GOVERNMENT

One of Tanzania's unique contributions to local administration has been to place both party and administrative authority in one office. In cells (households), villages, and wards (groups of villages), executive and party functions are merged. At the area and regional levels, the chief government administrator is also de facto the regional party leader. Rarely have local government systems put so many eggs in one basket.

Regional and area commissioners are appointed by President Nyerere. The TANU party organization has only such power as the president concedes to it. Although the distribution of power appears to be managed in a bureaucratic framework, political bargaining ultimately determines the fortunes of party leaders or of particular ministries. Despite the egalitarian, self-sacrificing tenor of the Arusha Declaration, rural development policies do not emerge from the deliberations of individual Tanzanians in their village communities. Rather, they emerge through a kind of national negotiating system in which the area occupies a focal position.[20] At the center of the bargaining process is Nyerere and his closest advisors—men who have been with him since the independence movement and also younger, well-educated political or administrative technicians.

Presidential appointments of party leaders as area commissioners make sense as a continuation of British practice and as a means to establish the political authority of the independent TANU regime. Historically, the commissioner was responsible for coordinating area-level functions, which included policing and security, taxation, and formulating area development plans. Originally, after the 1962 post-independence reforms, the intention was that commissioners could implement party and government objectives and could do so within the framework of their political base in the TANU hierarchy. President Nyerere described the single-party system as one that he hoped would inhibit factionalism but still allow elections to the local councils and to seats in the national parliament to be strongly contested (as they were from the beginning).

To some extent, Nyerere's hopes were realized regarding a competitive, single party without factionalism. Voting turnouts have been high compared to elsewhere in Africa—around 50 percent of the eligible populace. In the absence of a second party, candidates vie for TANU nominations, with two candidates selected by party leaders standing for a general primary. Overall, Tanzanian politics has been free of the rife conflict experienced by many other African nations.

Nonetheless, a certain amount of factionalism has occurred, and TANU local organizations have been one vehicle for it. In a country where the public sector has been chiefly responsible for economic investment and for redistributing private wealth, government employment has acquired a particular attractiveness. Following nationalization in 1967, government employment was the principal type of white collar work that was expanding rapidly enough to provide opportunities and the possibility of security to recent high school graduates. The result was that economic incentives heightened political competition at both the local and national levels.

Often electoral and administrative competition interfered with the continuity of authority by encouraging a high rate of turnover among local and national officeholders. In some areas, TANU area commissioners were unable to control competition without resorting to discipline. For this they often needed and received cooperation from high-level party bureaucrats.

After a decade of independence, criticisms of government policies by local officials still could get lost in the party bureaucracy. Rumors that the government had its own "eyes and ears" in the village helped to undermine TANU's image as the people's avenue to Dar es Salaam and promoted administrative solutions to problems of local governance.[21]

Simultaneously with the TANU's transition to ruling party came the erosion of the commissioners' positions within the government. The new subordinate post of administrative secretary was created. The secretaries were senior civil servants who might have been commissioners except for their lack of political credentials. Since 1972, as directors of development, the administrative secretaries have headed a group of officials that is ultimately accountable to the regional administration office in the prime minister's office.[22]

Regional and area directors are responsible for implementing their respective development plans *in consultation* with development committees. The development committees are, in turn, made up of elected representatives and officials.

Neither the committees nor the TANU party branches were to do more than to indicate their general priorities for development expenditures. Decisions about specific activities were to be made by the directors and by the specialized bureaucrats who worked under them. Elected district councils were abolished.

LOCAL "TYRANTS"

The 1972–1973 reform, officially described as "decentralization," that created the office of development director did not decentralize. In reality it was a move toward less concentration of administration and minor policy decision-making in Dar es Salaam. Fiscal powers, policing functions, and budgetary decisions still resided in the hands of national officials. Moreover, throughout the continued reorganizations, the national regime's fundamental orientation toward local politics was consistently maintained. First, the regime has insisted upon symbolic popular participation in local government, through elected representatives on the development committees and the TANU party committee. Second, it has been reluctant to allow the growth of autonomous local power centers. Thus, in his published comments about the decentralization, President Nyerere pointed out:

> Nor is it the intention . . . to create new local tyrants in the persons of the Regional and District [Area] Development Directors. . . . The decentralization exercise is based upon the principle that more and more people must be entrusted with responsibility.[23]

When was an area politician behaving as a local "tyrant"? When was he assuming his *proper* responsibilities? The answers to these questions were left entirely to the discretion of national politicians and bureaucrats. As a general rule, the dividing line fell where a local official moved from enlisting local support for national policies, however unpopular, to attempting to revise or even subvert national policies, or pursuing enforcement with glaring disregard for local conditions or human dignity. The imprisonment (and consequent death) of some delinquent taxpayers by local officials was an example of such excessive zeal.

Ironically, even after the decentralization program, development fund allocations remained largely in the hands of national politicians—specifically, in the prime minister's office. In fact, perhaps the most important impact of the 1972–1973 changes was to bring the specialized national ministries under the scrutiny of the development directors. And, thus, through the bureaucratic channels of the regional administration office, they came under the scrutiny of the prime minister.

The 1972 decentralization also was an attempt to curb the competition among ministries for public resources. Claims on public resources were made through the ministries, often originating in local demands for particular development projects. The objective of the decentralization program was more to curb bureaucratic politics than to increase participation in policy-making. The complexity and flexibility of the party bureaucratic network meant that participatory politics and bureaucratic politics had become inextricably intertwined.

In the "old days" of commissioners and administrative secretaries, for example, competition between the two often was strong and inevitably affected their behavior in the field. An administrative secretary, anxious about his status, was inclined to settle into his area headquarters and not risk being away from the "center of things" (meaning communications to and from Dar es Salaam). Area commissioners, by contrast, were often former politicians. Their backgrounds were in farming or commerce, and they spent more of their time traveling through the rural areas. An area commissioner was a political jack-of-all-trades, who was expected to stay clear of the specialized ministries' operations. He could also be shifted by the party to other regions, and thereby be prevented from gaining a strong local power base.

The structural constraints against the acquisition of disproportionate power by any one office at the area level also have created a political hiatus between the area and the village. As in the case of the administrative secretary, the system of checks and balances that stimulated competition among area officials and among area and national officials contributed to the officials' preoccupation with one another. This precluded the area officials from becoming involved in village affairs. Ideological commitment to rural development and to expanding popular participation encounters numerous hurdles in practice; one of the most persistent is this mid-level bureaucratic competition.

The possibility of realizing the commitment to rural development lay upon TANU more than upon the bureaucracy. The party enjoyed a degree of legitimacy after independence that was not true of the administrative machinery, and had more grass-roots power. During the last days of the colonial period, TANU became a widespread organization that linked villages to towns and chiefs to school teachers. Throughout the first decade of independence, the single-party regime managed to hold elections that offered voters a choice of candidates and yet did not become deadlocked in conflict. The success of this system depended, at the grass-roots level, upon the entrepreneurship of the party's village leaders.

Some of their responsibility for political order fell to the local politicians by default. This de facto decentralization was a result of the unresolved conflicts over policy-making at the area level. While the commissioners were political representatives (and therefore the logical persons to whom local disputes should be referred), they were reluctant to assume this kind of responsibility. By interfering in local disputes, a commissioner perforce would be taking a position on the issues or interests involved. Commissioners wanted to avoid that as much as possible because it created political risks. The commissioners' futures ultimately lay in the president's hands. If, as the representative of national authority, a commissioner took an unpopular position, the president would be implicated in that decision also. The commissioner could then expect to be reprimanded, if not relieved of his post. Thus, to the degree that the commissioner was constrained to use his power conservatively, he also was effectively isolated from local affairs. At the village level, consequently, there was potential for local tyranny.

VILLAGERS AND VILLAGE POLITICIANS

"Tyranny" could be expected of the more enterprising party leaders were it not for the existence of other groups and power centers. Organizationally, the local party includes virtually the entire population and is broken down into ten-household cells. Party leaders are called upon for a wide range of decisions; their roles are reminiscent of the traditional roles of chiefs, headmen, and elders.

Judging by the scope of authority they have assumed or acquired, TANU leaders do have entrenched positions in village political life. Many of their tasks, however, are only marginally relevant to development.

Norman Miller reported on the more common requests made of a particular TANU rural branch.[24] Most requests involved hearing disputes—including marital disputes—and determining what appropriate compensation should be paid. Disputes heard included a bar quarrel, settlement for dog bite injuries, and a woman's complaint against her husband for mistreatment. In response to the first dispute, the party took no action; the second brought a ten-shilling settlement; and, in the last case, the chairman sent a letter to the husband "ordering him to improve his behavior." A similar list could be made of complaints relating to property and debts.

The chairman's response to several complaints was simply to issue a warning to the errant person. The high incidence of compliance with the party officials' warnings could be attributed to three factors. First, disputes were likely to be heard in community meetings and, thus, had the sanction of public opinion behind them. Second, the party officials' judgments were generally preferred to that of government officials who were "outsiders," for the leader's opinion had both local and area support. Third, party chairmen occasionally resorted to threats and intimidation, although by doing so they risked being reported to the area party office.

The nature of the abuse of power by village chairmen was a consequence of the dilemmas and opportunities they met as local party leaders. For example, the chairmen were enjoined to build up party resources by collecting party fees from their constituents. This was a particularly unpopular task, especially when it was not the party but the specialized ministries that controlled development expenditures in the villages. To make up for his lack of positive sanctions, the village chairman contrived unauthorized methods of eliciting party support. According to the examples provided by Miller, the chairman's "innovations" often involved finding ways to enlist or force others to comply with his decisions. Sometimes that meant holding "court" to fine villagers who did not cooperate with the party. But for doing this, the local leaders could be admonished by area officials.

In one reported case, a local court magistrate complained that he had been pressured by the party leader to find a person guilty of criticizing the party. Apparently, however, the magistrate's complaint to officials in the bureaucracy about this not-so-public strategem was never acted upon.

These examples indicate that, rather than being behaviorally distinct, the politics of mobilization and of regime stability are very much enmeshed at both the strategic and tactical levels. The local party leaders, the local complainants, and the higher officials who were asked to arbitrate were all attempting to balance two separate objectives: first, to keep conflict under control and maintain a reasonable balance of power and, second, to advance the interests of the political community as they saw them. The methods they selected similarly combined the innovative and the traditional.

This is then an "organization of complexity," where political actors seek to establish priorities that comply with their own perspectives. In it can be found the explanation for another instance of empty authority within Tanzania's development regime—the development committees. In 1963, development committees were created for each territorial unit and were strengthened by the 1967 and 1971 reorganizations. The committees had a mixed membership of appointed and elected officials and thus were combinations of popular councils and interministerial consultative committees.

The *village* development committee's role was to be particularly crucial. Self-help was the original organizing principle of Tanzanian development. The village development committee, and later the ward development committee, was to be responsible for transforming the self-help idea into a sequence of concrete projects. Once the proposed projects had taken shape in the committees, they were to be passed on to the district level for approval and possibly for funding. In practice, the committees did not assume active roles in the planning process, despite this apparent opportunity for village improvement. Nor did they even exist in some localities.

The problem lay not so much in the mixture of politicians and bureaucrats on the committees, officials who were as yet uncertain of and still testing the limits of their authority, but in the substantial authority officials held in other local agencies. Local cooperative society directors, the party chairmen, and the ministries' field representatives—all had opportunities to influence the allocation of public resources in the villages.

TRACTORS, TAXES, AND COOPERATIVE SOCIETIES

Another particularly important local institution in rural Tanzania was the agricultural cooperative. Tanzanian cooperatives engage in a wide range of activities—from organizing production to processing agricultural commodities to serving as middlemen in the market. Cooperatives also distribute farm machinery, seeds, fertilizers, and technical assistance. Hence, at the local level cooperatives often have a greater impact upon villagers than any official government agency.

Cooperative society leaders are politicians and bureaucrats at the same time. Members of local cooperatives elect local officers, who then are expected to conform to the dictates of the cooperative hierarchy. These dictates can be quite at odds with the immediate interests of local farmers. Liaisons between cooperative society officers and local farmers take place, but they are often extralegal.

Tax collection has been one source of conflict between farmers and cooperatives in Tanzania. Until 1969, when the local "cess," or tax, on agricultural produce was abolished, Tanzanian cooperatives were also revenue agents.[25] Cooperative society officers collected the cess at the same time that they purchased produce from the farmers. The revenues collected were then sent on to the district executive officer. A second tax, the "local rate," or head tax, was collected by the village executive officer.

Neither collection process, however, was particularly successful and both were eventually replaced by a sales tax on nonessential commodities, presumably because it was easier to collect. Both peasant farmers and the urban poor were exempted from this new tax.

The problem of collecting taxes was not unique to the cooperatives; it reflected the fundamental and continuing question of the ability of the government to extract any tax from the Tanzanian citizenry. As a result, the major proportion of Tanzanian national revenue comes from indirect taxes, particularly from levies on foreign trade. For example, in 1963–1964, indirect taxes were 51 percent of national revenues.

The local cooperatives were first and foremost marketing organizations. In fact, they were the only legal channel through which Tanzanian farmers could market their produce. Whatever price the farmer received—at least in the *legal* market—was determined by the cooperative society.

In general, agricultural prices were set with a view toward (1) providing incentives to encourage farmers to develop their land, (2) providing incentives to encourage farmers to produce specific crops, and (3) the political acceptability of these prices to domestic consumers. Consequently, the cooperatives' prices for specific products often were lower than the prices farmers could obtain on the black market.

With the removal of the cess, a major disincentive to selling through the cooperative was eliminated. But since price setting problems remained, national agricultural policy was still the product of a variety of interests that often diverged from the specific interests of the farmers.

In 1966, the Special Presidential Committee of Enquiry into the

Co-operative Movement and Marketing Boards was convened as a result of complaints that the cooperative societies were proving to be altogether too vulnerable to bureaucratic pressure. One of the complaints registered before the committee was against the overhead charged by the cooperatives for their marketing activities. The farmers argued that the differential between the price paid to the producer for a bag of maize and that received by the National Agricultural Products Board was at least 100 percent.[26] But despite complaints and enquiries, government intervention continued.

Throughout the 1960s, the national regime attempted to keep control of those regional cooperative organizations that had been active during the preindependence period. The largest of these, for example, was the Victorian Federation of Co-operative Unions. This cotton purchasing and ginning cooperative was finally taken over by the government in 1967. So by 1969, a group of foreign advisors to the government reported that farmers had become seriously alienated. They were unwilling to support the cooperatives and help them fulfill their mission, as a result of the lack of farmer control of cooperative policies.[27]

There are also examples of the intervention of local politics into "cooperative business." Cooperative officials were encouraged to allocate agricultural equipment to one locality rather than another. They were also induced to overlook discrepancies between what a farmer produced and what he sold to the cooperative—the difference being his black market transactions. In many such cases, the intermediary and/or the beneficiary of the favor was a local party official.

The Tanzanian system of regional administration is quasi-colonial.[28] That description fits particularly well the operations of the cooperatives during the cess tax period; in such a colonial system, local cooperative officials and politicians play the roles traditionally played by the village headmen. These headmen were rewarded to the extent that they could keep the local peace. Contemporary TANU district leaders are no more pleased with an incautious party chairman who allows his part in the system to be exposed and criticized than were the earlier chiefs with overly ambitious headmen.

SUMMARY—RECONCILIATION AND POLITICAL BUREAUCRATS

Tanzania's experience with regional administration is instructive. It indicates that the combined objectives of rural development (organized in Tanzania through the public sector and controlled by TANU), self-help, and popular participation make it quite unlikely that there will be much conflict between local bureaucrats and politicians. It is not simply that the lines of responsibility between TANU and the bureaucracy are blurred. In addition, lines of responsibility within TANU and within the administrative hierarchy are also indistinct. And, finally, Tanzanian institutions that mix elected officials and appointed officials, and appointed officials with different bases of accountability are prevalent. All these factors make role distinctions less apparent.

Even in the most judiciously planned development regimes, conflicts arise over access to resources and participation in allocative decisions. Such conflicts must either be reconciled or ignored. National regimes have often tried to deflect such competing claims upon scarce resources by increasing the number of formal decision-making sites and trading formalistic participation for real influence. At the same time, these regimes try to leave the lines of political accountability sufficiently vague so that no one appears to have actually achieved a dominant position. Tanzania's development committees and the cooperative organizations in Tanzania are examples of this symbolic reconciliation approach.

During the past one or two decades, the ultimate effect of symbolic reconciliation in Tanzania has been the bureaucratization of politics. As the number of educated and experienced Tanzanians available to the civil service has grown, the bureaucratization process has been extended towards the grass roots. This is the process that has come to be called "decentralization."

The Soviet Union — A Case Study in State Planning and Local Politics

Local government in the Soviet Union is a product of that country's state-centered development. Within the rubric of a state that is committed to industrial growth, political stability, and achieving a minimum standard of living for all its citizens, local government plays several critical roles. Local government in the Soviet Union generally has broader duties, although fewer legislative powers, than it does in many other countries. Its extensive duties are commensurate with the more extensive scope of government at all levels in the Soviet Union.

First, local government in the Soviet Union affects political recruitment in the system as a whole. In practice, local offices are training grounds for potential leaders at the *oblast* (provincial) level. Local councils also provide ethnic minorities formal representation, even though the offices themselves may lack effective power.

Second, local government in the Soviet Union includes local citizen groups. Communist ideology envisages local groups as part of the absorption of the state into the populace.

Finally, local government in the Soviet Union is expected to make more tolerable the dislocations associated with industrial growth and the rapid development of cities. Local authority over social policy and social control in the Soviet Union includes providing housing, health care, and some police services. In general, these local functions—

shared with national ministries—are those which are expected to ameliorate the effects of industrial growth, urbanization, and social change rather than those directly promoting economic growth.

Urbanization has brought to the Soviet Union many of the social and administrative problems associated with a large and dense population. As a result, sociologists there have begun to discuss with their colleagues from other countries what they call the "universal urban culture," although they still draw a distinction between socialist cities and other types.[29] The issues that the Soviet urban sociologists have been confronting, however, are primarily labor force related, and not issues within the jurisdiction of local authorities. Central political elites, on the other hand, are concerned about local governmental performance.

Local authorities include Communist party officials and members of the (elected) soviet and its executive committees. These authorities are immediately responsible for alleviating social problems and for fulfilling their own economic plans, as well as the national plan, within their jurisdictions. As a result of its important functions, local politics has been treated as a highly sensitive area. For example, a United States specialist in Soviet urban policy, David Cattell, undertook research in Leningrad on municipal government and found that many of the activities of local governments were classified as state secrets.[30]

One especially sensitive question about local politics is also very basic: Who makes decisions? In practice, politicians at higher levels have been heavily involved in Soviet local politics; thus, the local political arena is subordinate and lacks defined boundaries. For example, only one candidate is fielded for the position of local deputy and that candidate is selected by extralocal party leaders. This frequent participation of higher authorities in local government—more specifically, the participation of the party organization in recruitment and decision-making —is another indication of the significance of local political decisions to extralocal elites. The fact that extralocal elites are so involved in local politics is a fairly reliable indicator of the stakes that local decisions represent for them. Moreover, the fact that particular officials have developed a specialty in local administration and management indicates that local management has come to be regarded as a distinct and valuable political activity. Michael Frolic's analysis of the biographies of Soviet urban officials, for example, concludes that they were becoming increasingly specialized.[31]

One of the arguments that this case study advances is that *local government in the Soviet Union is very political.* The political nature of Soviet local government means that Soviet administrators often behave like politicians; they wheel and deal outside their organizations, but through their own organizations, in an effort to gain influence in the wider political system. In the Soviet Union, the political nature of local government means that local leaders are very deeply involved in "who gets what."

SCARCE RESOURCES AND POLITICAL BUREAUCRATS

The stakes of local politics (the "what" of power) have often been defined in the Soviet Union in terms of economic growth and modernization. The object of the political process in the Soviet Union, as far as state leaders are concerned, is not simply to preserve ideological unity on behalf of the Communist party, but also to maximize the returns from public investments in industrial and agricultural production, in social services, in infrastructure, and in military preparedness. Consequently, local officials and managers gain political influence and are promoted to higher positions to the extent that they are able to relate their activities to the advancement of the growth objectives of the national elites,

The executive committees of the local soviets include party bureaucrats and ministry technocrats, along with local elected representatives. The complexity of the economic planning process and administering urban policy has given the party and ministry officials a strong position on the executive committees. At the same time, their roles have become politicized.

Local administration is political in the Soviet Union because Soviet local administrators and politicians are involved in allocating a wide variety of political goods—in particular, public resources for economic production. As a result, *bureaucratic* politics—informal communications, patronage links, and reorganization struggles—is even more significant than *public* politics for students of Soviet affairs.[32]

Yet, despite the significant role that local authorities play within the context of the industrial state, they operate under very real financial constraints. The share of public revenues flowing directly into local coffers is limited—just 10 percent in Moscow, for example.[33] In addition, extralocal intervention in recruitment and policy-making limits the predictability of the local environment. Both of these limitations contribute to a fairly high level of uncertainty for local officials.

This uncertainty promotes political solutions to administrative problems. Political activity creates certainty from uncertainty; administration is using power within a clearer, better-defined framework. Accordingly, politicians form alliances wherever they contribute to the politicians' influence, while administrators, theoretically, confine themselves to hierarchical relationships. Thus, local politics in the Soviet Union is very political, in that policy outcomes are relatively uncertain. The uncertainty affects bureaucrats as well as politicians. Bureaucrats are encouraged by the indeterminacy of the local milieu to form alliances or build "understandings" with others outside their own organizations.

The decisions of local bureaucrats are backed up by quite comprehensive plans drawn up by authorities at the republic level. Nonetheless, these plans do not necessarily reduce the indeterminacy faced by local bureaucrats. In fact, they may increase it. When the economic plans are drawn up in an environment of scarce resources (which they inevitably are) and of high expectations for governmental performance, the difficult task of choosing among priorities is very likely to be "swept under the rug" until the last minute. For local officials, this procrastination means that they are given unrealistic production targets. Meeting these targets is often accomplished only through informal processes of influence-peddling and alliance-building among local officials—mainly among party leaders, administrative department heads, and managers of local enterprises.

LOCAL SOVIETS

These informal networks of influence typically do not include the local soviets, the equivalent of local elective councils. The soviets are one of three popular institutions at the local level in the Soviet Union which, theoretically, relate local demands to public policy outputs—the soviets, the party committee, and "citizens' action" groups. Volunteer organizations also have been formed as "comradely courts," housing committees, and street committees, but they have not been able to arouse much enthusiasm among their members.[34]

The soviets are at the center of a system of soviet committees that are to coordinate local administration. Soviets exist at every territorial level of government—from the village to the union-republics to the center. A soviet's executive committee comes the closest to exercising responsibility for policy; its membership reflects that responsibility. Department heads serving at the local level serve also on the soviet executive committees, where they have coordinating roles.

By contrast, the function of the elected soviet members is mainly to formally represent the citizen to the government, not to make policy. The primary criteria for the selection of these deputies are representativeness, service to the state, and technical competency.[35] Accordingly, in the soviets turnover is high among the elected deputies, and participation levels are high. In fact, by 1972, 59 percent of all workers in the Soviet Union had participated in city soviets.[36]

Deputies elected to the local soviets have a place in local politics, but they are not politicians in the sense of creating order from uncertainty. Like local councils in many other countries, the local soviets—as distinct from their executive committees—play the role of ombudsman more than that of policy-maker. And the ombudsman role is played quite successfully. Since the soviet members are officials of the government, the complaints they handle acquire more legitimacy in the eyes of their superiors.

On the other hand, soviet deputies consistently mirror their constituents in terms of their social backgrounds. For example, deputies to local soviets reflect their constituents' occupational characteristics quite faithfully, while at higher levels, farmers and agricultural workers are overrepresented in comparison to industrial workers—just as farming districts were overrepresented in U.S. state legislatures prior to the one-man, one-vote ruling. This may be changing, however. A marked shift toward more representation for workers occurred between 1959 and 1960, apparently as a result of a deliberate move by the party central committee.[37]

The similarities among the soviets at the intermediate, republic level are so striking that there appear to be some standard, nationwide criteria applied to recruiting soviet members. There has been little variation from republic to republic in the percentages of soviet members who are (1) women, (2) Communist party members, and (3) *Komosomol* members. (In 1969, the percentages were roughly 44, 45, and 11, respectively.)[38]

Recruitment decisions also seem to have been made about representing ethnic minorities. Not all minorities are equally well represented. Regionally based ethnic groups have been favored for recruitment into local soviets; those who do not have a regional base are underrepresented. Of the former group, Jacobs finds three nationalities to be of particular interest—the Balkans, the Kalmyks, and the Cherkessy. What is significant about these three is that they are "deported nationalities" who were rehabilitated in 1957. Following their rehabilitation, they apparently were recruited into local soviets in disproportionate numbers to encourage their successful integration into the political process. On the other hand, assimilation of the Jews has apparently been assumed to be either undesirable or impossible; the Jewish population is "the most underrepresented national group in the entire Soviet Union."[39]

The memberships of the soviets reflect the regime's concerns about political integration in that they include both party and nonparty members, representatives of various ethnic communities, and local administrators. However, the soviets' integrative potential has not been developed as it might have been. The deputies serve on a volunteer, part-time basis. As a result, the deputies' commitment to their offices is limited, nor can they afford to spend much time with their constituents. Moreover, although the deputies themselves have been partially integrated into the local political system, their constituents' support for the soviets' largely symbolic position must be much more tenuous.

THE LOCAL POLITICAL-BUREAUCRATIC NEXUS

The Soviet local government system is among the growing numbers of local systems in the world that are functionally integrated. The membership and the responsibilities of local political, popular, and administrative bodies overlap in the soviet executive committees. The soviet executive committees are part of the local political network, although they are not at its center. In fact, it is difficult to find a center. Especially in city politics, it is more relevant to talk about a political-bureaucratic nexus. Heads of the local departments of republic and all-union ministries are members, for example, of the popularly elected local soviets, through the executive committees. Local party officials also have dual responsibilities; members of the local soviet executive committees often are members of the local party committees.

With such cross-cutting patterns of officeholding, it should be fairly easy to coordinate local policy; that is the intention. Yet, like all formal systems of coordination, this one does not always function according to the formal plans. The rapid turnover among local officeholders means that relationships among local officials must be constantly reestablished. Local administrators are anxious to get to the top and are therefore highly mobile. In addition, local officials are recruited on the basis of criteria other than their local political influence. Personal loyalty to politicians at higher levels also plays a role in the appointing of local officials. As a result, local officials have less of a political stake in developing the local political connections that would help them to coordinate policy. Legally, local department heads are elected to their positions on the soviet executive committee by the local soviets, from their membership. In fact, local department heads are chosen by individual ministries, on the basis of party recommendations, not by the local soviets, although the official subsequently is given a constituency that he or she legally represents in the local soviet.

In recruitment matters, it is apparent that the soviet's jurisdiction is subordinate to the influence of the party and the ministries. Despite its formal pluralism, local politics is not pluralistic in practice. In fact, some students of Soviet politics see the Communist party at the local level as relatively impermeable.[40] In order to wield effective influence in urban politics, party membership is essential.

But party dominance does not preclude local bureaucratic politics. In addition to the party secretary, heads of economic departments are influential. For example, intrabureaucratic politics enters into local appointments; the decisions are political in that they do not simply reflect how well the officials who are recruited can carry out ministry functions in some abstract sense. Rather, the recruitment decisions are made within the context of competition among ministries for resources and influence. There are local and extralocal dimensions to bureaucratic politics. A successful department head will be able to compete with other influential local administrators in order to satisfy his own superiors in the ministry.

Jerry Hough compares the Soviet province (oblast) to the prefecture of France and Italy, with the provincial Communist party secretary the equivalent of the prefect.[41] Both officials are expected to coordinate the activities of state agencies and production units within their jurisdictions. Hough argues that political control is only one function and often a subsidiary function of both European prefects and Soviet party secretaries. More significant is the coordination that they are able to bring about at the local level, so that specific issues are not passed up the hierarchy to overwhelm the central planning organs.

Specialization within the local party has been increasing and has been characterized as a "basic development" in the Soviet administrative system. Accordingly, the local Communist party organization in the Soviet Union includes specialized departments—"propaganda and agitation," "construction and communal services," "industry," and others. The party departments oversee the administrative departments.

Specialization also has affected the recruitment of the party secretary. The party leaders try to ensure that at least one secretary in each urban center will have previously held a high managerial post in industry or construction, so that they will have expertise sufficient for the task.[42]

The party secretaries' raison d'être is to implement the complex and specific economic production plans that are handed down from the center. The plans can only be implemented smoothly with a little "wheel-greasing" at the local level, and the party secretaries are the wheel-greasers. This is illustrated by the situation in housing. Housing is at a premium in the Soviet Union, and its adequacy has been and still is a major local issue. No sooner had the revolutionary Soviet government taken control in Moscow than it systematically began to reallocate housing. The wealthy were turned out of their commodious quarters; a half-million poor moved from "the cellars, doss-houses and barrack houses in which they had been living into (the) mansions and flats."[44] Sixty years later, the Soviet government still takes particular pride in its ability to provide adequate housing at minimal rents.

The regime's housing objectives are transmitted to local officials in the city Housing Department, under the jurisdiction of the local soviet. If insufficient housing is available for the workers in a projected industrial plant, for example, the party secretary is supposed to intervene and reconcile the housing resources with planned industrial expansion. This can be an extremely complicated undertaking in terms of the sheer numbers of agencies involved. In the city of Cherkassy, four construction trusts and more than thirty subcontracting organizations were involved in implementing housing plans.[45]

The party secretary is expected to reconcile conflicting interests through the secretary's "good offices," rather than by imposing party sanctions. The secretary's ability to do this depends upon the secretary's personal stature vis-à-vis the departments and industrial heads. The first secretary usually has the requisite stature, but his subordinates in the party may not. Hough tells the story of the director of a shale processing combine, who was also a member of the Estonian Central Committee. The director, A. N. Lebedev, dealt with the first secretary of the party's city committee (*gorparkom*), but the head of the industrial-transportation department was afriad even to talk with Lebedev.[46]

Despite the secretary's influence, there are ways to go around the party secretary should local bureaucrats want to do so. The shale combine director mentioned could request authority from his superiors for the combine to provide its own housing. Many choose that option. Approximately 60 percent of the urban housing in the Soviet Union is provided by industries, institutes, and centralized departments rather than by the local government.[47]

There is intense competition for resources among local leaders who are required to implement national plans. State economic planning makes local politics necessary. The stakes associated with implementing local plans encourage local officials to create their own networks of influence—be they plant managers or party officials.

Shifts in planning priorities have brought changes for local politics in their wake. During one period of rapid industrialization, for example, several experiments with decentralized planning were attempted. From 1957 to 1964 the country was divided into economic regions (*sovnarkhoz*). The *sovnarkhoz* were not long-lived, but they did indicate that union-level leaders, mainly Premier Khrushchev, felt politically secure enough to try a different approach to making economic decisions.

The abandonment of the *sovnarkhoz* took place simultaneously with a shift into consumer goods production.[48] One explanation for these concurrent changes is that the competing pressures on state resources increased. In the context of this increasing scarcity, the central authorities had more incentive to intervene and to make certain that political credit for consumer production was given where credit was due (i.e., to the higher party politicians).

Some local industries apparently have been taken over by local managers, but urban authorities still have much less control over economic decisions than they would like. This has occurred despite a 1957 reform that gave urban soviets more responsibility for urban planning.[49]

BUILDING POLITICAL ALLIANCES AT THE LOCAL LEVEL

In many situations, local competition for external resources is diminished because the party secretary and the industrial managers see their interests as overlapping and complementary. Party secretaries perceive their roles as local. They support investments and productive activities thought to be beneficial to their local constituency (pork barrel), as opposed to concerning themselves with the efficient distribution of *national* resources. The party officials' and managers' overlapping interests often are in local industrial expansion. According to one Soviet authority quoted by Hough, ". . . localistic tendencies are not always the result of subjective motives . . . of local officials. In a series of cases they are the result of a one-sided approach to the local economy and of a lack of information about the national need for a particular product. . . ."[50] Whatever the cause of the "localistic tendencies," they represent local alliances and cooperation, rather than competition.

In order to achieve their day-to-day objectives, city leaders in the Soviet Union are quite willing to form "working relationships" with local representatives of national ministries.[51] "Beggar bureaucrats," as Carol Lewis calls them, cannot afford to be particular about where they find support, and support is as likely to be from outside their own ministries as from inside. Officials of state industrial enterprises need cooperation from city leaders to fulfill their production plans; city leaders are anxious to attract industry to help share the costs of social services.[52] By extending mutual favors, both are able to better satisfy the expectations of their superiors.

According to Lewis, relations among local bureaucrats are "pragmatic, makeshift, flexible, and very different from the highly structured relations among city leaders and their superiors."[53] The actual operation of the party helps meet plan requirements, even if it is not bureaucratic and orderly.

The party secretary *within* local industrial plants often is a key link in the informal political network. While it is this secretary's responsibility to concern himself with general policy within the plant, he often subordinates this objective to the more immediate needs of the production process and to making the process function smoothly. Alliances among party and plant officials tend to foster efficient production. The party plant secretary is, in effect, an assistant to the manager. Reflecting the priority of plant interests over party policy, party secretaries often move into the position of plant manager, although movements in the other direction rarely occur.

The most common type of "under-the-table" deals have been those that overstate enterprise efficiency.[54] The coalitions among the industrial managers and the party officials that promote such arrangements leave the local soviets in a rather ambiguous position. The party secretary cannot be an impartial arbiter. He is encouraged to support local industrial interests. Informal accommodations are made between the managers and those soviet department heads who can offer the managers various facilities in return for their cooperation with municipal development plans. Local party secretaries have become involved in such arrangements, effectively discouraging the soviets from exercising their authority.

The elected soviet representatives, who are not also administrators, are relegated to the position of accommodating the personal demands and complaints of their constituents within the informal but nonetheless very real network of local influence. Meetings between soviet members and their constituents tend to be recitations of specific grievances—for example, the lack of a recreation room in an apartment house or the presence of a beer stall in a residential neighborhood. While the local party committees are inundated with specific requests from enterprise managers, the soviet members have the same relationship with their constituents.[55] If the party offices resemble a "dispatcher's office for production supplies," the elected members of the soviets are the consumer's dispatchers of first resort.

State plan priorities are communicated to local authorities through individual industrial managers, as well as through the ministries and the party. In some cities, industries function independently of the city government—a soviet version of the "company town." In those cities, industrial managers often are able to overrule local governments and party officials combined.[56]

BUREAUCRATIC LOCAL POLITICS AND URBAN FINANCE

Influence of a more pervasive kind comes from controlling public purse strings. Soviet local government is no exception to this rule. Among the various local departments and agencies, the representatives of the Ministry of Finance carry particular weight, as do the heads of the state banks. Reflecting their political influence, local Ministry of Finance officials tend to remain in their posts longer than do most other local administrators.[57]

The Finance Ministry has the particular responsibility for distributing to localities their share of the nationally controlled revenues that have been designated for local use. That power puts the ministry in an especially critical position—a position that ministry officials have apparently been able to preserve for a long time. Cattell reports, for example, that the ministry was able to thwart a 1959 law which would have authorized republic governments to control additional public revenues, including some designated for local governments. Finance officials have more authority, too, than do other local bureaucrats. The head of the finance department at the local level is a member of the executive committee and wields considerable influence over the committee.

In addition, through its control over the local budget, the Ministry of Finance serves as intermediary between the soviet executive committee at the local level and the ministries that do not fall under the soviet's jurisdiction. The finances of several local departments—including finance, security, architect-planning, construction materials, construction, and education—are specifically earmarked in the local budget but are underwritten by the central ministries. In addition, some industrial enterprises are not controlled at the local level, even formally, and initial investment decisions are made at higher levels. The most centralized agencies still have an important impact on local affairs, though, and their department heads often serve on the local soviet's executive committee.[58]

Because housing is a major issue in local politics, the agencies that handle housing resources exercise significant power at the local level. The State Construction Bank is a major source of funds for both housing and civil and industrial construction. As such, the bank occupies a position in Soviet cities at least as influential as that of the Federal Reserve Bank in Boston, for example. Consequently, local bank managers in the Soviet Union are subject to directives from the state bank as much as from the local executive committees of the soviet.

As a result of the influence of state organizations, like the banks, a municipal leader must take his case to officials in those state organizations if he wants to make more resources available for urban programs. At that level, state priorities determine the allocation of resources. Local requests receive more attention when they have come from some municipalities than from others. Resources, in fact, are allocated disproportionately among cities; allocations are at least partly indeterminate and political. One comparison of Soviet cities shows that Moscow and Leningrad, specifically, and Russian cities, generally, receive much more than their per capita share of national resources. The index constructed by Lewis, for example, shows Moscow and Leningrad at 225 and 200 percent, respectively, where 100 percent would be equal distribution.[59]

Inadequate finances for meeting local responsibilities appears to be as frequent a complaint among local leaders in the Soviet Union as it is in cities elsewhere in the world. Housing and other urban programs—pollution abatement, health and social services—fall within the purview of local government. The minimal budgets of local governments suggest that the regime gives them a low priority but would like to place the responsibility for that decision on local officials. The financial plight of the cities has been widely aired in the Soviet Union. Its origins are rather unique and grow principally out of the complex administrative structure that has been described.

Soviet cities have several sources of income. Most of the sources are shared by city governments with other authorities. City services are financed through (1) the turnover tax, (2) deductions from profits, and (3) "above-plan profits" from municipal enterprises—i.e., those enterprises that are under city control. The last, particularly, give municipal administrators and the managers of the enterprises ample incentive to cooperate with one another in order to lower costs and raise municipal revenues. However, the "above-plan profits" have not always been turned over to the cities. Lewis cites a number of complaints that these revenues have been siphoned off by extralocal agencies.[60] In one case, Ukraine Republic ministries gained access to the subordinate cities' surplus revenues.

One of the strategies that local actors have used to bargain for resources with the higher-ups has been to join forces with one another. Local alliances take place regardless of the degree of formal autonomy enjoyed by the prospective allies. Officials in agencies that are subject to central control are still potential partners in local coalitions. In fact, they probably are more likely partners because they can use allies outside their own agencies to increase their influence within the agency.

One example is the local militia in Moscow. The militia, according to Cattell, is budgeted locally, but its activities are subject to the union-republic Ministry of Security. Nonetheless, when the militia failed to get a satisfactory response to its manpower needs from its own channels, it turned for allies to the Moscow executive committee and the local press.[61] Thus, the fiscal system, too, stimulates alliances among local bureaucrats and politicians alike.

SUMMARY—PLANS AND BUREAUCRATIC POLITICS

Soviet local government processes are a good example of the artificiality of distinctions between political and administrative roles at the local level. The overlapping can be understood as characteristic of state planning, where the state bureaucracy performs the combined functions of promoting growth and keeping order. Within the Soviet national regime, local administrators are impelled to seek political means of solving their administrative dilemmas.

The potential influence of the party secretary is thereby enhanced insofar as the secretary's office can be used as a channeling device for political solutions. Some scholars maintain that it is the failure of political institutions at the local level that accounts for the bureaucratic politician's appearance. The Soviet case suggests that the explanation lies more in regime objectives. The promotion of rapid economic growth—coupled with the belief that centralized, rational planning is the means to achieve that growth—has been as much responsible for local bureaucratic politicians as have been the shortcomings of the local soviets.

The party secretary is highly influential largely because other local actors acknowledge the necessity for a local political network. And the network's importance, in turn, is a result of the acknowledged complexities of centralized economic planning. State plans placed such strains on local resources and organizing capabilities that the politicization of the party bureaucrat and department technocrat has become as intrinsic to the Soviet system as it has to more decentralized political systems.

Economic Interests in the Local Political Arena

5 Local politics is an integral part of the struggle for power and wealth in national politics. When M. Corpierre argued that "for Algeria as for China, economic development is not priority number one, but priority number three," an unnecessary and unrealistic distinction was made between economic growth and the consolidation of the state and of national regimes.[1] Economic growth is an integral part of contemporary nation-state politics. Economic security is an important part of state-building. Regime elites are particularly sensitive to the demands articulated by key economic groups and organizations. Through history, the establishment of political regimes has been pursued through state intervention in economic processes as well as through more explicitly political means, such as the bureaucratic politics described in the last chapter.

Local government and politics unavoidably are affected by economic growth and state planning. In the contemporary world, economic interests have contributed to the nationalization of politics and to the exercise of political control by national regimes on behalf of either state enterprises or private economic interests. Everywhere, the influence of local politicians has been limited by the economic decisions of national regime elites. The fiscal policies and development plans of national regimes affect different localities in dissimilar ways. For some, outside investment means an economic boom and a "politics of plenty." For others, higher taxes or declining industries spell the beginning of competition for ever scarcer resources and a "politics of scarcity."

In addition to influencing local politics indirectly through the local economy, elite consolidation and state economic planning directly stimulate local political change. For example, the new institutions and new programs created by state planners force local politicians to adapt their politics to new situations. The regionalization programs in France and Iran have brought state planners to the regions and have taken some economic functions away from local politicians and bureaucrats.

This sequence of national intervention and local adaptation produces the dependency and unpredictability of local political networks. The greater the intervention, the more competition that occurs among local politicians. The competition may appear to be part of a trend toward grass-roots democracy, but this competition has been for the support of regime elites rather than for the support of local constituents. It is an indication of dependency not democracy.

In the future, the intervention of extralocal economic interests in local politics is likely to increase, not diminish. Local politics is linked to the national economy directly through the economic activities of the national government and indirectly through private economic interests. For industrialized and nonindustrialized countries alike, government intervention in the economy is now regarded as legitimate and necessary. The alliances between state planners and economic interests upon which government intervention is based are not secret; they are expected.

The vast majority of governments in the contemporary world have been authorized to assume responsibility for several kinds of economic activities: (1) providing incentives, such as physical infrastructure (roads, irrigation, energy) to encourage economic growth; (2) organizing human services (education, public health, etc.); (3) redistributing wealth and income; and (4) maintaining economic stability. These are as familiar to local politicians as to state planners. Each of these activities brings local government and politics into contact with broader extralocal economic issues.

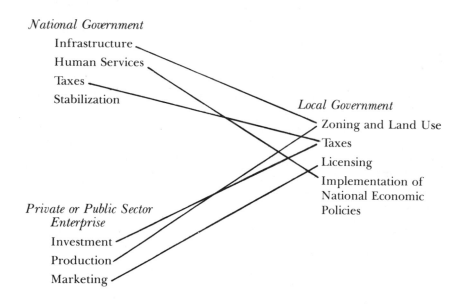

Diagram 2: The National Economy and Local Government

Diagram 2 illustrates the ways in which fiscal and development policies relate to local government authority. The diagram shows that local political economy clearly has a national dimension. For example, the finances of local governments are subject to significant influence by extralocal public authorities and private organizations. Outside investments in local industries, for example, change the tax base of local governments. At the same time, these investments create demands for local services—such as housing and transportation—beyond the capacity of local governments. Local taxing authority usually is limited. Although in some countries local tax *rates* can be changed by local governments, the authority to impose new *kinds* of local taxes usually is vested in state or national governments.

Grants-in-aid from extralocal authorities are commonly used to supplement local taxes. Grants-in-aid come from national tax revenues that are redistributed to localities for expenditures on transportation, public health, or other specific programs. Grants can be a boon to localities that receive them. They are not, however, a reliable source of revenue for local governments because their continuance depends upon decisions made outside the locality and often beyond the control of local officials. Local officials find that they are held accountable for local budget deficits even though they have minimal control over outside funding.

The strength and effects of links between local economic policies and extralocal actors (as indicated in the diagram) vary from one locality to another and from one nation to another. However, few local governments are so removed from national economic processes that they are unaffected by them. Village headmen face some of the same kinds of political dilemmas as do big city mayors; they too must respond to outside economic interests. In contemporary nation-states, interdependence of the agricultural and industrial sectors is such that rural towns are caught up in networks of production and marketing that extend far beyond town boundaries. Moreover, in recent decades, large-scale commercial farming has become increasingly widespread—involving large investments, mechanization, and national credit institutions. The integration of modern economies means that rural local politics can be as penetrated by and contingent upon national policies as city politics.

Economic interdependence does not guarantee political cooperation between national and local elites. Opposition from local leaders can make life more difficult for those at the top, and economic interdependence does not eliminate opposition. From the viewpoint of national policy-makers, *ideal* local authorities are passive agents in the administration of national economic policies. As Annmarie Walsh points out, "the amicability of intergovernmental relations and the extent of local power tolerated are contingent upon the degree of political stability . . .

of the ruling groups."[2] National political elites are most interested in controlling local politicians when their rule is shaky.

Ironically, local politicians find their constituents most dissatisfied during periods of rapid economic change. National regimes may have less material leverage with local politicians precisely at the time when it is most needed. Weak regimes become caught between responding to the demands of local politicians and to those of extralocal economic elites.

The efforts of national politicians to maintain amicable relations with local politicians and with economic elites are most often challenged by the issue of how government funds are to be distributed. Industrial leaders want to see government resources invested where they will simultaneously enhance industrial investments. Politicians in localities that are not experiencing economic growth prefer that the government's resources be distributed on the basis of political loyalty or populist considerations.

Another frequent conflict is over local politicians' demands to participate in formulating and administering national economic policy. Local politicians face pressure from their constituents to intercede in those policy decisions on behalf of local economic interests. When industry and national government officials fail to consult with local politicians, the national regime can lose allies that are valuable in other situations.

Finally, conflicts between economic interests involve local politicians directly. Small businessmen are active in local government in many countries. They often use local political arenas to oppose the interests of large industries and those national policies that support large industries.

The links between local politics and economic interests, then, are disparate regional growth, local participation in economic policy-making, and small business versus big business interests. To some degree the economic aspects of urban politics are distinct from those of rural politics. National politicians use similar political strategies in both settings. Regionalization and community development, discussed later in this chapter, are two such strategies, designed to reduce the conflicts between the demands of economic interests and of local politicians upon national regimes.

NATIONAL POLITICS AND URBAN POLITICAL ECONOMY

The priorities that policy-makers adopt for national development are based upon political realities as much as upon economic models. Thus, some national leaders devote most of their attention and resources to cities. This results in part from the fact that in many Third World countries city voters are typically the principal source of opposition to dominant national parties; rural voters are usually more acquiescent. Urban voters have opposed the Accion Democratica party in Venezuela, the Congress party in India, and, in its early years, the Republican People's party in Turkey. The late president of Algeria, Ahmed Ben Bella, once asked: "What African president has a majority behind him in his capital?"[3]

National regimes have relied upon a variety of means for controlling urban political affairs—some of which have contradicted the regimes' own economic policies. For example, where local power structures have been impervious to direct political intervention, national elites have used indirect economic tactics, such as manipulating import licenses and labor politics to strengthen their hand over local politicians. In addition, many national regimes decide to participate directly in local economic policy by creating quasi-independent agencies that they then superimpose onto the local political structure. The new agencies often have provided additional avenues for political mobility at the local level and stimulated competition among local politicians. In the short run, this competition facilitates external intervention in local affairs.

But in the long run, interventionist strategies often must give way to strategies that contribute more to local politicial stability. National economic growth objectives depend upon a stable environment within which private (or public) productive activities can be carried out. National regimes often respond erratically to this dilemma—first intervening, then withdrawing. In either case, the conflict between national control and local political stability shapes the local marketplace.

The recent experience of the Ghanaian regime is a case in point. In 1961, the government of newly independent Ghana moved to enlarge its control over the national economy and thereby to replace European investors. The first step was to create a monetary reserve system, managed by the national Bank of Ghana.[4] Subsequent measures included the nationalizing of certain foreign firms and raising taxes on the other foreign and private businesses.

The success of these efforts to nationalize economic control, however, had serious local repercussions for the Ghanaian town of Swedru, not far from the capital, Accra. The firms of Swedru that had been threatened with nationalization refused to serve as middlemen for local merchants by making loans and replacing stocks of goods. At that point, local politics became involved. The economic upheaval that occurred in Swedru as a result of nationalizations undermined the popularity of the Convention People's party in Ghana, the party of President Kwame Nkrumah. The party was founded upon a strategy that emphasized the importance of strong local organizations. But building and maintaining these organizations was more problematic in fact than in theory. Local party leaders tried to cut the party organization's losses by granting economic favors to businessmen who supported the party, again linking economic policy to political loyalty.

In the short run, the Convention People's party and the nationalization policies survived intact. A group of party "traders" appeared. These traders worked through the Ghana National Trading Company, the government's stand-in for the private suppliers that it had put out of business. Both the "old" organization, the party, and the new trading company proved to be willing and able partners to the ruling elite.

In time though, neither the party nor its leader, Nkrumah, withstood the pressures created by Ghana's faltering economy. Nkrumah's local allies were expected to play dual roles, as local economic managers and leaders. The Convention People's party national leadership constantly intervened through the local politicians—granting or withholding support and encouraging them to implement commercial policies that benefited particular groups. Little recognition was given to the need for more stable local leadership.

The political interests of national regimes often conflict with those of local economic groups. Local businessmen in many countries find themselves in the same insecure position as were Ghana's European firms, as a result of national regimes' typically strong commitment to economic consolidation. The case of local Peruvian businessmen opposing the large economic organizations favored by the national development plans was discussed in chapter two. Peruvian government planners viewed investments in small business as politically and economically risky. Small businessmen turned to local officials for protection.

Some political analysts think this preference for large enterprise is unwise. Where local political arrangements and local business are supported by national elites, argues Clifford Geertz, the vigorous entrepreneurship necessary for growth is more likely to emerge.[5] Local businessmen may, in fact, be bypassed by national planners, not for reasons of economic efficiency, but because they oppose the overall growth policies of the national regime. The majority of national growth plans formulated during the 1960s and 1970s were based upon technocratic ideologies that tended to support the short-run stability of national political regimes. In one southern Italian town, local tobacco factories were bought by a state agency, and jobs in those factories were made available to supporters of the Christian Democratic party.[6] That way, the local party head was able to control a significant portion of the local economy and consolidate Christian Democratic rule in that locality.

LOCAL POLITICS AND URBAN POLITICAL ECONOMY

Local economic growth is closely linked to local government and politics—as well as to state planning and national regimes. Cooperation between local government and business, either private or public, is associated with economic growth. Two cities in Colombia—Medellin and Barranquilla—have made markedly different progress in industrial development, in the level of public services they provide, and in the infrastructure they have built. Barranquilla, the less progressive of the two, was plagued by governmental instability—instability so pronounced that it became known as "the crematorium."[7] During one fourteen-year period, Barranquilla swore in a new mayor on an average of every four months and twenty-one days. Private sector leaders complained that investment in the city's development was impossible in view of the prevailing unpredictability of public affairs. They invested elsewhere.

In Medellin, by contrast, cooperation between local government and business prevailed. Public sector investments frequently supplemented projects that the private sector undertook. Business leaders participated in making government policy.

What accounted for the lack of cooperation and the political instability that apparently was endemic to Barranquilla? The case study of the two cities provides few explanations other than that of local "culture." Dent notes that Barranquilla relied upon nonlocal capital. This may well have been the cause of recurrent instability. And cycles of instability can indeed become so recurrent that they have a long-term impact on culture. Barranquilla's leaders viewed the world as "capricious." Such a view would be encouraged by the leaders' inability to influence the local economic process.

When local politicians do have some influence over economic policies—or when they hope to have such influence—much of their time and their contacts involve the business community.[8] The cooperation between government and business in Medellin did not include all sectors of the population. Business leaders are brought into formal municipal counsel on a regular basis in many regimes, whether they are businessmen in Medellin, Leningrad factory managers, or mill owners in Isfahan, Iran. In Leningrad, where the government owns the industries, industrial managers have much the same impact upon local politics as do private managers elsewhere.[9] Like managers in the private sector, government bureaucrats do not all share the same interests. Each responds to his own constituency and to superiors in his particular administrative hierarchy. Administrators in industrial states negotiate their differences, whether or not they are privately or publicly employed. The same imperatives of national economic security and local prosperity encourage cooperation among economic managers in publicly and privately run economies.[10]

In contrast, representatives of urban lower classes are almost never found in the paneled boardrooms of industry or otherwise in the company of influential leaders. Their impact upon policy is overt, in confrontation situations, or occurs through the mediation of political patrons, who characteristically handle only individual demands but try to influence overall policy.

Local business interests become more involved with local government than do extralocal businesses. This conclusion is illustrated by the evolution of company towns in the United States.[11] Over the years, local industries grew, and their interests came to transcend local boundaries. The economic necessity of "spreading their risks" was welcomed by corporate managers for political reasons too. According to Norton Long, "few corporations today regard it as desirable to have a major portion of the local labor force dependent on their payroll."[12]

One of the political advantages of spreading corporate operations more thinly is that the corporation cannot be held singly responsible for local economic problems, nor is the firm's welfare dependent upon that of just one town. Absentee firms are the "outsiders" in local politics; they lose the (former) support of the local police and merchants in labor disputes. Their local managers are transient and held to be "aliens" by the community. Nonetheless, because their operations are extralocal, they enjoy greater flexibility *and* the possibility of political support at the national level.

ECONOMIC ISSUES AND POLITICAL IDEOLOGY

Local officials, being relatively powerless, cooperate with organized economic interests. These organized interests, however, often hold opposing points of view. In their competition to influence local officials, they generate strong ideological positions about local government.

Urban land use and housing are political issues that typically create conflict among local interests. As more people move into cities, and now the suburbs in many countries, land prices multiply and create volatile political situations. Too many people without employment, high land prices, and the spatial organization of economic activities contribute to using land in very different ways from one section of a city to another.

Is scarce land to be used for "squatter housing," or is it to provide space for transportation arteries and/or commercial buildings? Much of the responsibility for providing living space for the poor falls upon the government. When housing is inadequate, local officials take the blame.

But others are just as heavily involved. The urban *cacique,* for example, comes into his own in land use and housing issues; getting licenses for squatter settlements is his specialty. In many countries, like the United States, private organizations also make decisions of major importance about land use and housing. Banks do this when they underwrite mortgages to property owners in some sections of cities and not in others.

When local officials attempt to bring their effective power into line with their authority, through such policies as buying land or adjusting property taxes, their efforts frequently meet with opposition from commercial and landowning interests, who have more political resources and experience than do the poor. In such circumstances, local officials are compelled to reaffirm their commitment to commercial and landowning interests rather than to meet the demands of their less politicized, but ill-housed, constituents.

City officials bargain from positions of uncertainty in these matters. Plans for metropolitan land use must be drawn up and implemented by city officials with little information about the level and direction of overall investments in the urban economy. In most countries, business managers are included in local government through various types of metropolitan advisory council mechanisms. But to actually coordinate the local economic activities of all the relevant public and private agencies is a politically impossible task.

One reason is that business managers in many countries prefer to work with local administrators rather than with local politicians. This was the case in southern Italy, where local managers of national corporations promoted the view that politicians were "inefficient."[13] The managers' ideology submerged the point that the politicians represented a different set of interests as electorally accountable party leaders.

Local business advisory councils tend to operate informally and rarely are subject to close public scrutiny. Decisions that affect local economic prosperity do not become matters of public record nor are they legitimized by legislative action. Members are coopted into the councils, and their meetings serve primarily as a sharing of information and mutual understanding rather than as an occasion for formulating authoritative policies. Their discussions serve as informal guidelines to members for making their own organizational decisions. For example, a survey of private firms operating in Malaysia found that participation in public project planning and government projects helped private firms make profitable investment decisions.[14]

Although their world of informal politics sometimes resembles a "never-never land" in its apparent lack of structure, local officials still are criticized for being too legalistic—particularly in their approaches to urban planning.[15] That image, again, has been promoted by interest groups that stand to gain from local officials' weakness.

Municipal leaders, in the midst of conflict over land use, use zoning regulations and city plans as power resources, not as sacred objects. In Iran, for example, Isfahan's city plan was framed in a locked case in the municipal building; its symbolism is much like that of the mace in the

British Parliament. But, above all, the plan was a bargaining counter for municipal officials in their struggle to control nongovernmental interests.

Land use policies are important to local officials because land is the major resource over which these officials have authority. They are not always able to use that authority effectively to control commerce and industry.[16] Occasionally, however, they can capitalize upon the appeal of local "autonomy" to increase their influence over land use decisions. That is one of the few cases of a local ideology that supports local officials in their quest for influence.

RURAL POLITICAL ECONOMY

Local networks of power in rural areas also have been structured around landownership and land control. Often land issues bring in national elites, not because they are interested in land itself but because land politics threatens regime security. For example, in India, national Congress party politicians were anxious to defuse the radical protest politics that grew out of landlessness and extreme poverty.[17] Land redistribution served that purpose. Government-sponsored land distribution and the creation of local cooperative organizations were used by the national elites to avoid a more fundamental political challenge—peasant separatism and subsistence agriculture.[18]

A second source of opposition to many contemporary national regimes has made land distribution very appealing. In addition to countering radical agrarian opposition, land distribution also has been used to curb the political and economic power of large landowners—a step seen as a necessity if the national leaders were to consolidate the political base of their regimes. Without distribution, landowners could control rural voters, food production, tax revenues, and at one time they could even raise local armies.

Without land redistribution, peasants under the influence of landed local elites have been a source of potential opposition to national regimes, particularly to modernizing, secular national regimes.[19] Peasant politics involves religious symbolism and regional or ethnic identities. Landed local elites can capitalize upon these attitudes and in behalf of their interests put the peasants in opposition to secular national regimes (see the discussion of Mexico in chapter two).

Land redistribution, accompanied by the creation of national cooperative organizations and political party branches at the local level, gives the national regime direct access to peasant leaders. National bureaucratic organizations are substituted to provide services traditionally carried out by the local political leaders.

These tactics affect local class structures, too, by depolarizing the landowner-sharecropper distinction and by creating a larger rural middle class. In all, the political and social effects of land redistribution are usually as significant as are its effects upon agricultural production. In most countries, small landowners behave more like small businessmen than did the sharecroppers before them. Cooperative organizations have been used more to capture produce for national markets than to increase production. Similarly, in many countries former landowners continue to play an important role in the economy—in commercial farming, industry, construction, and commerce. But their continued participation in national economic life does not detract from the success of land redistribution, which divested landowners of their exclusive control over peasants and, at the same time, turned the peasants into allies of the national regime.

Subsequent to land redistribution, national regimes employ local branches of national political parties to neutralize agrarian politics still further—to mobilize voters, recruit candidates for office, and provide forums for publicizing government policies. Through local economic intervention and political mobilization, the national regime may absorb local politicians into government parties and offer them access to government resources in exchange for their support of issues important to the regime.

Egypt's Arab Socialist Union, under the late President Nasser, recruited local politicians representing different groups at different times, depending upon their compatibility with national development objectives.[20] Owners of medium-sized farms, who were the chief beneficiaries of land reforms during the early 1960s, had an early foothold in the nominally populist Arab Socialist Union. Later reforms, initiated in 1965 by the union's secretary-general, Ali Sabri, envisaged the party as a mechanism for reaching the rural poor, and curbed the influence of the middle class in the organization.

The local branches of the Arab Socialist Union were vehicles for consolidating the regime's control over rural areas; the role of local branches in broadening popular participation was limited by their lack of control over public policy. Secretary-General Sabri's reforms did not insulate local farmers from the insecurities of agriculture nor did they eliminate rural inequality (see chapter six). The reforms occurred side by side with relatively conservative agricultural development policies. The combination kept the poorer farmers from improving their position, but removed the middle class from power.

COMMUNITY DEVELOPMENT AND UNDERDEVELOPMENT

In the process of regime consolidation in urban and rural localities, significant economic inequalities among localities often must be confronted. In poorer localities, party and administrative organizations, linking national and local politicians, often have been supplemented by community development programs that are promoted as "development from below."

During the late 1950s and early 1960s, the community development idea found advocates among United Nations specialists, national government officials, and a variety of private development institutes. The theory behind community development was that local economic growth rates could be improved by the poor themselves, their heightened incentives to become productive would make up for their lack of capital. Community development was an "integrated approach to development." Local citizens would first realize that they wanted their lives to change, then they would participate in local development decisions and work together cooperatively on local projects. Community development was the adult world's "little engine that could." Outside "change agents" would contribute capital—in amounts small enough that it would not "be wasted."

Community development *without* outside political control is, essentially, a subversive activity. It assumes a high degree of local autonomy in finding solutions to poverty and would threaten existing political organizations. *With* outside control, however, community development is highly supportive of regime stability.

Much of the political support for community development, therefore, came from the fact that, when controlled by outsiders, it promised a low-cost solution to the "problem of poverty." Community development emphasized low-cost capital—investing local capital acquired from "hidden" savings and "wastefully" consumed income, using underemployed labor for community projects, and creating cooperative organizations to replace ordinary commercial organizations.

One rationale for community development was that the "culture of poverty" prevents the poor from using what economic and political power they have. Edward Banfield, an advocate of this view, described the culture of the impoverished southern Italian town, Montegrano, as one of "amoral familism."[21] According to Banfield, amoral familism precluded cooperation among different families toward long-term development goals.

The political side of amoral familism was the politics of poverty. National political parties vied for votes in Montegrano by offering money for votes. But none of the parties' candidates proposed major social or economic reforms. Townspeople, for their part, saw few material benefits coming to them through the national political system. Few saw virtue in political competition, and many looked back fondly to the fascist period of the 1920s to 1940s, when at least order was brought to southern Italy and political corruption was kept to a minimum.

When a community development program was tried near Montegrano, it failed—foundering on the poorer townspeople's strong distrust of outsiders. A long history of unfavorable experiences with contacts between the town and the outside lay behind that distrust. The town's small upper class—the doctor, the druggist, the landowner—were the townspeople's main link with the world beyond Montegrano. All of them were seen by the poor as exploiters.

Montegrano's history was typical of many settings that face similar poverty. The distrust of outsiders complicated the task of outside change agents. In almost all cases of successful community development, leaders have come from within the community.[22]

Despite the fact that indigenous leaders have been linked to successful community development, national bureaucrats typically maintain tight control over development programs. As a result, community development projects sometimes appear to be only a way for the poor to "let off political steam." Referring to the national government of independent Kenya, Henry Bienen wrote, "it has preferred local participation through concrete self-help projects to participation in competitive politics expressed electorally."[23]

Community development has been for the poor, especially and exclusively. At low levels of wealth and power, calculations of risk tend to have a conservative bias; impoverished and powerless people look for longer-run guarantees for their investments than do those with high income and considerable power. When national regimes refuse to invest much capital in community development and to put development projects under local control, community leaders are likely to react to the programs with skepticism.

REGIONALIZATION

Economic regionalization is another development strategy that has as much political as economic significance. Regionalization has been promoted as a means to equalize or rationalize the distribution of investments and production. Most regionalization programs are intended to confront political problems, too (see the French case, in particular).

Regionalization is politically similar to community development. A major motive for regionalization, as for community development, is to remove accountability for regional economic difference from the national regime, while continuing the regime's political control over the region. Regionalization is accompanied by political decentralization in theory, but rarely in practice. Bureaucratic agencies established to implement regionalization plans typically include national as well as regional and local representatives, and link the two levels in other ways.

Regionalization sometimes leaves local officials less powerful, and is quite different from decentralization. This has been particularly true in metropolitan regions that consolidate the functions of municipal and suburban town governments. Creating a metropolitan regional authority promises an administratively efficient framework for urban development and has political appeal for national leaders. Within metropolitan agencies, the power of city and suburban officials is diluted. These officials, in turn, tend to rely increasingly upon alliances with national politicians to enhance their local influence.

Metropolitan regional planning has been stimulated by the increasing trend of industrial plants locating outside cities. Suburban locations are attractive because they are comparatively free from pollution, taxes, and welfare programs. City politicians consequently must balance their lesser influence within regional organizations against their interest in sharing suburban wealth. The threat of protest by the urban poor creates an incentive for city politicians to cooperate with regional authorities. Even the informal alliances that exist among city politicians, on one hand, and financial and business managers, on the other, can be perceived by local politicians as a way for them to influence extralocal economic decisions.

Metropolitan regional authorities and alliances first arose in response to economic growth issues. Significantly for the evolution of local politics, many city politicians devote the largest share of their time and resources to their relationships with financial and industrial groups.[24] As a consequence, demands for improved social services often have been carried to the national level. Increasingly, more dependency upon national politicians grew out of the conflicts of urban politics.

SUMMARY—PLANNING AND LOCAL POLITICS

Regionalization is a response to both politics and economics. Where regionalization has been implemented, it has given rise to further changes in local politics within the region. Specifically, regionalization has tended to break down local power networks and stimulate political alliances among local and extralocal actors.

Other policies, in addition to regionalization, that affect local politics are similarly political and economic in character. The local political arena is a significant dimension of the national political economy. In local politics, for example, the issue of the equity of state economic planning priorities is often raised of inequalities within and among localities, and among regions. In fact, local politics highlights the inseparability of economic growth, regime consolidation, and economic redistribution.

Governmental and nongovernmental actors use local politics in order to advance their own political and economic interests as well as the interests of the locality as a whole.

Local government and politics has been especially valuable to managers of small businesses, urban landowners, and other economic interests whose power essentially is local. At the same time, national politicians intervene in local politics to weaken the influence of those groups with primarily local political and economic resources because the interests of these local groups are seen to be incompatible with the economic and political consolidation of national regimes.

Regionalization, community development, and local "institution-building" have been initiated and evaluated in terms of their economic objectives. But the effects that these policies have had upon local politics make it clear that they have not been politically neutral planning techniques. Local politicians typically react to such development policies as if their own *political* influence were at stake; it almost always has been.

France—A Case Study in Local Politics and Growth Policies

Government at the local level in France is a combination of a highly centralized bureaucracy, represented at the district level by the prefect (an appointed governor), and local, popularly elected councils at the commune (municipal) level. These French communes differ widely in size, although many are very small. There are 38,000 communes in all, and 88 percent have no more than 2,000 inhabitants.[25]

The formal responsibilities of the local authorities are largely the same regardless of the size of the commune. The politics involved in administering individual communes, however, are quite different. One of the most important political relationships within this authoritative framework is that between the prefect and the local authorities. The local council and the mayor (both elected) serve with the (appointed) prefect as the point of contact between the central bureaucracy and local government.

These political contacts and the legal authority of local officials give them some influence over the services that they provide and the way in which those services are financed. The legal duties of local authorities are of four types: obligatory, permissible, forbidden, and "subject to approval by the State." Many of the communes' responsibilities fall into the category of permissible. French communes enjoy the same home rule rights vis-à-vis the national government that towns in the United States do within the federal system.[26] Those policy areas deemed *outside* the legislative competence of communal councils must be specifically enumerated. But the origin of local authority is legislation by higher authorities.

Those local activities that are subject to approval by national authority include the construction of municipal facilities and municipal civil service regulations. This oversight is known as *tutelle*. For many years, *tutelle* was exercised over the budgets of smaller communes and over unusual budgetary expenditures in communes of over 9,000 inhabitants. By 1974, the requirement of budgetary *tutelle* had been abol-

ished.[27] Still among the obligatory duties of local authorities is funding the communes' basic services, such as fire and police service, and for the maintenance of schools, but there is more flexibility in other parts of the budget.

The overall ability of municipal leaders to influence the development of their communes is severely limited by extralocal decisions on the locations of large industrial and agricultural organizations and the policies of central government planners with regard to public investment expenditures. Nonetheless, within that framework, French communal authorities become involved in numerous activities that have an impact upon the development of their communes. Among the commune's permitted functions are building industrial parks, housing, and public recreational facilities, and maintaining roads and schools. The performance of these communal functions may vary among the communes according to party and bureaucratic politics.

This case study illustrates ways in which local officials in France develop areas of political influence within the context of centralized authority and national economic planning. The alliances that local officials create with national bureaucrats is one link through which that influence is acquired. The electoral politics of the French multiparty system is another source of leverage for local officials. The conclusion of the case study is that French mayors are both local political leaders and, at the same time, rather firmly entrenched figures in the machinery of the state. Consequently, part of the case study is about local politics, part about national economic planning and national political competition.

URBAN POLITICIANS AND NATIONAL BUREAUCRATS

The relationships between local politicians and national bureaucrats have been one source of influence for local politicians. These relationships have been influenced only indirectly by partisan issues. Theoretically, in a centralized political system like that of France, local party politics would make little difference to the performance of local governments whose options are limited by decisions made at the center. However, in practice, municipal performance varies considerably. This variability is illustrated by Jerome Milch's study of public policy in two French cities.[28] In one, Montpellier, conservative partisan politics corresponded to the local government's record of financial conservatism. By contrast, Nimes had both a socialist government (and later a communist one) and fiscal policies that were directed more toward providing public services than toward balancing the budget.

These policy variations occurred in part because municipal income is subject to influence by municipal authorities, as well as by the central government. For example, local property tax rates are set by local councils. Thus, in the two French cities studied, quite different proportions of their public revenues were drawn from the property tax, or *centime.* Montpellier obtained 18.6 percent of its operating budget from the *centime* in 1969; whereas for Nimes the *centime* represented over 42 percent of the operating expenses.[29]

Aside from the direct tax, municipalities also raise revenue from indirect taxes and fees for public services such as water, garbage collection, and sewerage. Lastly, subsidies and loans from the central government provide local governments with the means to underwrite local budget deficits.

Each of these categories of revenue can be influenced by local officials. In the case of central government financing, their influence is informal, but it exists nonetheless.

As a result of these financing flexibilities, local officials in Montpellier and Nimes were able to mold local expenditures into different patterns, even though neither municipality was completely self-financing. Consequently, the public services that Montpellier provided and the distribution of the financing burden for those services were quite different from those in Nimes.

The thrust of Montpellier's performance has been toward financial conservatism. Montpellier officials, for example, accepted lower levels of risk on expenditures for subsidized facilities like public housing. Montpellier's authorities strongly emphasized self-financing, while those of Nimes relied more on the central government to underwrite their deficits. The communal government of Montpellier also provided fewer public services than did that of Nimes.

The variability of local government performance observed in Montpellier and Nimes was a result of the interaction among central bureaucrats and local officials, as well as of the party identification of local officials. For example, the greater number of public housing units constructed in Nimes, as contrasted with Montpellier, was the product of an alliance—a result of shared priorities between national housing bureaucrats and local Nimes officials. Decisions about total housing expenditures within municipalities were essentially cooperative decisions arrived at by the housing authorities and local officials. Municipal public housing in France is financed by the central Ministry of Construction and Housing through the local Habitations à Loyer Modérés (HLM), which are directly accountable to the prefect. Municipal authorities can influence specific decisions about the location of housing units and prefects' appointments to the HLM boards.

Particularly noteworthy in this example is the fact that the Nimes government was communist, in opposition to the centrist coalition ruling at the national level. Despite that partisan difference, the housing bureaucrats and Nimes officials lobbied together to obtain funding for public housing. It was to their mutual advantage to finance more public housing—the HLM would have a higher budget and more projects, a bureaucratic advantage, and the local communist officials would be able to meet their election promises.

The options for municipal and district officials to make these kinds of alliances and cooperative arrangements are somewhat more limited in smaller communes than they are in larger ones. The larger municipalities have commensurately larger numbers of local civil servants with expertise in specific policy areas. This expertise helps them to outline project plans and to lobby successfully with central bureaucrats to fund those projects.

In addition, the sheer weight of numbers gives local officials in the more populous cities more bargaining strength with national politicians. When France's large cities turned in a heavier vote for the socialist-communist left in 1977 than before (see chapter one), the national centrist coalition began to reconsider an entire range of policy options—from new international economic policies to regional development programs. Local politicians could use federal funding for those "target" cities.

The mayors of large cities usually have direct access to Paris. That access is important to them because one of the chief sources of the mayor's influence within the commune is his ability to finance public projects. As we have seen, local public projects are carried out by the communal government and are subject to the mayor's approval. Expenditures on such projects represent a substantial proportion of all government expenditures. One estimate places them at 13 percent of total government expenditures in 1967.[30]

The mayors' influence over "spoils" is exceptionally important because it provides them one of the few viable roles that they play in a centralized political system. The mayors are not in the position to directly control local public works projects. What they can do is influence who benefits, locally, from any related construction. Also, they try to influence the availability of public works funds through the prefect and through national politicians from their districts.

Their influence is variable, so mayors tend to be extremely sensitive about their position in the wider political system. They buttress their influence with extralocal alliances wherever possible. Mayors and members of Parliament, for example, have more contact with each other than do local and national politicians in many political systems. This is partly an outgrowth of their career patterns. It has not been uncommon for mayors to serve also as members of Parliament, either successively or simultaneously.

The alliances within this "club" were once cemented by such formal arrangements as the mayors' membership in the presidential electoral college, side by side with national officials. The change to direct elections in 1962 removed this important prerogative from the mayor's office.

For a short time thereafter, mayors still had a collective political organization through which they enjoyed direct access to the national bureaucracy. Their Association of French Mayors held annual congresses and gave its members privileged access to the Ministry of Interior.[31]

This source of influence was also lost, however, in an episode in 1965 that Mark Kesselman has dubbed "the Revolt of the French Mayors." At an annual convention of the association, the mayors had included a number of issues on their agenda that in the view of the Interior Ministry were too political and thus too far beyond the mayors' authority. The association scheduled discussions on the French nuclear force and on civil liberties, as well as on the 1962 changes in the presidential electoral system.

In the mayors' view, the chief source of conflict between them and the Interior Ministry over the years had been the ministry's recurrent threats to restructure local government. Throughout the 1960s, regionalization had been a continuing theme of French development plans, and specific regionalization proposals involved restructuring local government. According to Kesselman's account, the mayors had received periodic reassurances that their offices would not be downgraded in the process. But the reassurances did not prevent an open split between the association and the ministry over the issue during the 1965 convention.

The mayors were responsible for initiating the split; the Interior minister was heckled throughout his speech to the Congress. But the split widened irrevocably when, subsequent to the convention, the minister offered to another organization all the privileges of access which had formerly been enjoyed by the association. Members of the new organization were provided with a lavish office and given lavish receptions. Communist mayors were discouraged from participating in the organization, the Welcome Bureau for Mayors and General Councilors.

Mayors have won some of their other political contests with the Interior Ministry. They have pursued collectively and most vehemently their official prerogatives and informal influence. Following the split with the Ministry of Interior, the original association received even more support from the mayors themselves than it had before. The minister who opposed the mayors lost his post after the 1967 parliamentary elections. Kesselman speculates that his falling-out with the association contributed to his dismissal from the cabinet.

Substantive policies have received less collective support from the mayors, and their bargaining position has been commensurately lower in those areas. Consensus can be achieved on interests they have in common, like the prerogatives of their office. However, questions of investment and growth priorities create divisions among them. The French national government's public investments discriminate among localities and stimulate conflict between the "have" and "have not" localities. As a result of these divisions, local politicians have little influence over economic policy.

Local politicians respond to the economic policies of the central government on the basis of their ideological orientations toward economic growth and their political incentives to cooperate with central bureaucrats. Like those in other political systems, local politicians in France tend to base their decisions upon relatively short-run assessments of political issues and on the material advantages to be gained for their localities from cooperating with central bureaucrats. Long-term economic trends are far harder to assess.

However, to construct political strategies that would influence economic policies, local politicians would have to consider long-run economic and social changes and how these changes would affect political alignments. This the local politicians do more rarely. According to a survey of French local elites in a marginally prosperous commune, they evaluated economic growth and modernization neither critically nor specifically.[32] The local elites equated economic modernization with expansion and progress, not with the specific effects that it would have on their commune.

Within their apparent ideological consensus that modernization was good for everyone, local officials did not value political organizations as means to affect decisions about economic policy or to structure alternative development plans. Instead, political organizations were used to preserve the local elites' traditional bases of influence.

REGIONAL POLICY AND LOCAL POLITICIANS

Because local officials take such great interest in the prerogatives of their offices, central planners have tried to enlist their support for particular policies by including them among the members of new institutions, such as the regional development councils. The councils were established in 1972; their specific mandate was to encourage private economic investments within their respective regions.

Representation on the councils did not give the local officials much real influence, though. First, the major sources of regional investments were not directly subject to the councils' authority. The Ministry of Finance and private industry, together, account for most of the regional development investment in France. Second, the most important regional planning apparatus of the government is centered in a national agency called Delegations for Spatial Planning and Regional

Action (DATARS). Although DATARS is formally under the authority of the Ministry of Interior, the Finance Ministry also has a major role in its decisions. Both ministries may be accessible to the mayors of major cities but not to local officials in general.

Within the central government's regional planning apparatus, political initiative rests with what has been described as technostructure.[33] The network of political influence among the technocrats at the national level involves both personal relationships and those established by more formal organizational structures. Civil servants, for example, often serve in elective offices too.[34] And businessmen and civil servants are connected through similar career combinations.

Through the civil servants' assumption of political and business offices, personal networks of influence can more easily be established among those three groups. No "hard" evidence exists that reciprocal socialization has, in fact, occurred as a result of these networks. However, civil servants-turned-politicians do belong predominantly to the conservative Gaullist party.

Regional planning and development policies are another test of the extent to which public and private interests overlap in the technostructure. Regionalization has political appeal to the national regime. But it is not so clear that private industry, for example, shares those interests.

Regionalization is politically attractive for several reasons. First, the rapid urban population growth and the concentration of industry in a few urban centers (especially Paris) strains public services in those cities. Second, and more significant, these regional imbalances and the attendant urban concentrations have been associated with the increasing number of leftist city governments (see chapter one).

If through the government's regionalization policies, industries could be encouraged to decentralize their operations or to direct new investments to less densely populated and industrialized regions, then the private sector's activities would complement the interests of the national governmental elites. The centrist ruling coalition appears to believe that regionalization would (1) help it stem the tide of leftist local election victories and (2) provide benefits to the coalition's traditional rural constituency.

Even though the central government has funded several regional development programs, many industries still prefer to locate in regions that are already industrialized, thus contributing to the cycle of industrial concentration.[35] Hugh Clout reports that those industrial relocations that have occurred have not been noticeably responsive to government incentives. His findings showed that half of the industrial relocations since 1955 were "accomplished without state aid and the pattern of job creation is almost the reverse of the map of (government) financial assistance."[36] The regional development programs have produced numerous "comités, commissions, et bureaux," but they have not actually devolved economic planning to the regions.

In contrast to the imbalanced regional distribution of private industrial investments, the direct expenditures of central government ministries on social services—housing, health, and education—have been
evenly distributed throughout the regions.[37] Nonetheless, the regional
discrepancy has continued. Social services are not a substitute for investments in production in fueling regional growth.

Sidney Tarrow tested two explanations for the pattern of distribution of central aid to local governments.[38] He concluded that the
economic productivity of a locality was a better indicator of the amount
of central aid which that locality received than were the political advantages that could be gained by aiding small, rural communities—the
government's "populist coalition." Tarrow concluded that the distribution of state aid can be understood in terms of a "productive coalition."
This coalition was made up of (1) localities that had experienced high
rates of population growth and/or increases in nonagricultural
employment, and (2) localities where more of the labor force was
occupied in the service sector. The alternative "populist coalition,"
which Tarrow hypothesized, was made up of those localities with high
proportions of small farms and farm laborers, agricultural employment, and provincial industrial employment.

If the productive coalition has indeed been the basis for the distribution of the central government's grants-in-aid, this explains the
phenomenon that Tarrow identified as a "revolt of the periphery."
Rural regions were becoming dissatisfied with the national regime's
support of the high-growth cities. Many of the localities in the "productive coalition," on the other hand, were among those cities that were
lost by the centrists in the 1977 local elections. There was no guarantee
that grants-in-aid would reverse the trend of leftist voting.

It appears that French governmental decision-makers at the national
level have defined their regime as basically technocratic and have been
moving away from their traditional rural constituencies. Political
losses—in elections—could arise from (mistakenly) (1) relying upon
the high-growth cities to remain with or return to the center and away
from leftist coalitions and (2) relying upon the traditional rural constituencies to remain essentially centrist.

The permanence of the center's productive coalition depends upon
the overall prospects for economic growth in France, as well as upon
stemming the revolt of the periphery. A slowing of economic growth
would limit still further the centrists' opportunities to reap political
benefits from their modest public investments in the cities. Those
investments could only be significant in the context of simultaneous
private sector growth.

The present pattern of public investment could be shifted, toward
the populist coalition, if the regime comes to view the political potential
for recapturing the cities as minimal. This would be a safe strategy for
the regime as long as leftist electoral strength was primarily a local

phenomenon, and it would shift the emphasis back to the periphery and its conservative role.

POLITICS ON THE RURAL PERIPHERY

Political activity at the local level in rural France tends not to be as partisan as urban politics, partly because political "distance" from national partisan politics leads the centrist regime to minimize the revolt of the periphery. The nonpartisan structure of rural local politics plays a significant part in the political strategies pursued by national elites and in the way that regionalization has developed.

French peasants have acquired an image of being little influenced by the outside world either in their farming techniques or in their politics. In Alexander Wylie's (southern) *Village in the Vaucluse,* in Edgar Morin's description of provincial western France, and again in Suzanne Berger's *Peasants Against Politics,* the French farmer is portrayed as an isolated, insular person whose political activities rarely extend beyond his town.[39] In addition, politics and public life are treated by the peasant with as much cynicism as is the "outside" world, although they are, simultaneously, of interest to all.

The peasants' insular political attitudes contrast with the strong influence that extralocal decisions have upon their livelihood. For example, farm produce is marketed at prices that are set in Paris and Brussels (European Community headquarters). French price support policy has favored the large commercial farms in the north and west. Despite this, organized political activities among the small farmers have been limited.

The agricultural syndicates and cooperative movement that could influence price policy on behalf of the small farmers have been weak. They have been continually plagued by their inability to formulate common negotiating positions on even a regionwide, much less a national, basis.[40]

Despite the farmers' political insularity and independence from extralocal organizations, they usually have turned out to vote in national elections in substantial numbers.[41] Urged to the polls by their priests and teachers, the traditional issues for rural voters (aside from the personal reputations of the candidates) have been those relating to the place of the church in politics and society. In many localities, rural voters have supported the church and opposed communism, forming a natural constituency for the center coalition against its leftist (and secular) opposition.

Beyond an underlying consensus on church-state questions and communism, few national issues evidenced a mutuality of interests between the small farmers and the national regime. For example, as we indicated earlier, their long-term economic interests appear to diverge.

To the extent that the basic structure of the national regime has become technocratic, the small farm has a bleak future. The small farm cannot compete—in the market or in politics—with the better-organized large farm enterprises. Neither the syndicate nor the cooperative organizations have developed sufficiently to provide the small farmer with a substitute for the corporate organization.

Were the small farmers' organizations to provide such a structure, they would need to be organized vertically and become involved in both production and marketing.[42] The leaders of the organizations have stressed, instead, grass-roots participation and have tried to make the organizations more open at the village level. They also have emphasized the breadth of their membership and have formed groups in sparsely populated areas. Their weakly organized populism has brought them little power.

As a result of the organizations' local strengths, the interests of specific farmers are represented in local politics. The syndicate and cooperative organizations have been most useful, perhaps, to those who have staffed them and have used their positions as a base for entering local office in order to acquire extralocal influence. When elected mayor, the former syndicate leader becomes enmeshed in what has been called the "honeycomb structure" of establishment politics—consisting of local officials, interest groups, and the territorial agents of the state.[43] At that point, the mayor's political influence becomes linked as closely to central bureaucrats as it was earlier to his local status among the farmers.

Local officials, particularly in France's rural communes, have relatively secure positions in the national political hierarchy. Even though voting turnouts in rural local elections have been high, local political competition has not been commensurately vigorous.[44] And, as we have seen, mayors have successfully resisted efforts to lower their status either by amalgamating small communes into larger units or by shifting significant power to the regional level and away from the prefects with whom the mayors have working relationships. Finally, national politicians have been able to appeal to the mayors by offering them limited access to the bureaucracy. Rural mayors, in particular, have had cooperative relations with the Ministry of Interior.[45]

The combination of their local political security and the center's ability to accommodate them by not directly undermining their authority probably makes the mayors somewhat less than effective in adapting to socioeconomic change. The status quo at least preserves their political privileges.

At the same time, local demands usually are channeled through local leaders. This gives the revolt of the periphery a conservative twist and also inhibits extralocal political organization. One agricultural syndicate leader, M. Tanguy-Prigent, is quoted as saying that the syndicates would be more successful "only if we first arrive at the unity of the peasantry, which [local] nobility tried to block."[46]

A community's level of political participation is in some measure dependent upon the relationship between local notables and their clients.[47] In the classic rural commune, voters are guided by their patrons, and it is extremely difficult to organize them politically without the patron's support. Local notables can control party and syndicate activities. The experience of the syndicate organizations has been that peasants have been less willing to vote for their peers than for persons with higher status.

The difficulty of organizing French peasants along issue lines rather than patron ties is reinforced by the political culture of the peasants, as well as by the absence of any concrete policy alternatives that their leaders might offer them. French farmers, according to Tarrow, were coalesced into a "national class of smallholding peasants" by the French revolution.[48] But this "class" has not been a homogeneous force on economic issues. The smaller farmers and farm laborers have been split by factional conflicts. Consequently, how much support a political party receives in specific communities depends upon the extent to which the party recruits candidates of high status and emphasizes local issues in campaigns—issues that do not, in the long run, affect economic growth policies.

SUMMARY—TECHNOCRATS AND MAYORS

Economic issues—economic growth and the distribution of public resources—have influenced French local politics in several significant ways. The development of the French technocratic structure has produced a notable discontinuity between the objectives and operation of that structure and traditional national-local political linkages. Localities with more entrenched positions in the national economy have received more than their share of public resources. As a result, in those localities the connection between local and national politicians has been strengthened. By contrast, alliances between national and local politicians in less productive localities have been weakened as a result of the fact that neither local nor national politicians have much to offer one another.

Despite technocratic priorities, local politics continues to have a distinct identity as a subsystem of French national politics. In providing public services, as in Montpellier and Nimes, local officials make decisions that reflect their different political ideologies and constituencies. The process of influencing national policies enhances the significance of local office and, from local factions and extralocal alliances, creates the uniquely diffuse roles of local politicians.

In some localities, competitive politics has become a means to register futile protests against national economic policies. In many, local factionalism has been the milieu in which politicians compete for national resources. In fact, what is perhaps the most distinctive characteristic of French local politics is that local politicians depend less upon partisan electoral strategies to create areas of influence for themselves than they do upon bureaucratic bargaining.

Iran—A Case Study in National Development and Local Politics

Bejgerd is an Iranian village—a village in a rapidly industrializing country where the future of village life is uncertain. There are many signs of that uncertainty—as apparent to the visitor as they are to the villager. The village's alfalfa fields are ringed by barren hills; agriculture provides only a marginal living in this semiarid region. The village itself—a collection of some four dozen mud houses, three shops, and a school building—depends upon the irrigation ditches for its water and upon its few trees for fuel. Bejgerd is linked to the outside world by a one-lane track, still narrower where the track has eroded and fallen away into the gullies. Twice each day, buses come down this road from the city of Falavarjan and, beyond that, from Isfahan—a city of more than a half-million people. Three hundred people live in Bejgerd. The distance by road (fifteen miles) between Isfahan and Bejgerd is much less than the material difference between city and village life. Like many villages, Bejgerd has no mosque and only a still pool of water as a public bath. Kerosene lanterns take the place of electric lights. The two-room school house accommodates the small boys during the day and those men and youths who are students in an adult literacy program at night.

Farmers who attend the evening literacy classes learn to read from a text that describes common crop pests and how to deal with them. Not all the students will spend their lives farming, however. Farming is declining in this region of Iran, especially in contrast to the extensive agribusiness complexes growing up in other provinces—particularly Khuzistan and Khurasan. The older men of Bejgerd complain that their sons have left the village to find work in the cities, and that their sons would have stayed if the government had invested more in agriculture. But that is not the future of most small villages like Bejgerd. Instead, the plan is to gradually merge villages like Bejgerd into larger units. Basic public services could then be provided more efficiently and cheaply, conserving the remaining resources for industrialization.

Bejgerd has already been affected by the industrialization of Isfahan. Isfahan has long been a major textile manufacturing center, but other industries have begun to move in also. Isfahan's new steel mill competes for water with Bejgerd's crops. Isfahan is the center of Iran's

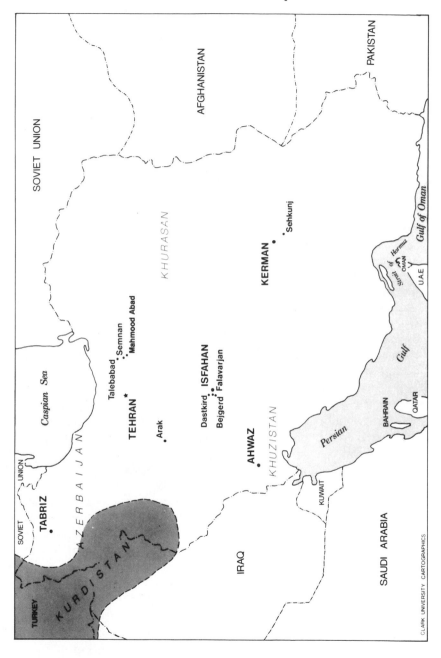

aircraft and electronics industries. The population of the region is much more heterogeneous than it once was. Skilled laborers were brought in from Azerbaijan in northern Iran to work in the steel mill; the steel and aircraft plants, respectively, employ Russians and Americans.

The changing economy of the Bejgerd/Isfahan region, as well as of other areas of Iran, has affected local politics in both the city and outlying villages. Through history, Iran's villages have been neither isolated nor completely self-sufficient. In recent years, they have become more integrated into urban life, the national economy, and—most important—the state. In the face of these changes, local political leaders have found themselves powerless to control development, and their constituents recognize that powerlessness.

Iran's evolution during the past century from a city-state to a nation-state has perhaps had its greatest impact upon the outlying villages. This case study illustrates the ways in which local politics in Iran has been influenced by the imposition of state control over the economy. For example, economic policies are implemented at the local level through a unitary administrative system. The national administrative framework is organized on the basis of provincial, governorate, and district subdivisions. At each of these levels, the chief executive officer is an appointee of the national Ministry of Interior. Village headmen (*kadkhodas*) and city mayors also are linked to national politics. In theory, local executives are elected, but in practice extralocal national regime elites strongly influence their selection.

Other linkages between national and local politics were created in the state-building process. At each level of government, from the grass roots to the province, elected councils share the executive officers' authority, although their collective influence is primarily symbolic. The ineffectiveness of the councils (like other characteristics of local politics) results from the intervention of regime elites into local politics. For many years, the national regime, dominated by the Shah, depended heavily upon the loyalty of local officials and upon their willingness to cooperate with the regime's economic objectives. As a result, the stakes of local political competition were high, and the democratic processes formally legislated rarely were allowed to operate.

VILLAGE POLITICS IN IRAN

In Iran, as elsewhere, social and economic relationships span the urban-rural "gap," and the processes of change affect both city and village. John Connell describes two villages in the province of Khurasan—Mahmood Abad and Talebabad—as being well integrated into the economy and the social life of neighboring Semnan—a city of some thirty thousand inhabitants to the east of Tehran. If village and city life are indeed part of the same economic system, what happens in the village is a result of changes elsewhere. Connell concluded that "social criteria are of more value to understanding rural change than are spatial criteria; a more useful differentiation is between local and national rather than urban and rural."[49] The crucial issue for village development was national economic consolidation.

The villages' economies were not self-sufficient; they were instead the base upon which provincial economic life depended. For example, Mahmood Abad's fields produced mostly cotton, and its entire crop was contracted to the cotton factory in Semnan. The factory also used workers from the village. In fact, so many villagers commuted to the factory that commuter buses ran daily to and from Mahmood Abad.

Villagers traveled to cities for their official business as well as for jobs. Semnan was where they could find the district commissioner (*bakhshdar*). The commissioner occupies the lowest rung on the national administrative ladder and is the court of first resort for villagers in their dealings with the state. Villagers make special requests of the *bakhshdar*—such as for additional village facilities or, more frequently, for assistance in dealing with the state bureaucracy. The *bakhshdar* has more status in the administrative hierarchy than does the *kadkhoda;* Bejgerd's *kadkhoda,* for example, was continually reminded of his dependence upon the *bakhshdar.* Nonetheless, the *bakhshdar* is the lowest official in a highly centralized system. Most local requests and issues are sent on to provincial governors and the national ministries. Such centralization removes much of the incentive for cooperation between village leaders and the *bakhshdars;* neither can expect to get much effective support from the other.

In Bejgerd, the *kadkhoda* is constantly criticized because he is unable to get any results from visiting the *bakhshdar.* The *kadkhoda* has little leverage with the *bakhshdar;* nor has the *bakhshdar* funds available for building his influence in Bejgerd, as most of the development funds go to the cities. Bejgerd lies in the shadow of the steel mill both politically and geographically. It has neither its own cooperative society nor its own health corps. The *kadkhoda* is a leading citizen, but he has little status among his constituents.

Village development projects that depend upon local initiative bring out the weakness of local authority. Legally, village and city development projects must be initiated locally and financed from a combination of local tax receipts and external grants. For village projects, the combination is determined by a formula that varies with the nature of the project. For example, villages are required to raise 40 percent of the cost of roads and 60 percent of electricity project costs.

The concept behind this village development strategy is that projects should depend upon local support and initiative as well as upon national resources. But a *kadkhoda* finds that support hard to obtain. For example, Bejgerd's *kadkhoda* found it difficult to respond to his constituents' demands for a new public bath, one with running water. Even with their ostensible interest in a new bath, he was unable to collect all the local taxes that were due—despite the fact that, on one occasion, he had pursued villagers into the bathhouse itself.

In extreme situations, the response of local officials to their powerlessness has been to abdicate responsibility entirely. For example, Paul English reports that officials in the southern village of Sehkunj were reluctant to become involved in making the most important local decision—how irrigation water was to be distributed.[50] Available water was scarce in Sehkunj, so farmers took hourly turns using it, with the order of use determined by lot each day.

Elsewhere in Iran, by contrast, water customarily was allocated through more structured procedures—usually in meetings of the water owners, whose decisions were administered by "the bailiff of waters." The bailiff, along with the "cropwatcher" and other village functionaries, was chosen with the agreement of the land and water owners and the farmers or sharecroppers.

Sehkunj was an example of a village where public authority broke down in a situation of extreme scarcity. Local opinion did count for something, but it counted in the "politics of survival" rather than in the "politics of growth." The future of Sehkunj, Bejgerd, Mahmood Abad, and other villages like them is uncertain. They have been cut off from provincial and national development funds because they are small and not within areas designated for intensive agricultural development.

Occasionally, national grants have financed development projects despite the lack of local resources. "Model villages," like "model cities" in the United States, are selected for improvements which are underwritten with national funds. Situated on the other side of Isfahan, away from the steel mill and Bejgerd, Dastkird became such a model village. As a result, it enjoyed a new cooperative society building—simultaneously used as a nursery school, a town hall, and a guest house.

Model villages like Dastkird have been integrated into the state marketing system through local cooperatives. Consequently, the local cooperatives' influence upon the local economy is pervasive. From its headquarters, the Dastkird cooperative society supervised the transport of sugar beet, opium, and wheat crops from the fields to the markets. The society ran the village store where rice, tea, and manufactured consumer goods could be purchased. The local two percent tax on agricultural production (abolished in 1977) went into a cooperative loan fund.

Where these cooperative activities run efficiently and smoothly, politics does also. The district commissioner, *bakhshdar,* has a solid base from which to bargain with extralocal authorities for additional development funds, and the cooperation of local officials, in turn, is valued by the commissioner. The value of cooperation between the commissioner and local officials is determined largely by the contribution that local production makes to the national economy—through the marketing structures imposed by the national regime.

The *bakhshdar* also is involved in village politics through his intervention in the recruitment of village officials. Although village offices are filled through local elections, the outcomes of elections are rarely in doubt. *Bakhshdars* suggest candidates for village councils, and they appoint the *kadkhoda* from among local candidates. (Prior to land reform, the *kadkhoda* was appointed by the village landowner and was his representative to the village.) Officers in the cooperative society also are recommended by the *bakhshdar*. In fact, often the same person occupies council and cooperative society offices simultaneously.

Local elections became more competitive after land redistribution. But at the same time, the commissioner's role in the nominating process was strengthened. The overall effect has been a kind of tutelary democracy. Local council members have little real power.

Land redistribution, begun in 1963, served mainly to increase the peasants' political and economic dependence upon the state and externally controlled farming corporations. For example, sharecroppers have always sought loans through landowners or bazaar credit facilities; now the alternatives are the cooperative society or regional banks.

REGIONALIZATION AND LOCAL POLITICS

To replace the traditional sources of credit, Bank Saderat (Iran's major commercial bank) has established a large number of branch banks—in most provinces and also in many small towns. However, these branches have not increased liquidity in most of those peripheral regions; instead they have channeled local capital into the national market. In response to different investment opportunities in various localities, they have shifted funds from less-developed regions to a few growth centers—especially Tehran, Ahwaz, and Isfahan.

The example of Bank Saderat reflects the larger socioeconomic changes underway in Iran. Iran's cities were once havens for landowners, markets for agricultural products, and stopovers on major land trade routes through Asia. Iran's major cities have now become financial and industrial centers. The city's changing role has affected certain provincial cities as much as it has the capital city of Tehran.

Tehran's size—more than five million people—has created serious economic and social problems. Iran's Fourth Development Plan (1968–1972) emphasized the establishment of other regional industrial centers. Four cities—Isfahan, Tabriz, Ahwaz, and Arak—were chosen as the alternative sites for locating industries.

In concept, Iran's regionalization program has several objectives other than spreading industry more evenly through the country. One is the decentralization of regional development planning; another, to improve social welfare in poor regions, is an objective given more prominence during the Fifth Plan period (1973–1978) than it received earlier. Iran's oil-fueled growth exacerbated regional inequalities to such an extent that the regime has to confront them publicly.

These several objectives were added one by one to the initial growth centers concept. Iran used regional planning during earlier periods but in more specific ways, for example, as a means of delimiting experimental development projects, and of pinpointing disaster areas and directing national resources to them.[51] During the Fifth Plan, regionalization came to be understood as an all-encompassing concept for initiating, implementing, and evaluating public policy. And a set of new governing institutions was established to help implement the new planning concept. In practice, however, the individual objectives never formed one coherent program nor had much significance in actual regionalization decisions.

Social welfare, for example, was the dominant criterion for allocating funds for the "special projects" administered by provincial Plan and Budget Bureaus. Two-thirds of these project funds went to social security, education, and rural development.[52] By contrast, those development funds distributed through *national* projects went into oil, and water projects.

Decentralization has remained a subordinate objective. Regional plans still must be approved by the national Economic Council; regional planning agencies are not autonomous. Only 11 percent of the national development funds was allocated to provincial Plan and Budget bureaus. The remaining 89 percent was allocated to the central ministries. As long as oil revenues are available to the national government, it can continue to control development spending without having to share those decisions with local authorities.

In administrative and political terms, regionalization has meant that regional planners implement national social programs but not economic growth policies. Major regional investments in industry and agriculture still are national decisions implemented by national officials.

Under the rural development projects, villages like Dastkird were designated model villages. Within the context of state planning, many of these development projects also are national projects in that national resources fund them. Villages, like Sehkunj, that have not been singled out for development in state plans have remained stagnant or grown poorer. Regionalization has affected neither the politics nor the administration of those villages.

City politicians too, have as little autonomy as they did before regionalization. In fast-growing cities, like Isfahan and Ahwaz, industrialization projects have as yet only increased the number and kinds of demands upon local governments and local politicians, not the influence of local officials.

For the municipality of Isfahan, for example, national industrialization projects vastly complicated local officials' tasks in providing social and public services and keeping social conflict to a minimum. At the end of the Fourth Development Plan, in 1972, Isfahan's annual population growth was estimated to be about 8 percent. The need for public services and food was vastly inflated by the city's rapid growth.

Land speculation on the outskirts of Isfahan increased as the demand for housing expanded. The industries that were introduced as part of the regionalization program located just beyond the municipality limits. So the plants neither expanded the city's tax base, nor were they subject to the city's pollution abatement regulations. Yet, the industries' employees usually chose to live within the city, so that housing, schools, and public services had to be made available to them.

Much of Isfahan's population increase was a result of immigration from rural areas and other provinces. The immigrants' heterogeneous backgrounds created various social problems. For example, the capacity of the courts was strained, according to municipal officials, by the increase in petty crime and personal violence. At the same time, Isfahan's new professionals complained about the lack of modern housing and recreational facilities.

Although the economic changes in Isfahan have created problems for local officials, alliances with national politicians offer local elites opportunities to increase their influence in local affairs. Whatever interest in local autonomy elites had when external ties created new obligations, they were glad to have those ties threatened by local competitors. During the 1940s, for example, Isfahan's textile mill workers were organized into labor unions, some sponsored by the (communist) Tudeh party, others staunchly anticommunist. Labor conflicts were frequent, and a serious lockout finally occurred in 1944.[53] Frightened by the situation's potential for labor violence, the mill owners retracted their earlier opposition to the shah's rule in return for his support against the Tudeh unions. The particular mill owner involved in the lockout had previously been one of a number of local industrialists who had urged the young shah (Mohammed Reza Pahlavi) to adopt a more passive role than had his father, Reza Shah. But with the labor crisis, his views changed. The mill owner's "fear was: no Shah, no army; no property."[54] As a result of that episode, a bill was proposed in the national parliament to allow governors to impose martial law in the event of industrial strikes.

The crisis cemented an alliance between public and private elites that lasted until the 1970s. The strategic value of the alliance to its members was that it established a basis for recruiting local officials. The case of one Isfahan city councillor is illustrative. The councillor began his career during the early 1950s as an anticommunist union leader. By 1973, he had become a prosperous, though not wealthy, businessman. He served simultaneously in the Isfahan guilds chamber council, the Isfahan provincial Iran Novin party committee, on the city's property tax assessment committee, and in several lesser capacities on city council committees.

The semiofficial links between national and local elites have been more important than those maintained through political parties. Party competition, particularly during the years 1950 to 1977, was virtually nonexistent. For most of that time, two political parties predominated—Iran Novin and Mardom. Neither had much more than a nominal organization; their local branches in rural areas consisted of the parties' parliamentary representatives. The Mardom party ran candidates for offices in only a limited number of constituencies. Iran Novin, the government party, consistently won parliamentary and local elections in all the major cities and in the vast majority of provincial towns and villages.

Iran Novin had little impact upon politics, and in 1974, the nominal two-party system was abolished at the shah's behest. It was replaced by a single party, *Rastakhiz* or "resurgence." The Rastakhiz party was intended to be a vehicle for mass participation in politics. Rastakhiz branches were to be established throughout the provinces. Local politicians were encouraged to use the party meetings to criticize the performance of national bureaucrats at the local level. Still, the resulting local party organization was not as effective a power base for local politicians as was an influential ally higher up in the bureaucracy or in the private sector.

The fluidity of local politics in Iran is partly attributable to the centralization of economic planning and the increasing centralization of the state. Regionalization is not likely to eliminate that fluidity within the next few decades. Under the Pahlavi family's rule, the national regime was strongly committed to industrialization. According to that regime's ideology, local autonomy and political competition impeded industrialization. And in the shah's view, they could give expression to antimonarchist sentiments.

URBAN POLITICS—CONTINGENCY AND GROWTH IN ISFAHAN

The regime contributes to a wide gap between authority and power in municipal politics. Local influentials do not typically hold elective city offices. Elected city council members rarely are involved in major decisions—for example, those regarding local development planning. National bureaucrats serving at the local level and local industrial elites make urban policy. The dominance of national bureaucrats in local decision-making is evidenced by their representation on local ad hoc and semipublic organizations—and occasionally on city councils and local party committees as well. Local politics in Iran, as in France, lacks distinct boundaries. It is characterized by a multiplicity of links between local and national officials. The capital, Tehran, has been governed by the national bureaucrats to an even greater extent than other Iranian cities. For example, in 1975, foreign consultants were brought in under government contract to advise the Tehran Development Council, whose secretary-general, Abdol Majid Majidi, was simultaneously director of the national Plan and Budget Organization.

Like the Tehran Development Council in the capital, provincial cities have groups that coordinate urban policy. This author has visited Isfahan and studied its development over recent years. Isfahan's politics is a good example of local urban politics in Iran. In Isfahan, various government officials were part of a group that, although not formally constituted, regularly met during the early 1970s to discuss development plans. That group, through its members, was a direct link between national and urban politics. Seven members had high appointive government posts, four in Isfahan and three in Tehran. The eighth was the city council president, who was from one prominent Isfahan landowning family, had married into another, and was the brother of Tehran's mayor.[55]

Local networks of contact and influence have been particularly active in Iran, where city councils have been prevented from participating actively in policy-making. The tight control over political competition maintained by the national regime has contributed to the growth of informal influence.[56] Politicians have been particularly cautious about assuming responsibility for decisions within such a circumscribed environment. Informal networks of influence flourish in such a climate.

Formal authority also brings together different agencies and offices. The Isfahan provincial committee of the former governing party, Iran Novin, included the Isfahan bureau heads of national ministries and city councillors. The city committee charged with assessing property for tax purposes included a local representative of the Ministry of Finance, a city councillor, and an official of the *edare-ye sabt* (office of the notary public). Army officers (some retired, others not) occupy positions in the municipality as well as in other public sector organizations such as the *otagh-e asnaf* (the central guild committee) and the *ogaf* (the religious endowment organization that is a major landholder in the city).

Diagram 3 shows the linkages between official and unofficial groups in Isfahan that existed in the early 1970s and underscores the direct

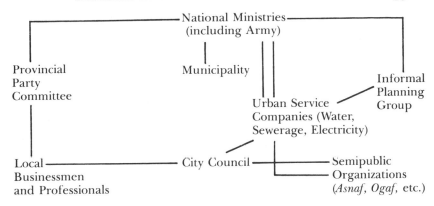

Diagram 3: Linkages between Municipal Actors

involvement of national institutions in municipal affairs. Through the agencies' overlapping memberships, two groups existed, one surrounding the ministries and the other surrounding the city council. The city council was involved primarily with the party and the local business community (through its members) and secondarily with the planning group and the guilds (with one council member in each). The council had very little to do with the national ministries or with urban service organizations. The council was isolated from the most important decision-making arenas. The only exceptions were the councillors' personal contacts on the provincial party committee, but the committee itself played no leadership role.

The nationalization of city politics also has had the effect of limiting the influence of city council members to more specific "grievance politics" (see chapter three). Mayors and city councillors have served more as sounding boards for complaints than as policy-makers. Elective officials have had to adapt to the uncertain context within which they find themselves. For example, the chairman of Isfahan's city council had to cope with complaints about the housing shortages and high food prices that were intensified by the steel mill and a new helicopter base. His skills as an intermediary between individual demands and national development policies were repeatedly tested as he attempted to stretch the municipality's scarce resources and his equally limited power into both areas.

As long as local elected officials limited themselves to praising the national regime and to satisfying individual demands, they enjoyed a measure of security and status within the local community. The formal institutions of local democracy, in turn, were symbolically useful to the national regime. For example, Isfahan city council meetings received regular publicity in the local newspaper, but these meetings usually consisted of little more than laudatory speeches on a holiday, when a prominent official visited from Tehran, or when a public project was completed in the city.

Serving on city councils was an extraprofessional, voluntary activity carried out in addition to a councillor's usual career. Many of the council members in Isfahan have been small businessmen, medical doctors, or government officials, both active and retired. Besides the anticommunist union leader, only one member actually had "worked his way up" from laborer to councillor. A textile worker and community organizer, he was active in the provincial party organization of Iran Novin. His nomination to the council was intended to symbolize the regime's commitment to improving the lot of working-class Iranians.

Sometimes city councillors have been able to improve their own economic positions or to help others do so. Isfahan council members are continually in contact with the business community in the city. In the past they have been able to intervene in municipal decisions on behalf of particular individuals. They have usually intervened to seek exemptions from municipal ordinances for their constituents—adjusting zoning regulations, taxes, public health restrictions, and regulations governing the use of public space (sidewalks, for example, were commonly used for selling merchandise in the past). This intervention was one way in which businessmen, both on and off the council, could enhance their security by earning reciprocal favors.

Local offices could be used more effectively to meet individual demands if the local politicians had national allies. City councillors welcomed the intervention of national officials in city politics when it was on behalf of the councillors' own clients. On the other hand, councillors resented external intervention when it undercut their own local authority and/or when it gave their constituents opportunities to circumvent the municipality.

Many decisions in Isfahan were affected by the city councillors through informal contacts with local businessmen—for example, contacts at the Rotary and Lions clubs or the Chamber of Commerce. Municipal officials in Isfahan also had been in a more competitive position vis-à-vis the guilds when the latter came under the control of the national government. According to the national regime, the guilds were "outdated" economic organizations, and inefficient. In actuality, the guilds were a center of antimonarchist politics. Local guilds and religious authorities often cooperated with one another and were politically very active in Iranian city politics.

State intervention in local politics has made the city council and the guilds more competitive with one another than they once were. Both the council and the guilds try to use their national allies to gain influence over each other.

In 1973, the councils and guilds lobbied in Tehran for authority over price control courts. The prices of food and other retail goods were controlled under state authority. Local guild courts enforced the price controls. Municipal officials argued that they would be more effective generally if they could reacquire the authority to adjudicate price violations that they had lost to the guilds some years ago. The guilds strongly opposed such a change; they were anxious to retain whatever remnants of their traditional power that they could.

SUMMARY—STATE PLANNING AND LOCAL POLITICIANS

As long as the Iranian regime evaluates its performance against the standard of the presently industrialized states and as long as oil revenues permit the regime to pursue rapid industrialization, economic planning will emphasize the role of state elites in investment decisions. Over the past decade, many bills were passed by the Iranian parliament that laid the groundwork for economic and political decentralization, but such objectives were outweighed by the imperatives of state planning.

Economic and political processes operated simultaneously to keep local politics dependent upon regime priorities. The regime's political insecurity reinforced its inclination to intervene in local politics. The centrifugal forces of Iran's historical city-state politics caused the national regime to "lie uneasily." The political stakes of encouraging local autonomy were, as a consequence, very high.

Local politicians (and local politics) operated within this framework, making use of national allies when they could and of their local influence at other times. Local elective office did not provide its occupants with significant power to make public policy. But it did afford them opportunities to influence specific decisions and to introduce some flexibility into state plans.

6 Redistributive Issues in Local Politics

Social and economic inequalities are at the heart of much local political competition. Local politics involves redistributive issues in two ways. First, these inequalities are often the source of jurisdictional disputes between towns and states or wards and cities. Second, within local political arenas, contests are waged over the formation and implementation of specific redistributive policies.

Local politics often is class politics. Looking at local politics within the framework of redistributive issues makes it easier to see the relevance to the national political economy of formal institutions of local government, local leadership strategies, and local political participation. Local politics plays a specific role in national redistributive politics; it often *defuses* conflict over such issues.

In concept, redistributive policies are those that have a direct impact upon economic inequalities. They alter economic structures and influence the economic security of relatively disadvantaged groups. In terms of actual policy results, the distinction between redistributive and other kinds of policies is not an easy one to draw. The previous chapter discussed local politics in the context of economic growth. As that chapter indicated, policies implemented in the name of growth can be redistributive as well, particularly in their differential effects upon particular geographical regions. Urban development programs, as a case in point, affect the distribution of income both among and within cities.

A distinction between growth and redistributive policies that has more empirical value is the *political* distinction that includes the perceptions of policy-makers as well as actual policy results. Do the parties to a political conflict perceive the issue as redistributive? In contemporary politics, for example, education and welfare policies characteristically are regarded as redistributive even though their redistributive effects are often questionable.

Theodore Lowi initiated the contemporary discussion in political theory of redistributive politics.[1] According to Lowi's definition, redistributive policies are (1) those that affect, or potentially affect, the relations among broad categories of people and (2) those that are concerned with the "equal possessions" rather than the "equal treatment" of these categories (or classes). In contrast, Lowi describes growth policies as "distributive." The critical difference between redistributive and distributive or growth policies is that the latter are made in a context of more abundant resources, and as a result, conflicts over the shares received by each class do not arise.

Patronage, for example, is a distributive policy process. It is cooptive, not conflictual, and does not affect broad categories of people. On the other hand, redistributive policy processes are highly conflictual. Because redistribution threatens the privileged, redistributive policy is made in a much more closed setting—a setting in which a regime's "command posts" take an active role. Distributive, or growth, policy may be made in a casual and haphazard fashion; redistributive politics is planned and deliberate, and closely held by the "haves."

Lowi's understanding of the distinct characters of the two policy processes is helpful in understanding the dynamics of national intervention in local politics. Local politics has come to be identified with the politics of privilege—as the last outpost of the "haves."

Michael Crozier has argued that redistributive policies fare better at the national level than they do in local political processes.[2] In his study of comparative bureaucratic processes, Crozier argues that the United States' political system is more decentralized than many, with a proliferation of authorities at different levels of government. This complexity makes it possible for "willful individuals to block the intentions of whole communities for a long time; numerous routines develop around local positions of influence; the feeble are not protected so well against the strong; and, generally, a large number of vicious circles will protect and reinforce local conservatism."[3]

Politicians, like scholars, have argued that centralization is a necessary prerequisite for redistribution. But this chapter argues the reverse, that *redistribution has been a prerequisite for centralization and state-building.* This means that national decision-makers have supported redistributive policies only to the point where redistribution has facilitated state consolidation and no further. Conversely, local conservatism often finds support at the national level. National intervention in local politics in support of redistribution has been at least equally matched by deliberate nonintervention in support of local conservatism. Local politicians rarely deserve their jaded reputation among reformers.

The roles that social welfare policies and local politics played in the development of European nation-states suggest that it is not valid to *contrast* the performance of national and local politics. Local political systems are part of national political systems. Accordingly, the policy outcomes in each system are interrelated. Redistributive politics is contested seriously in both national and local political arenas. At the national level, coalitions are formed around redistributive issues in such a manner that the "command posts" of the political system are protected.[4] These coalitions, for example, keep redistributive issues out of the public arena wherever possible.

Local politics often contributes to this protective strategy by defusing redistributive demands at the grass roots—particularizing general class demands through modified versions of pork barrel and through coopting lower-class leaders into public office. Conflicts arise between national and local politicians over redistributive issues, but such polarized conflicts have been exceptional, not customary. And national politicians have opposed local support for redistributive policies as often as they have opposed local support for conservative policies.

STATE-BUILDING AND SOCIAL POLICY

The history of social welfare programs in Europe indicates that more is involved in redistributive politics than the issues of central or local control. The poor laws of seventeenth- and eighteenth-century Europe were local laws; they committed the local community to sharing responsibility for indigent persons. Poor laws were rudimentary extensions of informal and community obligations from earlier days. These community welfare programs usually involved "means tests" of some sort; recipients of the community's charity had to be declared poor by the administrators of the funds before they could share in them. Social insurance programs, which extended help to broader groups of the population than the indigent, did not exist in most industrialized countries until the late nineteenth or early twentieth century.

The early poor laws were motivated by a combination of paternalistic community responsibility for poverty and the necessity of maintaining order. Accordingly, the justices of peace in England administered "43 Elizabeth" (or the 1601 Act for the Relief of the Poor) with an eye to keeping paupers off the streets. Local authorities exercised considerable discretion in dealing with paupers; compulsory employment of the poor was common.

The relationship between police and welfare functions was, at that time, an obvious fact of political life. The tardiness with which French welfare policies developed in comparison to those of England, for example, has been attributed to the efficiency of the French police.[5] A regulation adopted by the Paris *Parlement* as early as 1532 ordered "all beggars be seized and made to clean streets and work on fortifications and bridges."[6]

In other European countries, the usual alternative to "outdoor relief" was the poorhouse. Local police were responsible for enforcing the poor laws. Almost two centuries after the Elizabethan act, the Prussian Civil Code of 1794 specified that "the Police Authority of every place must provide for all poor and destitute persons, whose substance cannot be ensured in any other way."[7]

For many years the local authorities in Prussia did just that; they provided public employment from local funds for those who were able to work. Comprehensive welfare programs were not adopted in Germany until the end of the nineteenth century, when industrialization and the political interests of Bismarck combined in the establishment of a highly centralized welfare system. (One final venture into locally funded welfare programs was attempted in 1854, but it was short-lived.)

Following the beginnings of welfare programs with the poor laws, both England and France went through a period during which public commitments to social welfare diminished. The neglect of welfare programs was encouraged by the popular doctrine of economic liberalism, the dependence of national labor markets upon a mobile labor force, and the new industrial elite's interest in undermining the influence of traditional authorities over the poor. One of the chief disadvantages of the poor laws had been that they were local community programs. From the standpoint of the industrializing societies, their local character hindered labor mobility. In agrarian Europe, the interest of employers was to keep farm laborers attached to the farms, and locally administered poor laws contributed to these attachments. Later, labor mobility was more highly valued, and poor laws, as a consequence, were attacked as remnants of traditional and backward social institutions. For many years, there were no substitutes for them at the national level.

The equivalents of the European poor laws can be found today in many developing countries. In many countries, local governments administer local welfare funds that are allocated to the poor on a case-by-case basis. In Iran, for example, a proportion of municipal budgets is designated for spending on local welfare cases. Part of this fund is transferred to the Red Lion and Sun Society—an Iranian organization equivalent to the Red Cross—for distribution. The remainder is allocated to individual families, who argue their need to municipal officials.

The same kind of "welfare program" can be found in India. In India, as well as Iran and many other countries, the sums distributed are small compared with the inequalities of wealth and income that exist. The variations among Indian localities in the amounts spent on welfare are significant. Some towns spend virtually nothing. At the same time, national social insurance programs are being adopted in certain cities and especially in the Indian government and larger industries.[8] The progression in European nation-states from local poor laws to national insurance programs is being replicated in new states like India.

SOCIAL WELFARE AND STATE-BUILDING

Most industrialized states had begun to implement national welfare programs by the middle of the twentieth century. In fact, some social insurance schemes began in Europe during the latter half of the nineteenth century. The first social welfare programs were stimulated in part by the increasingly vocal socialists who advocated thorough-going redistributive policies. But programs were enacted, for the most part, by conservative leaders like Bismarck and Napoleon III, who sought to preserve their power by making at least minimal concessions to industrial workers' security needs.[9]

Of all the early national welfare programs, Bismarck's has been used most often as an example of how social policies were structured according to the political objectives of the regimes that sponsored them. The regime could capture the loyalty of the groups who were covered by social insurance schemes.[10] So that the programs would accomplish these political objectives, they were nationally controlled and even structured vertically by industry, rather than administered by local authorities.

Bismarck's strategy has not become obsolete with the passage of time. In the context of contemporary development "theory," state-controlled social policies of all kinds are viewed as instrumental to the process of state-building. For example, William Platt wrote that developing countries must choose between the "centrifugal" effects of "parent-oriented" education and the more desirable "centripetal" effects of "future-oriented," nationally controlled education.[11] State-controlled educational systems have been justified by the need for manpower training to support industrial growth; it was argued that local and/or private education could provide neither the necessary skills nor the scientific training needed for technological advancement.

The redistributive issues connected with education tend to be submerged in rhetoric about the impact of educational policy upon economic growth. National education administrators justify many of their decisions in growth terms, even though their decisions may be of even greater redistributive significance. For example, the urban bias of public policy in many countries characteristically shows up in more schools and better-trained teachers for city children and fewer for children in rural areas. These policies are redistributive. In this case, they have not so much to do with the alternatives of "future-oriented" or "parent-oriented" education as with the political risks of ignoring city youth. Like Bismarck, contemporary national politicians prefer social policies that enhance the stability of their regimes.

Social policies found to be politically feasible often have been accomplished through national authorization and local implementation. Federal loans and grants made available to local school systems for science education in the United States in the post-Sputnik period are examples of such a mixture of authority. In Great Britain, national education inspectors regularly supervise the coordination of educational programs in schools throughout the country, while day-to-day control over schools remains in the hands of local authorities. The local education authorities are not autonomous from the central government by any means; they can be (and have been) abolished or have had their jurisdictions altered by the national Ministry of Education. The system as a whole is one of shared, rather than exclusive, policy responsibilities.

Similar examples of combined national and local policy-making can be found in Japan. Local school administration is often influenced by state-initiated changes in educational policy. After World War II, the Japanese educational system was restructured after the American model. As time passed, it became apparent to Japanese policy-makers that the imported educational system should be adapted to Japanese needs. In one instance, the middle schools that offered general education were to be restructured to provide more specialized programs. The national policy was to be implemented through local decisions, with national financial incentives to "sweeten" those decisions. In one community, three small middle schools were to be amalgamated as part of the program.[12] The major dispute in the town was over where the combined middle school would be located, not over the question of specialized education. The local school districts eventually authorized the consolidation. The conflict that arose locally only prolonged implementation; it did not prevent it. Mixed authority helped to avoid political confrontation along local-national lines.

LOCAL AUTONOMY AND REDISTRIBUTIVE ISSUES

Local autonomy often has been used as a "rallying cry" in attempts to block the adoption or implementation of redistributive policies. As a result, local autonomy has been seen as a symbol of privilege. As a variety of case studies shows, however, appeals for local autonomy have been made by specific interest groups that oppose redistributive policies. It is not local politics that inhibits redistribution but the particular groups that use local politics.

The question of whether to press demands at the national or local level is a tactical one. In Britain, during the post–World War II period, for example, the Labour party advocated public housing. The party's housing policy was enacted in national legislation and implemented by local housing authorities. Although the Labour party's original housing targets were subsequently scaled down, Conservative party opposition to the program continued to build up. Ultimately, in the 1972

National Housing Act, local authorities were required to increase the rents on the public units in order to bring them in line with private housing costs.[13]

This *national* retrenchment followed a period during which public housing had suffered various setbacks at the local level—at least one of which resulted from national legislation. A 1965 government reorganization act took the full authority for housing projects away from the metropolitan Greater London Council. It gave borough officials within the metropolitan area the authority to veto public housing projects within their jurisdictions. During the first three years after the reorganization, the number of housing units attempted and completed by different borough councils varied widely. Councils with Labour party majorities attempted to build almost 50 percent *more* units than did those controlled by the Conservative party.[14]

Party conflict over social policies occurred in both local and national politics. As the example of Britain's housing program indicates, the reduction of social policy commitments is by no means limited to decisions made locally; it involves other levels of government as well.

Where socioeconomic classes are residentially segregated, local jurisdictions do influence the politics of redistribution. Urban residential patterns within socially and economically stratified societies have been a major factor in establishing the political value of local autonomy to conservative politicians. Local autonomy as a factor in redistributive politics has depended upon the relationship between class and demography.

Political Parties and Redistributive Issues

Redistributive issues arise simultaneously in local and national arenas because of the political party and interest group organizations that link the two. These organizations serve as transmission belts in the formulating and implementing of political strategies and in the linking of the fortunes of local and extralocal politicians. For example, in the Federal Republic of Germany, Social Democratic party leaders at the national level pressured their state organizations *not* to support educational reform. The national leaders had concluded that a progressive state party position would cost the party votes in national elections.[15] Conversely, the beginnings of Sweden's present public housing programs can be traced to the initiative of Swedish Social Democrats in the municipality of Stockholm, initiatives which subsequently were transmitted through the Social Democratic party to the center.

In competitive-party systems, whether conservative or progressive views happen to be in the ascendancy at the center or in local politics depends partly upon the distribution of party support over time. The right and the left have both debated redistributive issues in national and in local political arenas. When conservatives are in minority positions at the center, they tend to concentrate on local politics. At the local level they often can find islands of popular support that give them a better opportunity to change or influence policy.

Most interparty conflicts in competitive-party systems are over relatively minor changes in redistributive policies and programs. When redistributive issues are brought into the political arena and taken over by party politicians, the issues typically are framed in incremental terms; they have lost much of their redistributive "punch."

In some countries, local governments have formal authority over a significant variety of redistributive policies. Robert Fried has examined three countries—the Federal Republic of Germany, Austria, and Switzerland—in order to determine what accounts for the differences among localities in their reactions to redistributive policies. He concluded that only slight differences could be attributed to differences among political parties. For example, the Swiss Radicals "are more to the left than the Marxists" with regard to "taxing, spending, municipalization, and public employment" but "further to the right than the Catholic-Conservatives" in their record on public housing.[16]

As an alternative to party-ideological explanations, Fried attributed some of the local variation to limitations upon the resources available to local governments. These resource limits imposed a de facto conservatism on local policy—a conservatism indicated by the similarity of local redistributive policies from the 1920s through the 1960s.

National social welfare programs in Western Europe have not changed much either. Relatively conservative social welfare programs proved to be a consistently valuable rallying point for state-building and for industrial development throughout Europe. Much of the partisan maneuvering for influence has been over specific questions about levels of financial commitment, benefit criteria, and program control.

A major political realignment in Europe doubtlessly would affect the relative roles of national and local authorities in social welfare policymaking. A review of *Politics in the Post-Welfare State* describes the rise of communalism, a variety of local autonomy, in the Swedish left.[17] Swedish educational reform and public housing programs were carried out simultaneously with a consolidation of local communes.[18] The consolidation was meant to equalize the size of electoral districts and to make the implementation of the social reforms more efficient. But by 1976, the national government had changed hands; the Social Democrats lost an election and a conservative coalition came into office. If the post-welfare realignment were to give conservative parties new national strength—as it appeared to have in northern Europe—the Social Democrats would need local political strategies to advance redistributive policies.

The interplay between political party competition and demands for local autonomy in Britain and Sweden illustrates the point that particular decision-making sites produce progressive or conservative outcomes only within specific political contexts. The incremental character of social policy in contemporary industrial democracies minimizes the distinctions among parties and between local and national policy processes. "The frontiers of European and American social policy are not a combat zone between pro- and anti-welfare state forces. In practice, there is no defensible line between the armies."[19] Without a "defensible line," one cannot stake out the contested ground. Theodore Lowi has argued that this vagueness is characteristic of redistributive politics; because the stakes are so high, the "combatants" try to camouflage the combat zone.[20] Attributing antiredistribution gains to the conservatism of local politicians does just that. The fundamental class differences at each level of government are dismissed as the idiosyncracies of local politics.

REDISTRIBUTION, LOCAL STYLE

In fact, local politicians are continuously involved in distributive politics. "The poor are the most grateful people in the world . . .," said Plunkitt.[21] Because they have been schooled in that wisdom, local politicians are very responsive to redistributive demands, in a political way. Redistributive issues, like others, must have some political implications for politicians to become involved. The more specific the incentives, the more vigorously politicians will promote the demands of the less advantaged—whether the politicians are national or local.

The type of involvement depends largely upon the extent to which redistributive policies are centralized under the jurisdiction of the national government. Where centralization is virtually complete, local politicians relate to redistributive issues by intervening on behalf of particular clients for particular benefits. On the other hand, where there are some opportunities for local initiative and where local demands for redistributive policies are politicized—politicians at the local level respond in a similarly substantive fashion.

Redistributive issues become more salient in local politics when economic growth slows and demands for redistribution actually threaten the privileged. Local politicians are the first to feel the pressure. The big city welfare squeeze is a local manifestation of the discrepancy between growth and equality. Local politicians have often simply passed demands made upon them for redistribution on to authorities at higher levels. At other times, they have used their control over local offices to seek reforms or to widen the scope of local government authority. Which alternative was selected depended upon the relationship between national and local politicians and the degree of politicization of the poor.

Local politicians have responded to redistribution demands in four ways: (1) seeking incremental benefits for their local clients from local resources, (2) seeking incremental benefits from national resources, (3) promoting increased local authority over redistributive policies, and (4) lobbying for redistributive policies at the national level. The third response is the riskiest because it challenges the political and economic structure of centralized regimes. Local politicians rarely have opted for that response unless they are certain that (1) the problem is structural, (2) incremental responses are irrelevant, and (3) extralocal politicians will not respond to redistributive demands. In other words, local politicians must decide whether they can avoid the growth-welfare political squeeze by appealing to national politicians, or whether they must look for more radical ways of preserving their power.

The presence of all three conditions was noted in a 1973 reevaluation of municipal fiscal policies of the Tokyo metropolitan government.[22] Under a section of their report entitled "Basic Concept," city officials pointed to the "collapse of the 'high growth' policy of the national economy" and "the crisis of local government finances." The fiscal side of the "welfare squeeze" was essentially that the business tax preferences granted by the central government were too high, and the property taxes levied against businesses at the metropolitan level were too low. Business taxes did not permit local revenues to meet the demands for social services that had accompanied the growth of the city. Local politicians were pessimistic about getting relief from national politicians. They had little hope that the state would neglect "State-encrusted" business in order to shift resources to urban social services. Local officials responded by advocating local autonomy, particularly local fiscal autonomy, as a basic step toward urban redistributive policy reforms.

Tokyo's municipal officials, representing a socialist-communist coalition, suggested a "civil minimum" concept to guide local redistributive policies after the groundwork had been laid by fiscal reforms. The civil minimum concept included social policies considered most crucial to collective life. The first two areas to be singled out were welfare and disaster prvention. (Disaster prevention included urban pollution and disasters resulting from excessive congestion.)

In the short run, the civil minimum detracted from state economic growth objectives. It sought to improve the urban environment by restricting the concentration of population and industry. The civil minimum proposal was made in the context of local officials' understanding that the structure of the state-industrial coalition was a fundamental cause of the urban crisis that the local politicians were confronting. At the same time, the Tokyo metropolitan government had been controlled by a leftist coalition for many years. The local officials' pessimism about the city's fiscal problems grew from their partisan differences with the Liberal Democratic national regime. If Tokyo's fiscal soundness depended upon the city getting more support from business and industry, local officials were certain that that support would come while they were in office.

Local officials had to work within the context of the alliance between the national government and the Tokyo business-industrial community. The fiscal autonomy of Tokyo under that regime was inextricably linked to conservative local policies. The socialist-communist coalition at the municipal level had little room for maneuver. From every standpoint, it was highly unlikely that national elites would bail out the city without its administration making unacceptable compromises.

Political structures vary, and it is for that reason that different local leaders behave differently in response to redistributive issues. *Caciques,* local political bosses in Mexico, often have been quite active in soliciting welfare benefits for their local constituents, and they receive payments from those same constituents in return for their services. By contrast, local communist trade union leaders in France often seem to have forsaken their "shop" constituents. They have failed to bargain on local benefits, turning instead to national politics, where the "bureaucratic phenomenon" has absorbed labor and welfare policy into the state apparatus.

The interest of French communists in politics and power at the center has not resulted in the neglect of labor interests. Labor demands have simply been pushed at the national level. According to Michael Crozier, French workers are as privileged as any in Europe.[23] Conversely, the brokerage of Mexican *caciques* had done little to alleviate the poverty of their clients. Mexico's rapid industrial growth has left many behind, particularly the Indian population. Except for land redistribution, "in no other major Latin American country has less been done directly by the government for the bottom quarter of society."[24]

Though less is done, there is no lack of political fanfare. The *caciques* are aware of the political stakes that the regime has in how well they serve as intermediaries in the poor communities. The *caciques* operate in a context in which welfare issues have been totally politicized, as is the "redistributive" system itself. The bulk of the social services made available to residents of poor communities have been available under the aegis of the ruling government party. Medical clinics were directly and visibly sponsored by the party; social workers were employed by the party; and the party sponsored the *Jornada de mejoramiento ambiental* (improvement Sundays), during which particular communities were singled out for vaccinations, fumigations, garbage pickup, food handouts, theatre, *and* political rallies.

At one of these improvement Sundays the master of ceremonies asked the audience to send letters to the president of Mexico requesting him to deal "firmly" with antigovernment demonstrators.[25] This was at a time when there were university student demonstrations, and the government hoped to encourage a backlash among the urban poor.

By linking social services, community improvement, and personal intervention to the state via the ruling party, national politicians hoped to balance the negative image of the state that was held by the poor. Cornelius reports that as high as 78 percent of the poor in one survey anticipated "bad treatment" from the police.[26] The police often were in the unenviable position of enforcing property laws, while the party's social service workers and the *caciques* were symbols of the regime's commitment to protecting the poor. The *caciques* defended squatters, and the social workers dispensed welfare benefits.

Despite the overwhelmingly bad reputation of the police—who are, after all, as much an arm of the state as are the ruling party and the *cacique*—Cornelius reaches a somewhat surprising judgment about the attitudes of the poor. He concludes that the migrant poor in Mexico City were satisfied with their relationship to the larger political system. The government's attempts to separate, in the public's view, social services and political control, while linking them strategically, were reasonably successful. The party-regime was more forthcoming with individual benefits than it was with collective benefits for poor communities. The local party intermediaries were thorough. Despite the complexity of the Mexico City "welfare" system, the majority of those poor interviewed by Cornelius could point to having received some personal favor or material benefit from the regime via the local leaders.

What helped make the Mexican welfare system work was the centrality of the ruling party to the regime. Local political support was important to the party leadership. The local party served as an exchange: social service for political support. The role of the politicians, consequently, was extremely important.

The sequence of political development has been quite different in Mexico than, for example, in Germany. As we have seen, the provision of social services by the German state preceded party politics, and social services were initially a product of the authoritarian regime of Bismarck. In the European context, where social services were absorbed at an early stage by the nation-states, those services could, during later periods, be influenced by institutional group pressure at the national level. In the early states, social policies were not subject to local political influence to the same degree that they were where partisan politics, regime support, and social services had coalesced within the same nexus of political calculations.

SUMMARY—LOCAL POLITICS AND THE DIFFUSION OF REDISTRIBUTIVE ISSUES

In single-party regimes, local politics is involved in redistributive politics to the extent that local politicians often bear the responsibility for preventing general redistributive demands from accumulating and

eventually being raised at the national level. In competitive-party regimes, when opposing parties hold office at the national and local
levels, redistributive issues often encourage local politicians to seek
more basic local governmental reforms (as has been the case with
Japan's "civil minimum" and leftist municipal governments). Finally,
outside organized party politics, redistributive issues are brought into
local politics by privileged communities that claim local authority to
protect themselves against redistribution.

In the same way that political strategies at the national level differ
among policy areas, as Lowi concluded, so redistributive issues in local
politics follow specific patterns according to the strategic interests
of the political actors involved. Local politicians are not "anti-
redistributive" or "conservative" because their constituencies are in-
herently conservative, or small, or "traditional" in some fashion. Local
politics contributes to conservative policy outcomes in the context of
national regime politics.

The two case studies that follow look at this conclusion from slightly
different angles. In the United States, local political activity is so visible
and pronounced that it is possible to talk about a local redistributive
policy. Egyptian local politics, on the other hand, takes place within a
highly centralized administrative system. The dominance of the national regime in the administration of public policy, coupled with the
intensity of redistributive politics under conditions of scarcity, gives the
question a different cast in Egypt. There, local politics has an impact on
essentially national redistributive policies. These two perspectives, one
local and the other national, illustrate a common point—that redistributive policy outcomes depend upon how the political process affects politicians' strategies, not upon whether the policies are made at
the national or local level.

The United States—The Class Case for Local Control

> In the United States a means has arisen whereby persons with financial
> resources can employ them to their children's benefit without having
> them spread over everybody else's children as well.[27]

The means by which that has been achieved is local control of schools.
The educationally privileged have used the ethos of grass-roots democracy which prevails in the United States to protect that privilege.

Jurisdictional questions have been less visible in social welfare programs than in education, but there too local control has been evoked in
order to influence welfare and housing policies. Although most welfare
programs are initiated at the state and federal levels, local politics has
influenced the way in which the programs are implemented.[28]

Not all localities have demanded control over social programs. Local
control has been demanded most frequently not in defense of the local
community against "creeping federalism," but in defense of the inter-

ests of prosperous local communities against their poorer neighbors. It is for this reason that federal control over social policies historically has been associated with egalitarian reforms in the United States.

Noting the almost sacred position of community and locality in American politics, one study concludes that in the United States, local government has been valued as an end in itself, one that excludes a "broad national purposefulness."[29] Jurisdictional issues are resolved in favor of localities more often in the United States than in political systems with stronger traditions of centralization. But the social policy record does *not* support the conclusion that this is a result of values rather than of tactical maneuvers. The variation in social policy outcomes within the United States has been sufficiently great to suggest that "local is as local does."

Jurisdictional demands are made when supporters believe that those demands will produce political gains for them. Local autonomy has often been advocated by opponents of redistributive social policies. The two are not theoretically or permanently linked, however. They are linked strategically through the actual workings of the political process. There *are* local variations in social policy performance. Local politics can play a vital role in class competition. But the impact of local politics on class competition can only be clearly seen if the two are kept analytically separate.

LOCAL POLITICS AND THE SCHOOLS

Sociologists Basil Zimmer and Amos Hawley asked local schools and government officials whether or not amalgamation of school districts would improve the quality of the schools.[30] The answers that they received varied with whether the official represented an urban or a suburban community. Seven out of eight *urban* officials responded that amalgamation would improve the quality of schooling; six out of seven *suburban* officials felt that it would not. The division was between the wealthier suburbs, which resisted attempts to alter the status quo, and the cities, which stood to gain from sharing the costs of schools with the suburbs.

The politics of education is highly salient from the standpoint of both numbers and doctrine; public schools have significant redistributive potential, and contests for control of them, as a consequence, have been intense. Schools in the United States are, when viewed through what Heidenheimer calls a "constitutionally idolatrous" lens, at the core of the "American way of life."[31] A much higher proportion of American youth (in the United States) attends public schools for a longer period of time than do youth in most countries. The equalization of school facilities has received support from disadvantaged groups within the population as a right to which American children are entitled.

By keeping metropolitan areas divided into separate municipalities, wealthier sections have been able to isolate themselves from less-privileged sections, and to provide themselves with better public services as a result of their greater resource base. Richard Hill's comparison of "separate and unequal" metropolitan areas in the United States shows that inequality of family income and of public fiscal resources was higher where the number of municipalites in an area was greater *and* where the size of the nonwhite population was higher.[32] Inequalities among municipalities also proved to be greater in "older, larger, and more densely populated areas."

Intrametropolitan inequalities have increased over roughly the same time period that education and welfare programs have evolved as measures to equalize opportunities for disadvantaged groups. It is not surprising, then, that political resistance to altering municipal boundaries and to taking jurisdiction over schools and welfare programs away from municipal agencies has intensified.

In the late 1960s, racial segregation in the schools became a political issue through the busing controversy. Redistributive demands also challenged the constitutionality of financing schools from local property taxes.

How education is financed has been a more tractable issue than has segregation. The trend has been toward using state funds, but not national, for public schools. In 1910, almost all public education expenditures came out of local property taxes, but by the 1960s, 40 percent of all public school financing came from the states.[33] Throughout, the federal share of public education financing continued to be insignificant (from 4 to 8 percent), although there were significant variations in the extent to which local property taxes were used. Greenville, North Carolina, for example, obtained 65 percent of its funds for education from extralocal sources; but Des Moines, Iowa, relied upon property taxes for 90 percent of its school budget—leaving only 10 percent for extralocal sources.[34]

The differences in school financing policies are only part of broader educational policy differences. One of the most controversial policy areas has been desegregation and local control. For example, in the name of participatory democracy and education reform, the Ocean Hill-Brownsville section of New York City began an experiment with decentralized school operations in 1968. For New York City, local control over public schools had different meanings at different times. The *citywide* school system had been in operation since 1896. Its beginning was itself a victory for educational reformers over the preceding ward system.

Each reform affected local educational policies. The real issue was determining which kind of local control would prevail. Still closer to the core of the conflict: To what extent would any reform involve a major reallocation of resources among the metropolitan area schools?

Local control of education became a major issue during the 1960s in the context of de facto segregation of schools in northern cities and the disparities in public educational expenditures within metropolitan areas. The two phenomena were virtually inseparable: white suburbs were the districts that could afford higher school expenditures; residential segregation in metropolitan areas was by income as well as by race.[35]

Black urban poverty was more persistent than white urban poverty. During the 1960s, city school children were disadvantaged relative to their suburban counterparts in terms of the public resources spent on their education. A decade earlier, the distribution of resources between city and suburb was the reverse, but throughout the 1950s and 1960s, center cities became poorer and blacker. Support in the wealthier metropolitan sections for segregating school jurisdictions had simultaneously become stronger.

The decentralization of public school systems like Ocean Hill was essentially a bargain struck between the urban (mostly black) poor and municipal leaders. Authority over educational policy was transferred to the community in exchange for the community's reducing demands on the municipal school boards to deal with intracity inequalities.

The nature of this bargain is illustrated by the politics of education in Detroit.[36] As a temporary tactic, decentralization was offered as a solution to Detroit's educational "problems" by some black leaders. It was promptly accepted, however, by much of the white population as a strategic alternative to prolonged conflict over busing. A few organizations refused to go along with the decentralization proposal when it first reached the state legislature in 1968. But opposition slowly dwindled after the National Association for the Advancement of Colored People (NAACP) recommended elected supervisory boards for each school. It became apparent that decentralization was a means to bring two quite opposite points of view together—that of the black community (articulated but not supported at the polls because blacks were a bare minority in the electorate) and that of the antibusing, antiintegration groups.

The reconciliation took a mere four years to accomplish, from the initial confrontation over de facto segregation in 1964 to the passage of decentralization legislation in 1968. In 1964, Detroit had elected a school board in which a majority of the membership appeared to be committed to equalizing existing education facilities. By 1968, that board had been recalled, and its replacement had fewer blacks on it than any school board in Detroit's recent history.

Local opponents of busing found support in two places besides city hall—the state legislature and the federal Supreme Court. What was happening in Detroit in the late 1960s was also happening in Lansing and Washington. The honeymoon of the modern reconstruction of the South was over, and the new Republican administration in Washington was facing pressure to put the brakes on the momentum for social change that had built up during the previous decade. The federal bureaucracy was under instructions not to demand local compliance with desegregation rulings. The courts took over the major responsibility for handling whatever conflict the schools generated. By the time the desegregation cases reached the Supreme Court, Nixon's appointees to the Court were able to overturn the lower courts' rulings in favor of redistributing educational advantages.

Ample evidence on pupil achievement has been accumulated to indicate that the stakes in desegregation and school financing politics are significant. A map of Detroit school districts showed the correspondence between pupil scores on standardized tests and levels of income in the districts. Race made a difference too. Black students were typically behind white students, and fewer were enrolled in college preparatory programs.[37] Redistributive educational policies, by themselves, are not likely to eliminate inequalities quickly, especially in the absence of other political and social changes. On the other hand, it is not surprising, in light of the maldistribution of educational opportunities, that the schools have been in the thick of the fray over the allocation of public resources.

Detroit and New York are just two examples of how symbols of local control have been manipulated on behalf of class interests. William Miller, a college professor who was also an alderman in New Haven during the mid-1960s, has written about how the busing issue developed in that city.[38] "Let them improve their own schools, instead of taking over ours" was one hostile reaction from his middle-class constituents. One of the crucial tests of perceptions of community is the way in which the terms *they* and *we* are used. In terms of class conflict in New Haven, local control meant neighborhood control. On other occasions, however, the municipality would become the critical line of defense against "outsiders."

OUR HOUSES AND THEIR HOUSES

Residential segregation lay behind de facto school segregation. Everyone quickly learned that fact in the tumultuous days of the mid-1960s when candidates for national and local office alike were expected to make their positions on busing clear. Conflicts like the busing issue had the effect of a "crash course" in class and community for new entrants into local politics. In the context of equal education, housing policy assumed a kind of instant centrality. Middle-class, mostly white, voters who were not completely opposed to the objectives behind busing still promoted the view that busing was simply the wrong way to go about integration. Integrate housing and the schools will follow suit, they argued.[39]

In many respects, that challenge became the urban issue of the 1970s. A major step toward residential integration had been taken with the "open housing" act of 1964, which prohibited discrimination by race in real estate sales and rentals. But antidiscrimination agencies and the courts faced practical problems in enforcing the act (for example, real estate agents could discriminate informally among their clients). Zoning and income inequalities too, effectively inhibit racial integration of upper-income sections. For those reasons, de facto segregation has continued in the housing market as it has in the schools.

In controversies over housing and land use, local control has been as vigorously defended as it has in education. And here too the courts began to play an important role in testing the extent of that commitment to local control. The specific issues that have arisen regarding housing and land use have been (1) the location of low-income housing; (2) "snob" zoning by cities and towns in an attempt to limit the in-migration of low-income groups; and (3) regional land use planning for conservation and environmental protection. This last issue is related to the point that local autonomy is a strategic, not a substantive, value. The same groups that have opposed local authorities when they have not promoted conservation have unequivocally supported home rule or local control when the issue was low-income housing or industrial zoning.

The question of using local political boundaries for exclusionary or restrictive purposes has been raised in numerous court cases, most of them during the period from 1970 to 1976. Several of the decisions limited the principle of exclusive local control of land use. In New Jersey, for example, a state superior court ruled that the community of Mount Laurel would have to draw up and implement an affirmative action plan for low-income housing.[40]

The Mount Laurel case, brought against the township by the NAACP, was a landmark decision in the history of exclusionary zoning. In the United States, and in many other countries, zoning and land use has been within the authority of local governments. So wealthy communities that wanted to exclude the poor seized the opportunity to do so even when that meant incorporating as townships in order to have zoning authority.

According to Michael Danielson's account of the case, a regional planning agency followed up on the Mount Laurel decision, using that momentum to encourage further zoning reforms. But court decisions like that of Mount Laurel have not always brought such positive local responses. In 1969, for example, the Chicago federal district court handed down a ruling in the Gautreaux case. The Gautreaux decision was to scatter public housing throughout the city, rather than centering it in low-income, predominantly black, neighborhoods.⁴¹ For years thereafter the Chicago Housing Authority and the City Council refused to implement the court decision. Local political foot-dragging prompted one lawyer involved to point out that "courts cannot build houses" and that without local political support, court intervention would be ineffective.

These court cases highlight the race and class issues involved in local zoning regulations. Many such cases never make it to court; they are resolved less formally. For example, when municipalities are required to provide low-income housing, they comply by constructing housing for the elderly.

Public housing became more of a local zoning issue when scattered housing became popular. When public housing first was promoted in national legislation in 1937, the approach to housing low-income families was to build large complexes concentrated in specific sections of cities. Then came the large-scale migration of southern blacks to the northern cities beginning in the 1950s and continuing over the next decade. The concentration of low-income housing became a concentration of black families in otherwise segregated cities. The resultant racial segregation carried with it the reality of high crime rates and the threat of civil violence. It was then that scattering public housing became a popular concept.

Efforts to integrate residential areas by income and race have progressed *incrementally*—as has so often been the case with social change in the United States. New Haven's experience with public housing, for example, illustrates the many tactics that can be used to impede change. Before scattered public housing could be built, the New Haven Public Housing Authority was required to hold public hearings in those wards that were prospective sites for its projects. Opposition at the ward level to a number of proposals to deconcentrate public housing was so strong that the projects were dropped.

Later, indirect rent subsidies were provided to low-income families, and the "scattering" of the poor took place—without the hearings and without the attendant storm of protest. Elsewhere, as in Chicago, where the scattering received more publicity and was opposed by a strong political machine, even scattering failed.

WELFARE POLITICS IN LOCAL POLITICS

The variability of political strategies and of local policy outcomes makes the local political arena of continuing importance in conflicts over the redistribution of public resources. The local politics of welfare policy adds another dimension to the incremental image of redistributive policy-making seen from the standpoint of jurisdictional disputes. Local control over education and housing has been used to inhibit redistribution. Welfare issues return our attention to politics within localities, rather than between localities. Some localities, and some states, have welfare records that are not explained by local control or federal prerogatives.[42]

Local variations in welfare performance have been possible in large part because federal poverty programs have authorized voluntary, rather than mandatory, participation from the states. On the basis of these local variations, it appears that certain types of social and political environments support welfare policies more than others. For example, in welfare (as in education), racial conflict has been a major impediment to increasing local commitments to welfare programs. Andrew Cowart's study of states' responses to federal antipoverty programs shows that those states with large black populations and/or those with significant black out-migration were less responsive to the federal programs.[43] The way the author interprets his finding is that antipoverty programs are associated with helping blacks, especially in states with large black populations. In these states (mostly) white policymakers are not likely to show any initiative in seeking resources for (mostly) black poor.

On the other hand, when black migration to northern urban areas culminated in high levels of urban unemployment and the threat of urban violence, local welfare rolls showed a dramatic increase.[44] Part of this increase, according to the same study, was a result of the greater awareness of welfare opportunities among the poor; part resulted from local authorities reducing the eligibility criteria, under the threat of unrest among the poor.

The study found local authorities to be quite responsive to the potential political demands of the poor, but the analysis did not look at local or regional differences. According to the legal provisions of national welfare legislation, all the states were off to an equal start in implementing welfare programs; in actuality, the start was unequal—politically, socially, and economically.

One explanation of incrementalism is that redistributive policies evolve slowly where redistribution is more threatening (i.e., where social cleavages are deep). Another is that the level of political support for redistribution policies may not be related at all to the intensity of the problems which they are designed to alleviate. Political support for redistributive policies may vary, in fact, inversely with inequality. The more entrenched the inequalities, the harder it can be to find support for remedial action. The states that spent little on welfare programs were southern, rural, and poor.

The principle "them that's got gets" applies to federal grants as well as to private wealth. In addition to their sizable black populations, those states that failed to respond to federal antipoverty programs were those that did not have well-established welfare programs and the welfare bureaucracies that go along with those programs. Their need for poverty programs was even greater than that of the states that went after the funds more determinedly. But the political pressure from welfare bureaucrats to get funding for welfare programs was in fact less.

The absence of established local welfare programs is both a symptom and a cause of the sluggish responses of some states to antipoverty programs. There is a very practical bureaucratic explanation for this. In order to seek out federal funds, state agencies need staff experienced in dealing with Washington bureaucrats. Those states that have welfare programs also had expert lobbyists.

In larger cities, leaders of welfare organizations and antipoverty officials operate within informal networks of welfare experts or specialists that extend beyond the city to other cities and to Washington. This bureaucratic network is useful for information and influence, and by belonging to it, city bureaucrats have a valuable political resource.

The maxim that a little welfare leads to more welfare has a political explanation. Welfare clientele may be politicized. Welfare recipients' organizations are additional sources of both pressure upon and support for welfare bureaucrats.

The fact that states with large black populations did not use federal welfare incentives illustrates the relationship among welfare, race, and local politics. Southern states made up a high proportion of the unresponsive states. The low participation of blacks in southern politics, in general, and segregated party organizations, in particular, would explain the unimportance of welfare programs for southern party leaders in the past. Where political participation has been open to black as well as white poor, welfare programs have been more attractive to local leaders. As a consequence, the inverse relationship between the size of the black population and the implementation of welfare programs found in the south begins to disappear. Krefetz's study of twenty-six cities where the poor are organized showed that client-oriented welfare programs did not correlate with the size of the black population.[45] The structure of local politics influenced welfare policy more than did the numbers of poor or blacks.

The Local Politics of Redistributive Policies

Local and state differences in welfare policy outcomes cannot be completely accounted for in terms of economic or demographic differences. If a particular welfare policy outcome is not simply a result of how rich a state or a city is (or how black a state or city population is), what does make a difference? The explanations that appear to be helpful are both *local* and *political*.[46] Machine politics, electoral strategies, and leadership style all have an impact on public policy.

Edward Banfield and James Wilson's classic study of Chicago politics argues that city politicians use welfare programs to enlist black support since the traditional patronage rewards system was undermined by the "good government" movement.[47] From the vantage point of black city-dwellers, however, welfare and patronage are vastly different. The patronage distributed through the old city machines provided more than income to the poor. Patronage also meant getting into the city administrative system and working into a network of political influence.

As Banfield and Wilson acknowledge, the scope of influence that black voters and politicians have had in city politics often has been quite limited. This has been particularly true in "reformed" cities with non-partisan governments in which black candidates for public office campaign for at-large, mostly white votes. One could speculate that immigrant workers had greater political mobility in city politics at the turn of the century than contemporary blacks have not only because of the economic expansion of the time but also because patronage allowed greater access to politics. From the standpoint of access, welfare was not a substitute for patronage.

Where the poor, especially the black poor, have electoral clout, decision-makers can and do respond to the poor with more comprehensive programs and with access to the welfare bureaucracy. Without that electoral power there is little incentive for those decision-makers to make more than moderate commitments to welfare programs or to opening participation in the implementation of welfare programs to representatives of the poor.

Baltimore and San Francisco both have municipal welfare programs. They also both have sizable black populations. However, Baltimore's municipal bureaucracy is 46 percent black. It also has a welfare program that takes in a higher percentage of the city's poor population.[48]

Krefetz, in her study of those cities' welfare programs, argues that municipal politics was responsible for the differences. Both Baltimore and San Francisco politicians want to stay in power, but in Baltimore politics, black voters have more influence. Baltimore is divided into wards for city council elections and the elections are partisan. San Francisco, on the other hand, has nonpartisan and at-large elections for the board of supervisors (council) and the mayorality—both of which lessen the weight of the black vote.

Like welfare, the issue of local jurisdiction over schools, zoning, and housing has been basically political, not legal. Despite overtures to grass-roots democracy in the United States, local authority comes from state governments, not from the towns. Municipal and town charters and attendant allocations of policy authority are approved by state legislatures and can be changed by state legislatures. For example, Boston's mayor, Kevin White, proposed a city charter "reform" in

1976; the Massachusetts state legislature defeated it. Legally, the state legislature was under no constraint to take either positive or negative action. Politically, the "grass-roots control over schools" doctrine favored burying the new charter in committee.

White's proposed reform included provisions to reduce the autonomy of the Boston School Committee by giving the municipality control over its budget. The proposal also would have enlarged the five-member school committee to fifteen members and provided for their election by district rather than by the present at-large system. Depending upon how the districts were drawn, the reform offered the possibility to black voters that they would carry more weight in the School Committee elections than they did under the at-large, small committee system. The district map that the mayor submitted to the council thus attracted much attention. It did accomplish the objective of breaking up segregated neighborhoods. However, before the reform itself was defeated in the state legislature, Councillor DiCara offered his own districting plan:

> I have cleaned up the lines from a racial point of view. I have put black people in districts which are all black and white people in districts which are all white. My purpose is to make it as representative a system as possible.[49]

Despite DiCara's objections to the violations of the "geographic integrity of a number of neighborhoods," he voted for the reform in the city council. The specific determination of district lines was to be made—after the legislature approved the reform in its entirety—by the council's Committee on Laws and Ordinances and subject to their interpretation of the Supreme Court's one-man, one-vote ruling.

The real political battles were yet to come, however. When the reform was turned down, widespread disagreement followed—with the various councilmen enlisting support for their particular positions from the grass-roots ethos, from interpretations of state legislative intent, and from federal redistricting formulas.

The home rule petition also included the stipulation that city council elections would be conducted on a partisan basis, rather than the previous nonpartisan arrangement. But the petition did not recommend establishing districts for council elections; it would be an at-large council. Hence, minority groups were skeptical that the council would represent their interests well in redistricting the School Committee.

Some efforts have been made to organize the poor at the grass-roots level, but organizers have had to compete with established political machines. One controversial community organizer named Saul Alinsky spent much of his time during the early 1960s experimenting with methods of building political organizations, especially among Chicago's poor. Chicago's Mayor Daley did the same but in different ways. Mayor Daley's organization seemed (to his opponents) virtually indestructible; Alinsky's was less powerful and less resilient. The Daley organization was in the business of getting votes and doing favors; Alinsky's organization was concerned with the multiple tasks associated with improving community life. The Daley organization's black machine occupied a dependent, but protected, position in the dominant urban political system. Alinsky's organization was created for the express purpose of severing that dependent relationship; accordingly, there were fewer immediate payoffs for his supporters.

Despite the apparent handicaps of the independent, largely black community organizations in Chicago, several gained recognition as political forces to be contended with in implementing urban renewal programs.[50] According to Chicago's urban master plan, the implementation of urban renewal was to be carried out in a decentralized fashion by neighborhoods. Decentralization was attractive as a strategy for avoiding conflict in prosperous neighborhoods. Decentralization permitted the poor to influence city policy as a whole.

By contrast, when Mayor Lee of New Haven was confronted by ward-level opposition to public housing, he responded at the *municipal* level. He marshaled his forces into a complex structure of political feudalism and bureaucratic competition. Early in his term, Lee fostered a new power base so that he could take the initiative from the local political establishment that existed when he took office. Mayor Lee was described as an unusual mayor—a politician with a "high need for power" and a drive to achieve in politics that encouraged him to create power at the local level for specific policy goals.[51] He also had one foot planted firmly in several "camps" in New Haven—the Irish political machine, urban renewal and business interests, and Yale University. He was comfortable in Washington too—at least during the Kennedy years. The four pillars of Lee's power permitted him to take a moderate reformer's position on urban problems.

CONSERVATIVE TACTICS AT THE NATIONAL LEVEL

Local politics has been blamed for retarding progressive welfare programs. The variability of political tactics pursued by conservatives and reformers alike raises questions about that relationship. Is it the localness of politics in the United States that accounts for the substance of its welfare policies? West Germany is a federal republic, and yet more of its gross national product goes to social welfare programs than any other Western European country's.[52] What has kept welfare at the "almshouse" stage—where welfare is for the poor exclusively, rather than for the whole society, as is common in Europe?

Some of the differences in social welfare performance have little to do with local politics. Trade unions in the United States, for example, have not campaigned as actively for comprehensive welfare programs. Welfare programs relating to labor—pensions, workmen's compensation, and unemployment insurance—were taken up at roughly the same time that unions were negotiating their general position in the political scheme of things—during the 1920s, 1930s, and early 1940s. It was not a time for broad-based welfare demands. It was a time for legitimizing the authority of unions to negotiate contracts and to write specific benefits into those contracts. For the fledgling unions, industrial control was the political imperative, and that priority diminished the pressures for overall welfare advances.

The U.S. federal government has not been a consistent ally of the poor, either. Antireform groups have lobbied at the *national* level, and government bureaucrats and politicians at the national level often have supported local inequalities and opposed redistributive policies.

The American Medical Association, for example, long an active opponent of national health insurance, uses *national* political strategics. When the national Medicare/Medicaid program finally went through Congress, it included "a payment plan that medical dreams could not have improved upon."[53]

Even more indicative of how local, class, and organized group interests can all be accommodated by national policies were the Nixon administration's proposals for Health Maintenance Organizations. These proposals would have provided more incentives to doctors to participate in Health Maintenance Organizations in the more well-to-do suburbs than in poverty areas.

Similarly, in the case of housing policy (discussed earlier), national politicians often supported local exclusionary zoning. President Nixon's advisors and the Congress were reluctant to override local zoning rights.[54] The Department of Housing and Urban Development under George Romney, for example, refused to use national authority to require suburbs to accept public housing. By 1973, the opposing pressures grew so strong that eventually the new housing subsidy program was simply halted. Meanwhile, congressmen representing the "exclusive" communities also were under pressure not to force integration. The result was that reform proposals, such as stopping water and sewer grants to segregated communities, never came out of Congress.[55]

As the example of the Nixon administration's housing program indicates, local autonomy has not been the only force standing in the way of a major redistribution of income and services. Local control has been advocated by proponents of the status quo when local jurisdictional boundaries coincide with class divisions, making it to their advantage to do so. But there is no inherent relationship between localism and conservatism on redistributive policies.

SUMMARY—LOCAL AUTONOMY AND THE POLITICS OF PRIVILEGE

In the United States, local politics has involved issues far more controversial than the "sewerage without tears" image of local politics. When politicians campaigned on behalf of community control, they may well have been appealing to class interests, not to local identities or grass-roots democrats. Through the issues of schools, housing, and welfare runs the undercurrent of racial and class conflict, and local officials are in the thick of that struggle. Curiously enough, this politically developed country (that appears to have resolved the requisite "crises" of national identity and national integration) reverts to local symbols and structures in the process of resolving its most prolonged and intense conflict of all.

Because many public services, such as schools and welfare programs, are administered by local governments, the United States is considered to have one of the most decentralized political systems in the world. Whatever national purpose does exist in the United States includes these local political institutions, institutions that have helped to preserve the political dominance of the advantaged

Nonetheless, where political incentives existed for local politicians to adopt redistributive policies, they have done so. Organized voting power has helped the poor gain access to city hall. Some local government reforms have undermined that voting power without touching the residential segregation upon which local conservatism depends.

Egypt—The Class Case for Central Control

In 1952, a military coup in Egypt replaced the monarchy and its civilian bureaucracy with a republic and its military bureaucracy. Under the late President Nasser, the new military-republican regime implemented several major socialist programs. President Nasser also attempted to consolidate the political foundations of the regime by establishing grass-roots organizations with links to Cairo. Consequently, the republican national regime was the predominant source of political power and public policy—including redistributive policy.

Public policy and political power overlap; they are not pursued independently. After the coup, public policy in Egypt was implemented with a view toward stabilizing the republican regime—a task made more difficult by severe economic scarcity and continuous wartime mobilization. The precarious base for the republican regime was in the largely bureaucratic middle class. This class, therefore, became a primary beneficiary of the socialist reforms.

In the context of scarcity and bureaucratic dominance, local politics has increased individual mobility more than it has class mobility—"distributive" rather than "redistributive" policy outcomes. The republican regime has used an administrative model of politics. Within that model, local politics has functioned as a safety valve. It has responded to demands of the most politicized Egyptians, who have, nonetheless, been left out of the mainstream of national political life.

Fewer redistributive issues have been raised and resolved at the local level in Egypt than in the United States. This appears to result from both the bureaucratization of Egyptian politics and the severe scarcity of resources. And without an active political organization like Mexico's ruling PRI party, for example, Egyptian local politics has been more directly accessible to the middle class than to the poor.

EGYPT'S BUREAUCRATIC MILIEU

Local politics in Egypt is dominated by the central bureaucracy—a bureaucracy that has been a factor in public life for decades. The influence of the bureaucracy in Egyptian politics results from the country's concentrated population and the early (and continuous) modernization policies of national leaders that emphasized the role of the bureaucracy.

Only a few areas of Egypt have remained untouched by the administrative system—either because of their remoteness or because of their marginal importance to the economy. Egypt is a small country with a large population. About thirty-five million people live on the approximately 3 percent of its land that is cultivable; the fertile Nile Valley has an average density of 650 people per square mile. One small portion of Egypt's land is both farmed and lived upon intensively.

Egypt began the process of state-building early. The Ottoman Turks governed Egypt uncertainly until the beginning of the nineteenth century. At that time, the Khedives (the Ottoman viceroys) asserted their independence from Constantinople and began a program of modernization. The Khedives strengthened Egypt against the further encroachments of outside powers; they also committed Egypt to a large and complex bureaucratic structure. Most notably, Mohammed Ali's reign, from 1805 to 1849, presaged the present republic in the way the bureaucracy was used to bring about national development. Domestic armaments industries were promoted, funded by a refurbished tax system. Higher education was secularized, and commercial farming was encouraged.

The Free Officer's coup in 1952 that brought President Nasser to power only increased the role of the government in the economy. Nasser's regime initiated land redistribution and committed the government to a number of agricultural development programs. Banks and industries in the modern sector also were nationalized. These policies and the government's concurrent commitments to expand education and public health services enhanced the power of the government ministries and agencies even beyond that enjoyed in earlier periods. By the late 1960s, the public sector accounted for more than three-fourths of all new investments.[56]

The national bureaucracy affects local politics in the countryside as well as the cities. The lives of rural Egyptians, approximately half of the population, are directly affected by the government bureaucracy in many ways. Most local administrators are national bureaucrats. National bureaucrats, for example, staff the agricultural cooperatives, operate the schools, and administer health programs. Provincial governors under the Ministry of Interior often intervene in village and town affairs. Their intervention is encouraged by the fact that few precedents exist for local self-government in Egypt, either through historic experience or as a result of the contemporary realities of bureaucratic power.

But, despite the bureaucratic bias of Egyptian politics and the absence of a tradition of local autonomy, local political life is active and political institutions at the local level are used by local politicians to defend a variety of interests. Political parties in Egypt, for example, have been as useful to politicians as they have to the national regime. During the monarchy, the Wafd party, an opponent of the British influence over the monarchy, was dominated in rural areas by local notables. Their local influence was buttressed by the party's nationalist position, but their main interest still was keeping their control over village politics.

The Liberation Rally, the National Union, and the Arab Socialist Union—the three parties successively created and dissolved since 1952—included locally powerful individuals in their ranks. None of these parties, however, was particularly powerful as a local political organization. In fact, some of President Sadat's critics argued that he deliberately tried to destroy the Arab Socialist Union in 1971, when he *decentralized* the process through which party leaders were chosen.

The Arab Socialist Union lasted longer than the others, although it too was finally abolished by President Sadat, in the autumn of 1976. Since President Sadat took over in 1970, the parliament has been reorganized into right, center, and left groups (in place of the former Arab Socialist Union).

Political influence at the local level in Egypt does not come from the formal authority of local officials or from local politicians' control over party organization. Rather, it grows from the scarcity of political and material resources in the central ministries. In other words, local politicians have exercised influence by default. In part, the political vacuum created by the ministries' lack of resources resulted from the regime's hesitancy to mix politics with administration—especially partisan politics. In effect, this hesitancy reduced the effectiveness of both the parties and the bureaucrats at the local level. The overall political power of the national regime was reduced, particularly in rural areas.

Local politicians, then, filled the gap between what the regime's bureaucratic officials could do and what they were authorized to do.

The formal separation of politics and administration at the top belied the "symbiotic relationship between government officials and political party cadres at the local level which was thereby encouraged with a view toward improving the effectiveness of the regime's policies. . . ."[57]

The Egyptian regime's administrative approach to politics created opportunities and incentives for local alliances. It also contributed to an environment in which redistributive issues were avoided in local politics. Without imperatives to maintain a grass-roots political organization, the demands of the poor were marginally less important than were those of the middle class.

REDISTRIBUTION IN SCARCITY

Egypt's continuing poverty makes it more difficult for politicians to confront redistributive issues. Redistribution is less common in the midst of severe poverty than in the midst of prosperity. The equality of income distribution tends to be directly related to per capita income in all but the poorest countries; the higher the population's income, the more equally it is shared.[58] In Egypt too, persistent and worsening population pressures and failure to achieve high rates of economic growth have affected redistributive politics, making it less explicit but more pervasive.

Land redistribution, agricultural development, and industrialization programs have had a significant impact upon the distribution of income and wealth.[59] A substantial redistribution of wealth and power from the upper class of royal Egypt to the contemporary middle class of republican Egypt has taken place. First, through land redistribution the largest agricultural landholdings were broken up over the period from 1952 to 1969. Second, the nationalization of banks and industrial establishments, particularly since 1961, eliminated another source of inequality of incomes.

These reforms benefited some segments of the population more than others—the landholding peasants more than the landless farm laborers and industrial employees more than the unskilled and unemployed. The proportion of land held in middle-sized farms, for example, increased with land redistribution. At the same time, farm laborers were turned off the large farms when they were broken up; the smaller farms did not rehire these laborers but used family labor instead.[60] Yet the rate of population growth among farm laborers continued at high levels, and the real income of those who were employed declined.

Under conditions of scarcity, it is exceptionally difficult to enforce redistributive laws. For example, ceilings were placed upon land rents by the land redistribution laws. But those official rent ceilings were only as valid as the demand for land and the government's ability to enforce them would allow. Despite the enactment of the rent ceilings, two prices for land rentals were common—the official (legal) rate and the market (illegal) rate.[61]

Although the unofficial rents undermined the intent of the legislation, local officials who were in a position to know about illegal rents had little political support for bringing them to the attention of officials at higher levels. The local influence of the large landowners disappeared along with their lands. But the middle-class peasants who replaced them were equally protective of their interests.

As long as severe poverty exists in Egypt, the middle-class beneficiaries of land redistribution find themselves in a defensive position. Accordingly, all political conflict in Egypt has redistributive undertones. Policies that encourage individual mobility have received more political support than have those that affect structural or class mobility. Redistributive politics in Egypt have been individualistic and subtle.

For example, educational policy has emphasized the expansion of higher education at the expense of primary schools. University enrollments have increased, and as a result, mobility has increased; some university students are the first generation of their families to receive higher education.[62] The universities have been expanded despite the enormous need for primary education.[63] In 1930, more than 94 percent of the population was illiterate; in 1973, 76 percent of the population still was illiterate.

Faced with enormous tasks and limited public resources, Egypt's republican leaders had to make choices about where to begin. In many respects, the decisions they made contributed more to individual mobility than to structural redistribution. The most politically expedient course of action was to emphasize higher education, a policy that appealed to the politicized middle class. Consequently, as far as individual Egyptians were concerned, the critical step in achieving mobility was to gain admission into a secondary school. From then on, the student's progress up the educational ladder was virtually guaranteed. The next step after a free university education was into the government bureaucracy where a guaranteed job awaited.

Stressing the growth of higher education meant that opportunities for intermediate education were limited. Those whose education was curtailed had far less political influence than did university students. The Egyptian National Assembly (parliament) reflected these power realities. A bill was introduced in the National Assembly, for example, in 1957 to require the government to provide a university seat to each and every secondary school graduate.[64] The law that finally passed was modified only slightly to guaranteeing secondary graduates either a university seat or one in a technical or professional school.

Social welfare policy, like educational policy, has been biased toward urban and educated Egyptians. For example, 20 percent of 1955–1956 government expenditures was allocated to social welfare. That proportion is extraordinarily high for any country. The term *social welfare* is misleading, though. A full 80 percent of that allocation was spent on pensions and cost-of-living bonuses for government employees.[65]

The advantages enjoyed by government employees in less-industrialized countries like Egypt result in part from the difficulty of covering a non-organized work force. Consequently, social security in nonindustrialized countries has been extended to workers in large firms and to government employees. So, in Egypt, social welfare largely meant promoting the welfare of government employees in the bureaucracies and public industries.

The emphasis placed upon the welfare of government employees and the educated, who live in the cities, points to one of the most serious inequalities in Egypt—that between Egypt's urban and rural populations. These inequalities are reflected both in wage differentials and in the unequal distribution of public services. From the perspective of Egyptian society, urban-rural income inequalities could be lessened by a more equal distribution of public services, as well as by directly intervening to redistribute either wealth or money income (through tax policies, for example).

The Egyptian government has responded to urban-rural inequalities by making many public services more accessible to the population. Some of these public services are administered by local officials; all are created by national authority. After 1946, the major vehicle for providing rural public services at the local level was the Combined Centres. The combined services centers were staffed by employees of the central ministries. They provided medical, school, agricultural, and social welfare services at the village level. The initial goal of the republican regime was to increase the number of centers rather than restructuring them entirely, despite the fact that the centers had been established under the discredited monarchy. Much was accomplished; by 1970, half of Egypt's villages had some public health services. Nonetheless, the difference between the two regimes was one of the scope and pace of reform, not an absolute difference.[66]

After land distribution, cooperative societies took over some of the centers' functions; rural municipal councils managed others. Local officials had only limited resources to provide the services they were authorized to provide. As a result, they were relatively ineffective in reducing the inequalities that still existed in rural Egypt. According to government figures, for example, significant inequalities still existed in mid-1960s in the number of hospital beds available, while very little difference existed in local administration revenues and expenditures.[67]

LOCAL POLITICS AND THE MIDDLE CLASS

Local political competition does involve redistributive issues even though local capabilities to influence distribution in a major way are limited. It has been the middle-class Egyptian who has been particularly active in local politics. Malcolm Kerr describes the reluctance of Egyptian middle-class professionals who had acquired some security under the republican regime to support broad, redistributive or social welfare measures.[68] It should not be surprising, then, that the local political process has also been used to protect the position of the middle class. In turn, particularly in the case of agricultural policies in rural politics, the priorities of national elites have contributed to the conservatism of policy outcomes at the local level.

Political outcomes at the two levels reinforce one another. Agricultural cooperative politics at the local level has been conservative, for example, because the cooperative system was seen by national elites as first and foremost a means to increase agricultural productivity and extract resources from agriculture to finance industrial growth. Farmers in the cooperatives were required to sell their crops to government buyers, to pay taxes, and to acquire cash obligations from the inputs available from the cooperatives. Given the government's priority of creating an agricultural surplus, cooperative policies reflected the interests of the peasants with larger holdings—those who were providing the largest surpluses. Their interests overlapped with those of the national regime.

The conventional wisdom about the democratizing effect of land reform on rural village politics is only partly true. Land reform did take power away from Egypt's large landholders. New faces appeared in local offices. New family names were recorded on the parliamentary roster in Cairo.

On the other hand, politics in redistributed villages did not automatically become an open process in which local citizens participated on an equal basis. There was more competition for local political office after redistribution. But local political competition was also dominated by the more prosperous peasants, as it had been by the large landholders before them.

There also were differences in the scope of the power of local officials. They did not employ as many nonfamily workers, for example, and consequently did not have dependent laborers as a reliable source of personal political support. More than earlier, the new local influentials also had to share their influence with the central government ministries that had programs in the villages.

Again, these differences were more of degree than of kind. Traditional local leaders had important sources of external support. Under

Egypt's "ancient regime," local political power usually resided in the hands of the village *umdah* (headman), who either exercised power on his own behalf or on behalf of an absentee landowner. The *umdah*'s influence was both personal and institutional; his office often was hereditary. In the town of Shubra, for example, the *umdah*'s office had been in the same family for three generations.[69] His family's influence was reinforced by its alliance with provincial and national politicians. Mustafa Samad, *umdah* of Shubra from 1927 to 1959, served on four provincial committees—including the *waqf* land committee (charitable land trusts, once largely in the control of Moslem religious authorities). The *umdah* often profited from renting this local *waqf* land, as well as from using the committee as a basis for establishing contacts outside his village.

Samad was able to influence votes on behalf of the political party he supported. These varied activities brought Samad into contact with provincial administrators, national bureaucrats, and notables from other localities. Local notables like Samad accumulated and exercised their power within the framework of extralocal politics under the monarchy, as they later did under the republican government. For example, when Mustafa Samad once failed to protect the absentee landowner's fields, the landowner (who happened to be a member of the royal family) was quick to request national police protection in the town.[70] Samad was convinced that he would lose his own influence if that happened. So he objected, through his political connections, and was able to keep the police out.

In this early period, local politics was far from conflict-free, and although individual local leaders were more entrenched, a politician's external alliances could tip the balance in his favor. Later, in the republic, extralocal alliances were still more important, while competition among individual local politicians increased too. New institutions of local government were established through which individuals sought influence. Village councils were created, and local committees of the ruling Arab Socialist Union were established. Old institutions were also expanded—for example, the cooperatives and the Combined Centres.

The new peasant politicians had many ways to acquire local influence without external intervention. First, because they tended to be wealthier than other villagers, they owned more scarce farm machinery. Second, they were a source of informal credit for the poor who could not obtain credit through formal channels. And third, many were politically ambitious and were skilled in political campaigning. Consequently, when it was time to elect the Arab Socialist Union local "committees of twenty," in many cases middle-class committees were elected.

In 1968, ostensibly because the committees of twenty had been dominated by the wealthier peasants and had contributed to local factionalism, the committees were reduced in importance by a reorganization of local government. In their place, party "leadership groups" were created. The new groups included both elected representatives and bureaucrats serving at the local level. Elections to the groups were more closely managed than the committee elections had been.

Prosperous peasants responded to potentially redistributive measures like the reorganization of the committees of twenty by trying to undermine the authority of any local agencies that threatened the local distribution of power. For example, small farmers (owning less than five acres) were guaranteed majorities on cooperative society boards. In response, prosperous farmers tried to reassert their control over the cooperatives by boycotting them. Eventually they were successful—the number of acres that were a prerequisite for cooperative leadership was again raised and cooperative politics returned to normal.[71]

Farm laborers have not benefited materially from the establishment of cooperatives. Cooperatives bid for farm labor, and consequently the interests of the cooperative managers are opposed to those of the laborers. For the managers and board members, the cooperative societies were a basis for extending local political influence.

The cooperatives controlled a variety of jobs, from mechanics and drivers to farm laborers. Cooperative leaders also influenced the distribution and use of machinery, agricultural chemicals, and loans. Cooperative boards worked under the close scrutiny of other community influentials, especially Arab Socialist Union party leaders. But politically active cooperative board members have usually been able to protect themselves against opponents. Iliya Harik gives two examples of how cooperative leaders fared in the face of opposition.[72] The first example involved a board that was strongly entrenched and able to resist pressures from the provincial governor to resign. In contrast, the board members in the other case were less politically involved and, consequently, were forced to resign.

The methods that local politicians have used to build local bases of support have not always involved distributing material rewards to individuals. Sometimes local politicians have implemented policies which have offered more generalized benefits to the local community as a whole while at the same time extending the politicians' influence. Harik reports that the town of Shubra's first (appointed) mayor and municipal council were able to get early action to create both a combined services center and a modern marketplace.[73] In 1966 and 1967, under another mayor, Shubra added a housing-renewal project and electricity. In both cases, the mayor behaved differently than did the traditional *umdah*. These mayors were interested in establishing their own networks of local influence. They sought to establish networks independent of the Samad family (who controlled the *umdah* position prior to 1960) and independent of a group of peasants that had its own links to the Agrarian Reform Administration. In order to build such a network, the mayors introduced innovations in the village that could attract support for them and thereby help them fill the party "leadership group" with their own men. In the process, the first mayor and council worked out a system of local deficit financing—something unheard of in the local politics of earlier days.

Many of the middle-class characteristics of rural local politics are true of local politics in the cities as well. Members of the parliament elected to office from urban constituencies have been predominately members of the middle class. The urban officeholders are primarily government employees, but smaller numbers of private businessmen are also elected.

Elective offices give businessmen prestige and also limited opportunities to protect their economic interests. The participation of small businessmen in politics was encouraged by the Arab Socialist Union leaders who hoped to gain their political support. The leaders of the new military regime wanted to wean businessmen away from the political organizations that they supported before the 1952 coup—the Wafd party and the Moslem Brotherhood being the major targets. For the businessmen, an official position in city politics was one reward for loyalty. Zoning and tax assessment decisions were under their discretion. Constituents' complaints about public services could be ironed out.

For many, the exchange was worthwhile, although local government officials shared their influence over local policy with officials in other institutions. In the cities, politics in the republican regime has been structured according to functional jurisdictions as well as local boundaries. Units of the Arab Socialist Union, for example, were organized in factories, in neighborhoods, and among young men and women.

For single-party states like Egypt, local territorial constituencies were important in electoral politics, while organizations in work places have been valuable for legitimizing the regime's economic policies. Because the Arab Socialist Union's grass-roots organizations had this legitimization role, they were limited to hearing the individual demands of their members rather than actually influencing redistributive policies. As important, by extending local party jurisdictions from geographic constituencies to functional constituencies, potential local power bases were divided. Competition among the party's functional units reduced the opportunities available to local leaders for organizing political influence from below.

The limited influence of grass-roots politicians and the intervention of the national regime in local affairs has prevented many redistributive issues from being raised. Although the republican regime has clearly indicated a commitment to socioeconomic reforms, economic growth also has been a high priority objective. Economic growth objectives have affected the redistributive impact of public policy.

At the plant level, industrial managers have incentives to cut costs, whether or not their industries have been nationalized. So, despite Egypt's unusually comprehensive labor legislation—from minimum wages to profit-sharing welfare schemes—the position of Egyptian laborers has not dramatically changed.[74] Improvements in workers' real incomes have fallen short of the legislation for three reasons. First, the minimum wages set by law have not always been an improvement over the de facto market wages; nor have they been uniformly enforced. Second, insurance or welfare funds have been primarily a means by which the government could force workers to save and then invest their savings in government-selected projects. Finally, the profit-sharing schemes did not automatically improve the workers' net real income. Some wages, for example, were forced down by the insurance schemes.

LOCAL GOVERNMENT AUTHORITY

Local government has relatively little authority or power to affect the economic growth priorities of the national regime. Nearly all of the effective restrictions upon the activities of local governments found in other countries also apply to Egypt.

In terms of its authorized functions, local government in Egypt is the classic case of local officials with little to do but administer national policies. Local authority is derivative, not autonomous; fiscal powers are dependent, and organized political competition is absent.

Municipal authority encompasses building and maintaining local roads and parks, slaughterhouses, and sanitation facilities, maintaining schools and hospitals, and several other functions. However, social welfare policy, for example, is under the jurisdiction of the national government. Current labor legislation for old age and sickness insurance, unemployment compensation, and compensation for work injuries all were enacted in 1964. The programs are administered by local authorities, but their legal provisions apply to all localities uniformly.

Under national legislation, there should be no local differences in social policy. However, as indicated by the example of Shubra's mayors, policies do vary from locality to locality according to the resources and actors involved, despite the centralization of formal authority. Local specialized committees, made up of municipal council members and others, have been created in social policy areas such as education, social services, and welfare management. Even if the committees simply act as checks on local executives, their individual roles produce somewhat different outcomes.

The influence of local politicians over policy has been further limited by successive reorganizations of local governments. Prior to 1971, local authority was vested in popular councils. Membership in the councils was mixed; some members were elected from the "active" members of the party and some were nominated by the Ministry of Local Administration on the basis of their community service. In addition, local representatives of such central ministries as Health, Treasury, Interior, and Education served on the councils on an ex officio basis. A reorganization in 1971 divided the popular councils into an executive body of bureaucrats at the local level and a "peoples'" council made up of local party representatives and local delegates to central party committees.

The original councils were influenced by national politics in numerous ways. Chairmen of the city councils, for example, were appointed by the president of the republic. Rural council chairmen were appointed by commissioners in the Ministry of Local Administration. Nonetheless, dividing the councils was criticized because it made it still more difficult for the locally elected councillors to supervise the nationally appointed bureaucrats. Without their physical proximity to bureaucrats, in the same council meetings, the popular representatives had fewer opportunities to exercise influence and no regular, formal occasions to discuss local issues with bureaucrats.

Another constraint upon the influence of popular councils has been their fiscal incapacity. Municipal budgets in Egypt are included in regional budgets and ultimately approved by the Ministry of Local Administration. The taxes on local property are all designated for use by regional and local authorities; none of the revenue is kept by the central government. On the other hand, allocations and expenditures made by municipal authorities that create deficits over local tax revenues must be approved by regional governors and then, together with the budgets of other municipalities within the regions, by the ministry in Cairo. The local spending above tax revenues that is approved is financed by loans and grants from the central government. The influence of private interests on local fiscal policy was significantly minimized when Egyptian banks were nationalized. Politically, national debt financing has limited the extent to which local municipal constituents can influence the levels and directions of financing by exerting pressure upon municipal officials. No taxpayers; no taxpayers' revolt.

SUMMARY—CLASS POLITICS AND REGIME CONSOLIDATION

As a result of these limitations upon local power, most of the competition over redistributive policies has involved national politicians. Yet, the images of politics held by the leaders of the republican regime have not always been conducive to the success of those policies. Redistributive policies, in the form of land redistribution and nationalization of industry, were accompanied by several grass-roots institutional innovations. These innovations were designed to enhance national economic growth under the new conditions created by these transfers of wealth. The new institutions—the single party, the cooperative society, and worker participation in industry—flourished when they offered political gains to those at the grass roots who were to make them run effectively. The national regime, which initiated the redistributive policies, had neither sufficient security to mobilize local political energies on a continuing basis nor sufficient direction to generate local activity under its own guidance. Either of these approaches might have challenged the middle-class basis of local politics. But, "we keep to the center of the stairs," runs one Egyptian expression, "neither up nor down."

Part of the explanation for this standoff is the illegitimacy of political conflict in Egypt. Apolitical politics is at the heart of the Arab socialism. Arab socialism emphasizes the wholeness of the community and interprets class conflict as conflict between the community and a minority of isolated "exploiters." Among the farmers that Harik interviewed, for example, Arab socialism evoked positive images of unity and equality rather than conflict and inequality.[75]

Harik portrays national leaders as "refusing to pay the price of politics locally."[76] President Nasser personified this rejection of politics. His complaint about union leaders typified that view:

> ". . . once elected, the members tended to their own business and generally omitted even to pay their membership fees to the union. Favouritism, ward-heeling, and above all, a complete dissociation from the people were the results. . . ."[77]

When James Heaphey quoted this remark by Nasser, he was arguing a case for decentralizing politics. Heaphey found Egyptian governors unable to assume the broader authority they were given under an official decentralization scheme because of this nonpolitical ideology. The governors had no effective powers although they had received new authority.

Similar lessons illustrating the necessity of confronting political conflict can be drawn from Egypt's more recent experience with local politics and redistributive policies. The conclusion that local political competition has been held in abeyance so that the national regime could carry out its redistribution policies is too simplistic. The national regime's two major redistributive acts have not achieved their objectives—in part because local politics have intervened. But this is the cost of the regime's priorities in its relations with local politicians—a cost that it has been either unwilling to bear or unable to avoid. Under the centralized republican regime, local power and influence still have been exerted more by middle-class segments of the local population than by the disadvantaged. Both redistributive policy and political mobilization objectives have been diluted by the priority that the regime has given to consolidating its rule.

7 Conclusion—Local Politics and Regime Security

... all kinds of relationships and interchanges may connect the center with the periphery, including some that may be offensive to discriminating tastes. ...[1]

If our "discriminating tastes" find politics objectionable— if we, for example, find Machiavelli more corrupt than insightful— then the local politician's domain will be particularly unappealing. His domain is at the political center of those "relationships and interchanges" that "connect the center with the periphery." A premise that this book shares with a growing local politics literature is that local political affairs are contingent upon national regime politics. Local politics is the political "periphery" and national regimes, the "center."[2] As a result, local politicians have to rely upon influence and bargaining—not authority and doctrine. The local politician's role is the most political of all.

Center-periphery relationships are colored by national regime security interests. Local politics varies within nations and among nations according to the nature of the regime security interests that are involved in local politics. For example, local elections and party politics often raise regime security issues. National regimes are distinguished by the ideological perspectives of regime elites that go beyond and are more significant than the elites' partisan identifications. Regime ideologies are more or less coherent images of the political economy as a whole.

It follows that local elections and party politics affect regime security most when they raise fundamental questions about the structure of power and wealth. For example, Ataturk's Turkey and republican Mexico looked quite different from the standpoint of the spatial organization of power. There was a difference despite the fact that (1) they experienced revolutions at the same time, (2) both were essentially single-party regimes for many years, and (3) both were large and potentially powerful nation-states. Local political pressures in both countries have challenged regime security and have encouraged regime elites to intervene in local politics. Yet, pressures from local politics have been absorbed by the Mexican *party* regime through its sectoral divisions and its local cooptive system. In contrast, opposition to Turkey's *bureaucratic* regime was able to mobilize peripheral support in one crucial decade.

191

The power of local politicians is quite practical. They are able to influence national policy and national elections. While the organizational basis of their power lies in government offices and party posts, the practical basis of their power is their identification of specific policies, localities, or local factions with political influence. For example, in Japan, the environmental issue became a vehicle through which local politicians could mobilize electoral support. In the process, the environmental issue acquired political momentum that it otherwise would not have had. In Turkey, the Democratic party's local organizations were strengthened by a popular rejection of "statism" and by Ataturk's secular bureaucracy. The "revolt of the periphery" began at the grass roots, where new, ambitious politicians challenged entrenched local elites and, at the same time, challenged the national regime. The Democratic party seemed to advocate fundamental changes—in that case a return to the Islamic state and a rejection of the republic and of state capitalism. Also in local campaigns, leftist parties in Japan and Western Europe raised issues more profound than specific policy questions, regarding the role of private capital and public choice.

Besides the potential to initiate debates about national policies, local politicians have another practical influence. They are able to influence whether policies are accepted, rejected, or accepted at very high cost to the national politicians who want to see the policies implemented. When local politicians are satisfied with the influence they have within the political system as a whole, they can help to shield national politicians from having to confront critical issues. This has been the case in political systems as different as those of India and the United States. In both countries, redistributive demands have been buried in local political conflict, and local politicians have served to protect the status quo.

It is precisely because the potential influence of local politicians over national policies is so significant that many national regimes have been organized to minimize that influence. One of the most political means of accomplishing that objective has been to organize power along functional lines (like the popular, peasant, and middle sectors in Mexico). Most national regimes also have limited the authority of local governments by controlling tax powers and the recruitment of local executives. The proliferation of national ministries and functional agencies in contemporary nation-states has discouraged political mobilization on the basis of local identities. Local politicians have had to accommodate their own political strategies and influence to the power of state bureaucrats.

ELECTORAL POLITICS AND DISTRIBUTIVE POLITICS

State bureaucrats serving at the local level have experienced almost as much uncertainty as local politicians. Formal models of administrative organization depict the lower-level bureaucrat's role as one of following orders and performing efficiently in a rigidly structured environment. Yet, state bureaucrats serving at the local level typically find themselves in situations where they are expected to implement policies that are not always popular and to implement them with limited resources. This "beggar bureaucrat" must be innovative as he tries to determine how the regime's policy objectives and limited resources can be brought into proportion. The bureaucrat, in sum, must be a politician and must create certainty from uncertainty.

One of the ways in which local-level bureaucrats have accomplished this has been to create a network of local alliances. These networks have included local politicians, local elites in the private sector, and other national bureaucrats. For example, the French case study showed the prefect, leftist mayors, and national housing officials in Nimes allied as a result of their mutual interest in spending housing money in "their" locality. The alliance helped the bureaucrat achieve his own career objectives by building up his ministry's commitment to the locality for which he was responsible.

Alliances among local-level bureaucrats, local politicians, and elites raise other kinds of problems, however. The paradox of local leadership discussed in the Tanzanian case is that the most successful local alliances tend to be those that are formed around *local* interests, defending the periphery against the center. At some point, the responsibilities of bureaucrats for implementing national policies conflict with their need to create local alliances.

Decisions about national economic policies, for example, affect national economic growth and, at the same time, local economies. The experience of bureaucrats at the municipal level in the Soviet Union is typical; they often have found themselves at odds with state industrial policies. This has been especially true when industrial location and production decisions have placed unusual burdens on their own local constituencies.

In political systems where local officials are more dependent upon local elections than they are in the Soviet Union, local officials still may ameliorate potential conflicts between regime and local economic interests, but not without extracting political concessions from the regime. In France, where local elections play a significant role in national politics, a continuing dilemma has faced national policymakers: how much emphasis to place upon cities that elect leftist governments, how much upon the centrist constituencies in rural communes, and how much upon the interests of the private sector—the regime's "productive coalition." In that dilemma, local politicians have served as buffers, easing the contradictions among these alternatives. The intransigence of local politicians, in the face of certain attempted local government reforms, has been intransigence in the face of local demands for a greater share of national resources. Local politicians protect their local influence against outside "reformers." They also protect, against local complaints, their extralocal influence with the prefect, members of Parliament, and even the minister.

THE LOCAL PORK BARREL

The distribution of resources within nations has become a major issue in contemporary nation-state politics. A characteristic response of national politicians to redistributive demands has been to rely upon local politicians to distribute pork barrel resources within their localities in order to contain redistributive demands at the local level.

The pork barrel system, however, has been of limited utility in containing demands for fundamental political and economic change. The pork barrel has been used most commonly to distribute resources from the national level to the local level, through political party officials and bureaucrats. It has been more useful in maintaining a well-functioning system than it has been in restoring a deteriorating one.

In Japan, for example, the pork barrel politics of the centrist regime and industrial interests in the city of Kariya were compatible. The economy of Kariya, based on Toyota's headquarters there, flourished for a time. During its prosperity, Kariya's residents voted conservatively, and its local politicians were part of the national pork barrel process. But the confluence of regime and local interests ended when Toyota moved some of its operations out of Kariya, and national politicians had to choose between Kariya and Toyota. The regime's political concerns and private economic interests began to diverge; national politicians tried to distribute public resources in such a way as to ameliorate the worst local economic hardships, but they could not prevent leftist electoral gains in many localities.

In France, the divergence between electoral and economic interests has been documented by statistics that show private economic resources and state investment in productive enterprises flowing to productive areas, while funds for social services are distributed more evenly among localities. Distributive politics is sometimes more compatible with electoral politics and at other times, less so. In all the countries discussed, national regimes are committed to rapid economic growth and to state intervention to control that growth. As a general rule, when local politics appears to be hindering economic growth, local politicians are quickly taken to task. For example, Korean national elites prorogued local elected councils in those cities that had the most revenues to distribute—the municipalities with the largest budgets.[3] The municipal authorities were accused of wasting their resources on local political priorities and impeding economic growth.

Local politics frustrates the growth objectives of regime elites in other ways. Local politics often has been used by small businessmen and commercial interests to protect themselves against national regulations. Small businessmen in many nation-states have valued the support of local politicians when national regime elites favored large industrial enterprises. Where multinational enterprises have been involved, the local businessmen's resistance has brought out the still more fundamental issues of indigenous versus foreign development strategies.

LOCAL POLITICS AND REGIME SECURITY

The imperatives of economic growth and electoral politics illustrate the basic point that local politics is far more than "sewerage without tears." Nonetheless, we have noted the large amount of time local politicians must devote to their constituents' grievances. Indian city councillors complained about that; they would have liked to spend their time making policy decisions rather than acting as intermediaries for constituents whose electricity is not working or whose landlords have overcharged them. That seems to be the nature of day-to-day local politics all over the world.

Despite the vital role that local politicians have had in making national political processes function smoothly, decentralization has remained more a topic for United Nations seminars than an active political force. National regime elites tolerate decentralization only when it is unavoidable.

The subject of regime security and local politics bears heavily upon hundreds of contemporary public administration issues and upon the functioning of nation-states. National regimes' economic growth strategies, for example, affect the way bureaucratic rule is imposed upon localities—local tax structures, the scope of local authority, and even local electoral politics.

Politically, the more secure a national regime is, the greater the willingness of regime elites to share power with local politicians. Decentralization is a political luxury. Where the stakes of political competition are high, regime elites intervene in local political processes more frequently. The "elasticity of control" that national regime elites exercise over local politicians is a function of the political consensus within the system generally.[4] The classical questions of politics—what is the "best" size for a political community and what is the "optimum" distribution of power within a nation-state?[5]—can only be answered in the context of specific regimes.

Local political processes are themselves subject to evolution and change. Sidney Tarrow concludes his study of French and Italian local politics with the observation that, in those two countries at least, local politicians have been giving increasing attention to collective issues (local public policy) over the individual bargaining characteristic of the past.[6] In so doing, they have contributed to building a national consensus through frequent, regular political interchanges with state bureaucrats and with local officials from opposing political parties.

By looking at the practical side of politics, regime elites may well be discouraged from intervening arbitrarily in local politics. The most interventionist states are not necessarily the most centralized. Given the critical political and administrative functions that local politicians perform, it could, in fact, be concluded that intervention brings decentralization in its wake.

At the same time, "reformers" may not find decentralization always to be a welcome change from state-centered politics. Under some conditions, local politics can be as useful to state elites as it is disadvantageous at other times. Local politicians very often are part of "a well oiled political and economic machine run by an elite committed to maintaining itself."[7]

Notes

Chapter 1

1. Mark Kesselman develops this contextual view of local politics within nation-states in "Research Perspectives in Comparative Local Politics: Pitfalls and Prospects," *Comparative Urban Research* 1, no. 1 (1972): 10–30.

2. Charles Louis de Secondat, Baron de Montesquieu, *The Spirit of the Laws,* translated by Thomas Nugeat (New York: Hafner, 1949), p. 16.

3. Francine F. Rabinovitz, "Urban Development and Political Development in Latin America," in Robert T. Daland, ed., *Comparative Urban Research: The Administration and Politics of Cities* (Beverly Hills: Sage, 1969), pp. 98–99.

4. Herbert H. Werlin, *Governing an African City: A Study of Nairobi* (New York: Africana, 1974), p. 26.

5. Ibid., p. 31.

6. Ibid., p. 192.

7. Norman N. Miller, "The Political Survival of Traditional Leadership," *Journal of Modern African Studies* 6, no. 2 (1968): 183–98.

8. Jerome E. Milch, "Influence as Power: French Local Government Reconsidered," *British Journal of Political Science* 4, no. 2 (April 1974), pt. 2: 139–61.

9. Because Peyranne is a small village in a poor region, the mayor's delinquency was ignored. See Lawrence Wylie, *Village in the Vaucluse* (New York: Harper and Row, 1964), pp. 164–67.

10. Roderick A. Church, "Authority and Influence in Indian Municipal Politics: Administrators and Councillors in Lucknow," *Asian Survey* 13, no. 4 (April 1973): 421–38.

11. *The New York Times,* September 4, 1977.

12. Ibid.

13. *The New York Times,* April 5, 1978.

14. *The New York Times,* September 4, 1977.

15. Fleur de Villiers, quoted in *The New York Times,* April 6, 1978.

16. Cynthia H. Enloe, "Internal Colonialism, Federalism and Alternative State Development Strategies," *Publius* 7, no. 4 (Fall 1977): 148.

17. *The New York Times,* November 16, 1976.

18. *The New York Times,* May 3, 1977.

19. James W. Fesler, "Approaches to the Understanding of Decentralization," *Journal of Politics* 27, no. 3 (August 1965): 539.

20. Ibid., p. 545.

21. Gabriel Almond and Sidney Verba, *The Civic Culture* (Princeton: Princeton University Press, 1963), p. 232.

22. Sidney Tarrow reexamined *The Civic Culture* findings in France and found them misleading. His research findings are reported in "The Urban-Rural Cleavage in Political Involvement: The Case of France," *American Political Science Review* 65, no. 2 (June 1971): 341–57. Also, see Bradley M. Richardson, "Urbanization and Political Participation: The Case of Japan," *American Political Science Review* 61, no. 2 (June 1973): 433–52.

23. Aristide Zolberg, *Creating Political Order: The Party States of West Africa* (Chicago: Rand McNally, 1966), pp. 93–108.

24. Anthony Downs, *An Economic Theory of Democracy* (New York: Harper and Row, 1956).

25. Joel Migdal, *Peasants, Politics, and Revolution* (Princeton: Princeton University Press, 1974), pp. 82–83, and James C. Scott, *The Moral Economy of the Peasant* (New Haven: Yale University Press, 1976), p. 8.

26. Luigi Graziano, "Patron-Client Relationships in Southern Italy," in F. C. Bruhns, F. Cazzola, and J. Wiatr, eds., *Local Politics, Development, and Participation: A Cross-National Study of Interrelationships* (Pittsburgh: Center for International Studies, University of Pittsburgh, 1974), p. 188.

27. Richard R. Fagen and William S. Tuohy, *Politics and Privilege in a Mexican City* (Stanford: Stanford University Press, 1972), pp. 132–43.

28. Robert Alan Dahl, *Size and Democracy* (Stanford: Stanford University Press, 1973), esp. p. 60.

29. Samuel Popkin, "Corporatism and Colonialism: Political Economy of Rural Change in Viet Nam," *Comparative Politics* 8, no. 3 (April 1976): 431–65.

30. Carlo Levi, *Christ Stopped at Eboli* (New York: Farrar, Straus, 1947), pp. 11–21.

31. The quote is from Alexis de Tocqueville, *Democracy in America,* edited by J. P. Mayer and Max Lerner, translated by G. Lawrence (New York: Harper and Row, 1966), vol. I, p. 73.

32. William L. Riordan, *Plunkitt of Tammany Hall: A Series of Very Plain Talks on Very Practical Politics* (New York: Dutton, 1963).

33. The "locust" simile is from Raymond E. Wolfinger, "Nondecisions and the Study of Local Politics," *American Political Science Review* 65, no. 4 (December 1971): 1063–80. For a careful conceptualization of local politics and power, see Krystaff Ostrowski and Harry Teune, "Local Political Systems and General Social Processes," in Terry N. Clark, ed., *Comparative Community Politics* (New York: John Wiley, 1974), pp. 395–406.

34. Richard J. Samuels, "Extralocal Linkages and Urban Politics in Japan," *International Studies Notes* 3, no. 4 (Winter 1976): 36–40.

35. Harold J. Laski, *A Grammar of Politics*, 5th ed. (London: Allen and Unwin, 1949), p. 411.

Chapter 2

1. David R. Cameron, J. Stephen Hendricks, Richard I. Hofferbert, et al., "Urbanization, Social Structure, and Mass Politics: A Comparison Within Five Nations," *Comparative Political Studies* 5, no. 4 (October 1972): 259–90.

2. Karl W. Deutsch, *Nationalism and Social Communication* (Cambridge: M.I.T. Press, 1966), pp. 170–81.

3. John Badgley, *Politics Among Burmans: A Study of Intermediary Leaders,* Southeast Asia Series 15 (Athens: Center for International Studies, Ohio University, 1970), pp. 83–86.

4. Malcolm W. Norris, "Ethiopian Municipal Administration, and the Approach to Local Government Reform," *Planning and Administration* 1 (1974): 47–74.

5. Amos H. Hawley, "Ecology and Human Ecology," *Social Forces* 22, no. 4 (May 1948): 398–405.

6. T. J. Keil and C. A. Eckstrom, "Municipal Differentiation and Public Policy: Fiscal Support Levels in Varying Environments," *Social Forces* 52, no. 3 (March 1974): 384–95.

7. Bruce London, "Functionalism, Marxism, and the City: Ideology Versus Science, or Competing Ideocentrisms?" *Comparative Urban Research* 4, no. 1 (1976): 26–29.

8. Edward W. Soja and Richard J. Tobin, "The Geography of Modernization: Paths, Patterns and Processes of Spatial Change in Developing Countries," in Janet Abu-Lughod and Richard Hay, Jr., eds., *Third World Urbanization* (Chicago: Maaroufa Press, 1977), pp. 83–86.

9. Richard Child Hill, "Capital Accumulation and Urbanization in the United States," *Comparative Urban Research* 4, no. 2–3 (1977): 39–60.

10. Carl J. Friedrich, *Trends of Federalism in Theory and Practice* (New York: Praeger, 1968), frontispiece.

11. W. Hardy Wickwar, *The Political Theory of Local Government* (Columbia: University of South Carolina Press, 1970).

12. Frank P. Sherwood, *Institutionalizing the Grass Roots in Brazil: A Study in Comparative Local Government* (San Francisco: Chandler, 1972).

13. Brij M. Sharma and L. P. Choudry, *Federal Polity,* 2d rev. ed. (New York: Asia Publishing House, 1967), p. 27.

14. John H. Herz, "The Rise and Demise of the Territorial State," *World Politics* 9, no. 4 (July 1957): 473–93.

15. William L. Ochsenwald, "Opposition to Political Centralization in South Jordan and the Hijaz, 1900–1914," unpublished paper delivered at the Fifth Annual Meeting of the Middle East Studies Association, Denver, Colorado, 1971.

16. The literature on political development includes several discussions of the crises of development that traditional political systems "inevitably" confront. National consolidation refers to the concepts of national integration and penetration as they have been described in Leonard Binder et al., eds., *Crises and Sequences in Political Development* (Princeton: Princeton University Press, 1971), pp. 3–72.

17. Robert C. Fried, *The Italian Prefects* (New Haven: Yale University Press, 1963).

18. Mark Kessselman and Donald Rosenthal, *Local Power and Comparative Politics,* Comparative Politics Series 5 (Beverly Hills: Sage, 1974).

19. Francesco Benet, "Explosive Markets: The Berber Highlands," in Louise E. Sweet, ed., *Peoples and Cultures of the Middle East* (Garden City, N.Y.: Natural History Press, 1970), vol. I, pp. 173–203.

20. Stein Rokkan, *Citizens, Elections, Parties: Approaches to the Comparative Study of the Processes of Development* (New York: David McKay, 1970).

21. Bryan R. Roberts, "Center and Periphery in the Development Process: The Case of Peru," in Abu-Lughod and Hay, eds., *Third World Urbanization,* pp. 176–94.

22. Advisory Commission on Intergovernmental Relations, *Significant Features of Fiscal Federalism,* 1976 ed. (Washington, D.C.: G.P.O., 1976), p. 3.

23. Nicholas Hopkins, *Popular Government in an African Town* (Chicago: University of Chicago Press, 1972), pp. 129, 201.

24. Michael Van Dusen, "Aspects of Agro-City Loyalties in Syrian Politics Since Independence," unpublished paper delivered at the Fifth Annual Meeting of the Middle East Studies Association, Denver, Colorado, 1971.

25. Charles Tilly, "Food Supply and Public Order in Modern Europe," in Charles Tilly, ed., *The Formation of National States in Modern Europe,* Studies in Political Development 8 (Princeton: Princeton University Press, 1976), pp. 380–455.

26. Hill, "Capital Accumulation and Urbanization," pp. 39–60.

27. Robert C. Wood, "A Division of Powers in Metropolitan Areas," in Arthur Maass, ed., *Area and Power* (Glencoe, Ill.: Free Press, 1959), p. 64.

28. Alexis de Tocqueville, *The Old Regime and the French Revolution* (New York: Doubleday, 1955).

29. Barrington Moore, *The Social Origins of Dictatorship and Democracy: Lord and Peasant in the Modern World* (Boston: Beacon Press, 1966).

30. Samuel Humes and Eileen Martin, *The Structure of Local Government* (The Hague: International Union of Local Authorities, 1969), pp. 38–41.

31. Ronald H. Grant, "Pegawai Role Perceptions in West Java: Implications for Politics and Economic Development," unpublished paper delivered at the Asian Studies on the Pacific Coast conference, Pacific Grove, California, 1976.

32. Fried, *The Italian Prefects*.

33. Mark Kesselman, *The Ambiguous Consensus* (New York: Knopf, 1967).

34. Wayne A. Cornelius, Jr., "Nation-Building, Participation, Distribution: Reform Under Cárdenas," in Gabriel Almond et al., eds., *The Politics of Social Crisis, Choice, and Change: Historical Studies of Political Development* (Boston: Little, Brown, 1973), pp. 392–498.

35. Mexico's land redistribution programs began two decades before those of most developing countries. See Hung-Chao Tai, *Land Reform and Politics: A Comparative Analysis* (Berkeley: University of California Press, 1974).

36. Ronald Rogowsky and Lois Wasserspring, *Does Political Development Exist? Corporatism in Old and New Societies* (Beverly Hills: Sage, 1971).

37. *The New York Times,* November 19, 1976.

38. Manuel L. Carlos, *Politics and Development in Rural Mexico: A Study of Socio-Economic Modernization* (New York: Praeger, 1974), pp. 26–37.

39. Ibid., p. 26.

40. This and the subsequent interpretation of why members of the *ejidos organizados* have not been recruited by the official peasant organizations is the author's, not that of Manuel L. Carlos. Carlos emphasized the lack of incentives for the farmers to join.

41. Richard R. Fagen and William S. Tuohy, *Politics and Privilege in a Mexican City* (Stanford: Stanford University Press, 1972), p. 52.

42. William S. Tuohy and David Ronfeldt, "Political Control and the Recruitment of Middle Level Elites in Mexico: An Example from Agrarian Politics," *Western Political Quarterly* 22, no. 2 (1969): 365–72.

43. Fagen and Tuohy, *Politics and Privilege,* p. 44.

44. Wayne A. Cornelius, Jr., *Politics and the Migrant Poor in Mexico City* (Stanford: Stanford University Press, 1973), p. 164.

45. Vincent L. Padgett, *The Mexican Political System* (Boston: Little, Brown, 1966), p. 151.

46. Fagen and Tuohy, *Politics and Privilege,* p. 22.

47. Ibid., p. 46.

48. Susan Eckstein, *The Political Economy of Lower Class Areas in Mexico City: Societal Constraints on Local Business Prospects,* Latin American Urban Research 5 (Beverly Hills: Sage, 1975), p. 126.

49. Jorge Balan et al., *Men in a Developing Society* (Austin: University of Texas Press, 1973), p. 302.

50. Donald W. Baerresen, *The Border Industrialization Program of Mexico* (Lexington, Mass.: D. C. Heath, 1971).

51. Kenneth F. Johnson, *Mexican Democracy: A Critical View* (Boston: Houghton Mifflin, 1971).

52. Charles W. Anderson, "Bankers as Revolutionaries," in William P. Glade, Jr., and Charles W. Anderson, *The Political Economy of Mexico* (Madison: University of Wisconsin Press, 1968), pp. 103–85.

53. Fagen and Tuohy, *Politics and Privilege,* p. 57.

54. Pablo Gonzales-Cassanova, *Democracy in Mexico* (New York: Oxford University Press, 1970), p. 29.

55. Fagen and Tuohy, *Politics and Privilege,* p. 136.

56. Ergun Ozbudun, "Established Revolution Versus Unfinished Revolution: Contrasting Patterns of Democratization in Mexico and Turkey," in Samuel P. Huntington and Clement H. Moore, eds., *Authoritarian Politics in Modern Society: The Dynamics of Established One-Party Systems* (New York: Basic Books, 1970), pp. 380–405.

57. Walter F. Weiker, *Decentralizing Government in Modernizing Nations: Growth Center Potential of Turkish Provincial Cities,* Sage Professional Papers in International Studies 1, 2007 (Beverly Hills: Sage, 1972).

58. Ibid., p. 27.

59. Serif Mardin, "Center-Periphery Relations: A Key to Turkish Politics," *Daedalus* 102, no. 1 (Winter 1973): 169–90.

60. Joseph S. Szyliowicz, *Political Change in Rural Turkey: Erdemli* (The Hague: Mouton, 1966), p. 49.

61. Ergun Ozbudun, *Social Change and Political Participation in Turkey* (Princeton: Princeton University Press, 1976).

62. Paul Stirling, *Turkish Village* (London: Weidenfeld and Nicolson, 1965), p. 281.

63. Walter F. Weiker, "Turkey: The Development of Modernizing Followers," unpublished paper delivered at the Tenth Annual Meeting of the Middle East Studies Association, Los Angeles, California, 1976.

64. Stirling, *Turkish Village,* p. 292.

65. Daniel Lerner, *The Passing of Traditional Society* (New York: Free Press, 1958).

66. Walter F. Weiker, *Decentralizing Government in Modernizing Nations.*

67. Szyliowicz, *Political Change in Rural Turkey,* p. 48.

68. Frank Tachau, "Turkish Provincial Party Politics," in Kemal H. Karpat, ed., *Social Change and Politics in Turkey* (Princeton: Princeton University Press, 1973).

69. Ozbudun, *Social Change and Political Participation in Turkey.*

70. Mardin, "Center-Periphery Relations."

71. Frederick W. Frey, *The Turkish Political Elite* (Cambridge: Harvard University Press, 1965), p. 187.

72. Walter F. Weiker, *Political Tutelage and Democracy in Turkey* (Leiden: E. J. Brill, 1973).

73. Szyliowicz, *Political Change in Rural Turkey.*

74. Ibid., p. 115.

75. Ibid., p. 124.

76. Ronald D. Brunner and Garry D. Brewer, *Organized Complexity* (New York: Free Press, 1971).

77. Peter F. Sugar, "Economic and Political Modernization: Turkey," in Robert E. Ward and Dankwart A. Rustow, eds., *Political Modernization in Japan and Turkey* (Princeton: Princeton University Press, 1964), pp. 146–76.

78. Fatma Mansur, *Bodrum: A Town in the Aegean* (Leiden: E. J. Brill, 1972).

79. Szyliowicz, *Political Change in Rural Turkey,* p. 125.

80. Frey, *Turkish Political Elite,* p. 96.

81. Paul Magnarella, *Tradition and Change in a Turkish Town* (Cambridge, Mass.: Schenkman, 1974).

82. Fatma Mansur, *Bodrum,* p. 91.

83. Majeed R. Jafar, *Under-development: A Regional Case Study of the Kurdish Area in Turkey* (Helsinki: Social Policy Association in Finland, 1976).

84. Ibid., p. 97.

85. Ibid., p. 114.

86. Ibid., p. 141.

87. *Area Handbook for the Republic of Turkey* (Washington, D.C.: G.P.O., 1970), p. 77.

88. Ozbudun, "Established Revolution Versus Unfinished Revolution," pp. 380–405.

89. Richard D. Robinson, *The First Turkish Republic: A Case Study in National Development* (Cambridge: Harvard University Press, 1965), p. 142.

Chapter 3

1. Nicholas Hopkins, *Popular Government in an African Town* (Chicago: University of Chicago Press, 1972), pp. 76–77.

2. Samuel Humes and Eileen Martin, *The Structure of Local Government* (The Hague: International Union of Local Authorities, 1969), pp. 129–43.

3. Lynn T. White, "Local Autonomy in China During the Cultural Revolution," *American Political Science Review* 70, no. 2 (June 1976): 479.

4. Harry J. Friedman, *Local Government in Third World Asia* (Morristown, N.J.: General Learning Press, 1973), p. 14.

5. Yasumasa Kuroda, "Ecology and Local Politics: A Citizen Movement in Japan," in F. C. Bruhns, F. Cazzola, and J. Wiatr, eds., *Local Politics, Development, and Participation: A Cross-National Study of Interrelationships* (Pittsburgh: Center for International Studies, University of Pittsburgh, 1974), pp. 116–26.

6. Heather Strange, "Community Leadership and Political Affiliation: A Rural Malay Example," unpublished manuscript, Department of Anthropology, Rutgers University, 1971.

7. Louis P. Benson, "Changing Political Alliance Patterns in the Rural Philippines," in Benedict J. Kerkvliet, ed., *Political Change in the Philippines*, Asian Studies at Hawaii 14 (Honolulu: University Press of Hawaii, 1974).

8. Chae-Jin Lee, "Urban Political Competition in a Developing Nation: The Case of Korea," *Comparative Political Studies* 4, no. 1 (April 1971): 107–16, and Young Whan Kihl, "Policy Output and Electoral Competition in Korean Cities," unpublished paper delivered at the American Political Science Association, New Orleans, 1973.

9. Mark Kesselman, "Research Perspectives in Comparative Local Politics: Pitfalls and Projects," *Comparative Urban Research* I, no. I (1972): 10-23, and Yasumasa Kuroda, *Reed Town, Japan: A Study in Community Power Structure and Political Change* (Honolulu: University Press of Hawaii, 1974), p. 75.

10. Kesselman, "Research Perspectives."

11. Friedman, *Local Government.*

12. Magda Talamo, "The Role of Industry in Local Politics: The Position of a Group of Italian Industrial Directors," in Bruhns, Cazzola, and Wiatr, eds., *Local Politics, Development, and Participation,* p. 25.

13. L. Gray Cowan, *Local Government in West Africa* (New York: Columbia University Press, 1958), pp. 18–34.

14. Nelson W. Polsby, "The Institutionalization of the U.S. House of Representatives," *American Political Science Review* 62, no. 1 (March 1968): 144–68.

15. Daniel Lerner, *The Passing of Traditional Society* (New York: Free Press, 1958). The conclusion that urbanization leads to participatory politics came from a bias toward modernization in the development literature in the 1950s and 1960s as much as it did from empirical evidence.

16. Sidney Tarrow, "The Urban-Rural Cleavage in Political Involvement: The Case of France," *American Political Science Review* 65, no. 2 (June 1971): 341–57; and Kuroda, *Reed Town, Japan,* p. 98.

17. Bradley M. Richardson, "Urbanization and Political Participation: The Case of Japan," *American Political Science Review* 67, no. 2 (June 1973): 433–52.

18. Tarrow, "Urban-Rural Cleavage," p. 344.

19. Richardson, "Urbanization and Political Participation," pp. 433–52.

20. Cynthia H. Enloe, *The Politics of Pollution in Comparative Perspective* (New York: David McKay, 1975), p. 224.

21. J. A. A. Stockwin, "Shifting Alignments in Japanese Party Politics: The April 1974 Election for Governor of Kyoto Prefecture," *Asian Survey* 14, no. 5 (May 1974): 887–89.

22. Michio Muramatsu, "The Impact of Economic Growth Policies on Local Politics in Japan," *Asian Survey* 15, no. 9 (September 1975): 799–816.

23. Kuroda, *Reed Town, Japan,* p. 133.

24. Ibid., p. 131.

25. Stockwin, "Shifting Alignments," p. 892.

26. Ibid.

27. Gary D. Allinson, *Japanese Urbanism: Industry and Politics in Kariya 1872–1972* (Berkeley: University of California Press, 1975).

28. Ibid.

29. Tosh Lee, "Tokyo Metropolitan Assembly Elections—1973," *Asian Survey* 14, no. 5 (May 1974): 479.

30. J. Reys Maeno, "Japan 1973: The End of An Era?", *Asian Survey* 14, no. 1 (January 1974): 52–64.

31. Kuroda, *Reed Town, Japan,* p. 123.

32. Tosh Lee, "Tokyo Assembly Elections."

33. The Korean War, for example, boosted Japanese industry and, simultaneously, the fortunes of the LDP in the prosperous industrial towns.

34. Kuroda, *Reed Town, Japan,* p. 103.

35. Muramatsu, "Impact of Economic Growth Policies," pp. 799–816.

36. Ibid.

37. Myron Weiner, *The Politics of Scarcity* (Chicago: University of Chicago Press, 1962).

38. Wayne Wilcox, "Madhya Pradesh," in Myron Weiner, ed., *State Politics in India* (Princeton: Princeton University Press, 1968), pp. 127–76.

39. *Economic and Political Weekly of Bombay,* July 10, 1976, gave the following figures for all-India landownership shares: 26.20 percent of the land was owned by 5 percent of the population; 69.64 percent of the land was owned by 25 percent of the population. These figures would leave 75 percent of the population with only 30.36 percent of the land.

40. Anthony Carter, *Elite Politics in Rural India: Political Stratification and Political Alliances in Western Maharashtra* (New York: Cambridge University Press, 1974).

41. In the county of Phaltan, Anthony Carter records the *vatandar* caste as making up 10.3 percent of the population and 41.0 percent of the officeholders (ibid., pp. 60–71). For more discussion of the politics of land in colonial India, see Rajat Ray and Ratna Ray, "Zamindars and Jotedars: A Study of Rural Politics in Bengal," *Modern Asian Studies* 9, no. 1 (February 1975): 81–102.

42. For more details about the composition of the block council, see Carter, *Elite Politics in Rural India,* p. 33.

43. Richard Sisson and Lawrence L. Shraeder, *Legislative Recruitment and Political Integration,* Research Monograph 6 (Berkeley: Center for South and Southeast Asia Studies, University of California, 1972).

44. R. C. Prasad, "Public Participation in Local Politics in India," in Bruhns, Cazzola, and Wiatr, eds., *Local Politics, Development, and Participation,* pp. 127–35.

45. Paul Brass, *Factional Politics in an Indian State* (Berkeley: University of California Press, 1965).

46. Frederick George Bailey, *Politics and Social Change: Orissa in 1959* (Berkeley: University of California Press, 1963), p. 96.

47. The wells that are made available through agricultural development programs, for example, often use the power-driven pumps that wealthy farmers can afford and prefer. Similarly, the national government has shown a preference for tractors designed for large farms. V. V. Bhatt, "Decision Making in the Public Sector: Case Study of Swaraj Tractor," *Economic and Political Weekly* [Bombay] 13, no. 21 (May 27, 1978): 30, 45.

48. Brass, *Factional Politics in an Indian State,* p. 125.

49. Carter, *Elite Politics in Rural India.*

50. Bailey, *Politics and Social Change.*

51. Lloyd I. Rudolph and Susanne Hoeber Rudolph, *The Modernity of Tradition: Political Development in India* (Chicago: University of Chicago Press, 1967).

52. Colin Rosser, *Urbanization in India,* International Urbanization Survey Report to the Ford Foundation, n.p., n.d., p. 73.

53. John P. Lewis, *Quiet Crisis in India* (Garden City, N.Y.: Doubleday, 1962), p. 188. Lewis describes the village rhetoric as "Indian development policy's genuflecting to the mystique of the village."

54. K. Matthew Kurian, *The Impact of Foreign Capital on the Indian Economy* (New Delhi: People's Publishing House, 1966).

55. Jawaharlal Nehru, *An Autobiography* (London: Bodley Head, 1953), p. 100.

56. Brass, *Factional Politics in an Indian State,* pp. 184–230.

57. Donald P. Rosenthal, *The Limited Elite: Urban Politics in Agra and Poona* (Chicago: University of Chicago Press, 1970).

58. Brass, *Factional Politics in an Indian State,* p. 187.

59. C. L. Sharma, "Changing Patterns of Leadership and Power Structure in Local Self-Government of a City in Rajasthan," *Indian Journal of Political Science* (1975): 80–94.

60. Rosenthal, *Limited Elite,* p. 14.

61. Prasad, "Public Participation in Local Politics," pp. 127–35.

62. Sisson and Schraeder, *Legislative Recruitment.*

63. Roderick A. Church, "Authority and Influence in Indian Municipal Politics: Administrators and Councillors in Lucknow," *Asian Survey* 13, no. 4 (April 1973): 421–38.

64. Henry C. Hart, "Bombay Politics: Pluralism or Polarization?" *Journal of Asian Studies* 20, no. 2 (May 1961): 271.

65. Donald S. Zagoria, "The Ecology of Peasant Communism in India," *American Political Science Review* 65, no. 1 (March 1971): 144–60.

66. Carter, *Elite Politics in Rural India,* p. 45.

Chapter 4

1. Ronald Loveridge, *City Managers in Legislative Politics* (Indianapolis: Bobbs-Merrill, 1971), p. 83; Roderick A. Church, "Authority and Influence in Indian Municipal Politics: Administrators and Councillors in Lucknow," *Asian Survey* 13, no. 4 (April 1973): 421–38.

2. K. J. Davey, "Local Bureaucrats and Politicians in East Africa," *Journal of Administration Overseas* 10, no. 4 (October 1971): 268–79.

3. Ibid.

4. Edward Schumacher, *Politics, Bureaucracy, and Rural Development in Senegal* (Berkeley: University of California Press, 1975), p. 196.

5. Cynthia H. Enlow, "Ethnicity and Militarization: Factors Shaping the Roles of Police in Third World Nations," *Studies in Comparative International Development* 11, no. 3 (Fall 1976): 25–39.

6. George E. Berkley, "Central vs. Local Police Organization in Western Democracies," in Jack Goldsmith and Gil Gunderson, eds., *Comparative Local Politics: A Systems-Function Approach* (Boston: Holbrook Press, 1973), pp. 194–211.

7. Enlow, "Ethnicity and Militarization," p. 36.

8. Karl Dietrich Bracher, "Problems of Parliamentary Democracy in Europe," *Daedalus* 93, no. 1 (Winter 1964): 179–98.

9. Frank P. Sherwood, *Institutionalizing the Grass Roots in Brazil: A Study in Comparative Local Government* (San Francisco: Chandler, 1972), p. 103.

10. Dan Fritz, "Bureaucratic Commitment in Rural India: A Psychological Interpretation," unpublished paper delivered at the Association for African Studies, Boston, 1974.

11. John Badgley, *Politics Among Burmans: A Study of Intermediary Leaders,* Southeast Asia Series 15 (Athens: Center for International Studies, Ohio University, 1970), p. 75.

12. Schumacher, *Politics, Bureaucracy, and Rural Development,* p. 226.

13. Aristide Zolberg, *One-Party Government in the Ivory Coast,* 2d ed. (Princeton: Princeton University Press, 1969), p. 347.

14. Ronald M. Grant, "Governing Indonesia: Role Perceptions and Orientations of Government Officials," paper presented at the American Society for Public Administration, Washington, D.C., April 1976.

15. Loveridge, *City Managers in Legislative Politics,* p. 52.

16. Mark Kesselman, "Overinstitutionalization and Political Constraint: The Case of France," *Comparative Politics* 3, no. 1 (October 1970): 21–44.

17. Ibrahim Mohammed Osman, "Local Administration System in the United Arab Republic," *Journal of Administration Overseas* 6, no. 2 (April 1967): 85–96.

18. Peter S. Cleaves, *Developmental Process in Chilean Local Government* (Berkeley: University of California Press, 1969), p. 2.

19. Juma Volter Mwapachu, "Operation Planned Villages in Rural Tanzania: A Revolutionary Strategy for Development," *African Review* 6, no. 1 (1976): 1–16.

20. District and area both refer to the basic unit in the Tanzanian territorial structure at which the national government operates. Above the district or area are (21) regions and below it are divisions, wards, villages, and cells. Clyde R. Ingle, *From Village to State in Tanzania: The Politics of Rural Development* (Ithaca: Cornell University Press, 1972), has a clear description of the territorial structure of the Tanzanian state.

21. Goren Hyden, *Village and State in Tanzania* (Ithaca: Cornell University Press, 1972).

22. James R. Finucane, *Rural Development and Bureaucracy in Tanzania: The Case of Mwanza Region* (Uppsala, Sweden: Scandinavian Institute of African Studies, 1974), p. 180.

23. Julius K. Nyerere, *Decentralization* (Dar es Salaam, Tanzania: Government Printer, 1972).

24. Norman Miller, "The Rural African Party: Political Participation in Tanzania," *American Political Science Review* 64, no. 2 (June 1970): 548–71.

25. Finucane, *Rural Development and Bureaucracy,* p. 64.

26. Ingle, *From Village to State,* p. 205.

27. Joel Samoff, *Tanzania: Local Politics and the Structure of Power* (Madison: University of Wisconsin Press, 1974), p. 172.

28. Finucane, *Rural Development and Bureaucracy,* p. 59.

29. Michael B. Frolic, "The Soviet Study of Soviet Cities," *Journal of Politics* 32, no. 3 (August 1970): 681.

30. David R. Cattell, *Leningrad: A Case Study of Soviet Urban Government* (New York: Praeger, 1968), p. x.

31. Frolic, "Soviet Study of Soviet Cities," p. 687.

32. T. H. Rigby, "Comments" on Jerry F. Hough, "Political Participation in the Soviet Union," *Soviet Studies* 28, no. 2 (April 1976): 257–61.

33. Frolic, "Soviet Study of Soviet Cities," p. 690.

34. Cattell, *Leningrad,* p. 65.

35. Everett M. Jacobs, "The Composition of Local Soviets, 1959–69," *Government and Opposition* 7, no. 4 (1972): 504.

36. Jerry F. Hough, "Soviet Urban Politics and Comparative Urban Theory," *Journal of Comparative Administration* 4 (November 1972): 311–34.

37. Jacobs, "Composition of Local Soviets," p. 517.

38. Ibid., p. 506.

39. Ibid., p. 515.

40. Michael B. Frolic, "Soviet Urban Political Leaders," *Comparative Political Studies* 2, no. 4 (January 1970): 443–64.

41. Jerry F. Hough, *The Soviet Prefects* (Cambridge: Harvard University Press, 1969).

42. Ibid., p. 73.

43. Ibid., p. 274.

44. William A. Robson, ed., *Great Cities of the World: Their Government Politics and Planning* (New York: Macmillan, 1975).

45. Ibid., p. 251.

46. Ibid., p. 105.

47. Carol W. Lewis, "Comparing City Budgets: The Soviet Case," *Comparative Urban Research* 5, no. 1 (1977): 46–59.

48. Cattell, *Leningrad,* p. 43.

49. William Taubman, *Governing Soviet Cities: Bureaucratic Politics and Urban Development in the USSR* (New York: Praeger, 1973), and Frolic, "Soviet Study of Soviet Cities," p. 690.

50. Hough, *Soviet Prefects,* p. 267.

51. Carol W. Lewis, "The Beggar Bureaucrat: Linking National and City Politics in the Soviet Union," unpublished paper delivered at the American Society for Public Administration, Washington, D.C., April 1976.

52. Taubman, *Governing Soviet Cities.*

53. Lewis, "Beggar Bureaucrat," p. 15.

54. Hough, *Soviet Prefects,* p. 118.

55. Ibid., p. 222.

56. Taubman, *Governing Soviet Cities,* p. 60.

57. Cattell, *Leningrad,* p. 79.

58. Ibid., p. 50.

59. Lewis, "Comparing City Budgets."

60. Ibid.

61. Cattell, *Leningrad,* p. 105.

Chapter 5

1. M. Corpierre, "Le totalitarisme africain," *Preuves* 143 (January 1963): 17.

2. Annmarie Hauck Walsh, *The Urban Challenge to Government* (New York: Praeger, 1969), p. 156.

3. Samuel P. Huntington, *Political Order in Changing Societies* (New Haven: Yale University Press, 1968), p. 438.

4. Maxwell Owusu, *Uses and Abuses of Political Power: A Case Study of Continuity and Change in the Politics of Ghana* (Chicago: University of Chicago Press, 1970), p. 271.

5. Clifford Geertz, *Peddlers and Princes: Social Change and Economic Modernization in Two Indonesian Towns* (Chicago: University of Chicago Press, 1963), pp. 153–57.

6. Luigi Graziano, "Patron-Client Relationships in Southern Italy," in F. C. Bruhns, F. Cazzola, and J. Wiatr, eds., *Local Politics, Development, and Participation: A Cross-National Study of Interrelationships* (Pittsburgh: Center for International Studies, University of Pittsburgh, 1974), pp. 181–205.

7. David W. Dent, "Cooperation and Community Development in Columbia: A Comparative Study of Two Urban Communities," unpublished paper delivered at the American Political Science Association meetings, New Orleans, 1973.

8. Robert C. Wood, "The Local Government Response to the Urban Economy," in James Q. Wilson, ed., *City Politics and Public Policy* (New York: John Wiley, 1968), pp. 69–96.

9. William Taubman, *Governing Soviet Cities: Bureaucratic Politics and Urban Development in the USSR* (New York: Praeger, 1973), pp. 99–107.

10. Charles E. Lindblom, *Politics and Markets: The World's Political-Economic Systems* (New York: Basic Books, 1977).

11. Norton E. Long, "The Corporation, Its Satellites, and the Local Community," in E. S. Mason, ed., *The Corporation in Modern Society* (Cambridge: Harvard University Press, 1959), pp. 202–17.

12. Ibid., p. 206.

13. Magda Talamo, "The Role of Industry in Local Politics: The Position of a Group of Italian Industrial Directors," in F. C. Bruhns, F. Cazzola, and J. Waitr, eds., *Local Politics, Development, and Participation: A Cross-National Study of Interrelationships* (Pittsburgh: Center for International Studies, University of Pittsburgh, 1974), pp. 3–45.

14. Fred R. Von der Mehden, "Interest Groups and Government Policy in Malaysia," *Rice University Studies* 64, no. 4 (Fall 1975).

15. Harry J. Friedman, *Local Government in Third World Asia* (Morristown, N.J.: General Learning Press, 1973).

16. Wood, "Local Government Response," p. 74.

17. Donald S. Zagoria, "The Ecology of Peasant Communism in India," *American Political Science Review* 65, no. 1 (March 1971): 144–60.

18. Hung-Chao Tai, *Land Reform and Politics: A Comparative Analysis* (Berkeley: University of California Press, 1974), pp. 360, 365.

19. Huntington, *Political Order in Changing Societies,* p. 438.

20. Iliya Harik, *The Political Mobilization of Peasants: A Study of an Egyptian Community,* Studies in Development 8 (Bloomington: Indiana University Press, 1974), pp. 63–80.

21. Edward C. Banfield and Laura Banfield, *The Moral Basis of a Backward Society,* 2d ed. (New York: Free Press, 1967), pp. 83–101.

22. Gove Hambidge, ed., *Dynamics of Development* (New York: Praeger, 1964), p. 57.

23. Henry Bienen, *Kenya: The Politics of Participation and Control* (Princeton: Princeton University Press, 1974), p. 57.

24. Wood, "Local Government Response," p. 95.

25. William Safran, *The French Polity* (New York: David McKay, 1977), p. 225.

26. Mark Kesselman, *The Ambiguous Consensus* (New York: Knopf, 1967).

27. Jerome E. Milch, "Influence as Power: French Local Government Reconsidered," *British Journal of Political Science* 4, no. 2 (April 1974), pt. 2: 139–61.

28. Ibid.

29. Ibid.

30. William Safran, *The French Polity,* p. 224.

31. Kesselman, *The Ambiguous Consensus,* p. 106.

32. Suzanne Berger, Peter Gourevitch, Patrice Higonnet, Karl Kaiser, "The Problem of Reform in France: The Political Ideas of Local Elites," *Political Science Quarterly* 84, no. 3 (September 1969): 436–60.

33. William Safran, *The French Polity.*

34. Vincent Wright, "Politics and Administration Under the French Fifth Republic," *Political Studies* 22, no. 1 (March 1974): 44–65.

35. Niles M. Hansen, *French Regional Planning* (Edinburgh: Edinburgh University Press, 1968).

36. Hugh D. Clout, "France," in Hugh D. Clout, ed., *Regional Development in Western Europe* (London: John Wiley, 1975), pp. 113–38.

37. Kevin Allen and M. C. MacLennen, *Regional Problems and Policies in Italy and France* (Beverly Hills: Sage, 1970).

38. Sidney Tarrow, *Between Center and Periphery: Grassroots Politicians in Italy and France* (New Haven: Yale University Press, 1977).

39. Laurence Wylie, *Village in the Vaucluse* (New York: Harper and Row, 1964); Edgar Morin, *The Red and the White* (New York: Pantheon, 1970); and Suzanne Berger, *Peasants Against Politics: Rural Organization in Brittany 1911–1967* (Cambridge: Harvard University Press, 1972).

40. Berger, *Peasants Against Politics.*

41. Sidney Tarrow, "The Urban-Rural Cleavage in Political Involvement: The Case of France," *American Political Science Review* 65, no. 2 (June 1971): 341–57.

42. Berger, *Peasants Against Politics.*

43. Mark Kesselman, "Overinstitutionalization and Political Constraint: The Case of France," *Comparative Politics* 3, no. 1 (October 1970): 21–44.

44. Tarrow, "Urban-Rural Cleavage," p. 344, and Kesselman, *The Ambiguous Consensus,* p. 25.

45. Kesselman, *The Ambiguous Consensus.*

46. Berger, *Peasants Against Politics,* p. 14.

47. Tarrow, "Urban-Rural Cleavage," p. 353.

48. Ibid., p. 354.

49. John Connell, ed., *Semnan: Persian City and Region* (London: University College, 1969), p. 83.

50. Paul English, *City and Village in Iran: Settlement and Economy in Kirman Basin* (Madison: University of Wisconsin Press, 1966).

51. Myong-Chan Hwang, *An Administrative Framework for Regional Planning* (Tehran: Centre for Research and Training in Regional Planning, Plan and Budget Organization and the United Nations Development Programme, 1974).

52. Ibid.

53. Ervand Abrahamian, "Factionalism in Iranian Politics: The 14th Parliament," *Middle Eastern Studies* 14, no. 1 (January 1978): 22–55.

54. Ibid.

55. Ann T. Schulz, "The Politics of Municipal Administration in Isfahan, Iran," *Journal of Administration Overseas* 14, no. 4 (October 1974): 228–39.

56. James A. Bill, *The Politics of Iran: Groups, Classes, and Modernization* (Columbus, Ohio: Charles E. Merrill, 1972).

Chapter 6

1. Theodore Lowi, "American Business, Public Policy, Case Studies, and Political Theory," *World Politics* 16, no. 4 (July 1964): 677–715.

2. Michael Crozier, *The Bureaucratic Phenomenon* (Chicago: University of Chicago Press, 1964), p. 247.

3. Ibid., p. 236.

4. Lowi, "American Business," p. 715.

5. Gaston V. Rimlinger, *Welfare Policy and Industrialization in Europe, America, and Russia* (New York: John Wiley, 1971), p. 24.

6. Ibid., p. 25.

7. Ibid., p. 94.

8. Vivek Bhattacharya, *Social Security Measures in India* (New Delhi: Metropolitan Books, 1970).

9. James H. Schulz, et al., *Providing Adequate Retirement Income: Pension Reform in the United States and Abroad* (Hanover, N.H.: Brandeis University Press and the University Press of New England, 1974).

10. Ralf Dahrendorf, *Society and Democracy in Germany* (Garden City, N. Y.: Doubleday, 1969).

11. William J. Platt, "Conflicts in Educational Planning," in James S. Coleman, ed., *Education and Political Development* (Princeton: Princeton University Press, 1965), p. 570.

12. Yasumasa Kuroda, *Reed Town, Japan: A Study in Community Power Structure and Political Change* (Honolulu: University Press of Hawaii, 1974), pp. 177–79.

13. Arnold J. Heidenheimer, Hugh Heclo, and Carolyn Tech Adams, *Comparative Public Policy: The Politics of Social Choice in Europe and America* (New York: St. Martin's Press, 1975), p. 82.

14. Ibid., p. 86.

15. Ibid., p. 59.

16. Robert C. Fried, "Politics, Economics, and Federalism: Aspects of Urban Government in Austria, Germany and Switzerland," in Terry N. Clark, ed., *Comparative Community Politics* (New York: John Wiley, 1974), p. 341.

17. Lars Gyllensten. "Swedish Radicalism in the 1960's: An experiment in Political and Cultural Debate," in Donald M. Hancock and Oiden Sjoberg, eds., *Politics in the Post-Welfare State* (New York: Columbia University Press, 1972), p. 297.

18. Heidenheimer, Heclo, and Adams, *Comparative Public Policy,* p. 60.

19. Ibid., p. 276.

20. Lowi, "American Business," p. 715.

21. William L. Riordon, *Plunkitt of Tammany Hall: A Series of Very Plain Talks on Very Practical Politics* (New York: Dutton, 1963), p. 37.

22. Tokyo Metropolitan Government, "Toward Achievement of 'Civil Minimum,'" *Tokyo Municipal News* 26, no. 7 (November/December 1976).

23. Crozier. *The Bureaucratic Phenomenon,* p. 246.

24. Roger D. Hansen, *The Politics of Mexican Development* (Baltimore: Johns Hopkins Press, 1971), p. 87.

25. Ibid., p. 206.

26. Ibid., p. 213.

27. James S. Coleman et al., *Equality of Educational Opportunity* (Washington, D.C.: G.P.O., 1966), p. viii.

28. Sharon Perlman Krefetz, *Welfare Policy Making and City Politics* (New York: Praeger, 1976).

29. Herbert Jacobs et al., *Values and the Active Community: A Cross-National Study of the Influence of Local Leadership* (New York: Free Press, 1971).

30. Basil G. Zimmer and Amos H. Hawley, *Metropolitan Area Schools* (Beverly Hills: Sage, 1968), p. 286.

31. Arnold J. Heidenheimer, "The Politics of Public Education, Health, and Welfare in the U.S. and Western Europe: How Growth and Reform Potentials Have Differed," *British Journal of Political Science* 3, no. 3 (July 1973): 315–40.

32. Richard Child Hill, "Separate and Unequal: Governmental Inequality in the Metropolis," *American Political Science Review* 67, no. 4 (December 1974): 1557–68.

33. Arnold J. Heidenheimer, "Local Control and Equal Opportunity in British and American Education," in Heidenheimer, Heclo, and Adams, *Comparative Public Policy,* p. 134.

34. Thomas R. Dye, "Governmental Structure, Urban Environment, Educational Policy," *Midwest Journal of Political Science* 11, no. 3 (August 1967): 353–80.

35. Hill, "Separate and Unequal."

36. William R. Grant, "Community Control vs. Integration—The Case of Detroit," *Public Interest* 24, no. 3 (Summer 1971): 62–79.

37. Heidenheimer, "Local Control and Equal Opportunity," p. 137.

38. William Lee Miller, *The Fifteenth Ward and the Great Society* (Boston: Houghton Mifflin, 1966), pp. 50–83.

39. Ibid.

40. Michael N. Danielson, *The Politics of Exclusion* (New York: Columbia University Press, 1976), p. 212.

41. Ibid., p. 91.

42. Krefetz, *Welfare Policy Making*, p. 186.

43. Andrew J. Cowart, "Anti-Poverty Expenditures in the American States," in Richard I. Hofferbert and Ira Sharkansky, eds., *State and Urban Politics: Readings in Comparative Public Policy* (Boston: Little, Brown, 1971), pp. 413–28.

44. Frances Fox Piven and Richard Ceward, *Regulating the Poor: The Functions of Public Welfare* (New York: Random House, 1971), p. 190.

45. Krefetz, *Welfare Policy Making*, p. 200.

46. Other studies have come to different conclusions. One looked at the ratio of local taxation to local expenditures: Brian R. Fry and Richard F. Winters, "The Politics of Redistribution," *American Political Science Review* 68, no. 2 (June 1975): 508–22. The authors conclude that wealth and demography were more important in determining variations among localities, but their aggregate data don't account for the incremental nature of local political decisions.

47. Edward C. Banfield and James Q. Wilson, *City Politics* (Cambridge: Harvard University Press, 1963), p. 296.

48. Krefetz, *Welfare Policy Making*.

49. *The Christian Science Monitor,* February 7, 1977.

50. Alexander L. George, "Political Leadership and Social Change in American Cities," *Daedalus* 97, no. 4 (Fall 1968), pt. 2: 1194–217.

51. Ibid.

52. Theodore Marmor, "Why Medicare Helped Raise Doctors' Fees," *Transaction* (September 1978): 17.

53. Ibid.

54. Joseph P. Fried, *Housing Crisis USA* (New York: Praeger, 1971), pp. 55–56.

55. Danielson, *The Politics of Exclusion,* p. 239.

56. Howard S. Ellis, *Private Enterprise and Socialism in the Middle East* (Washington, D.C.: American Enterprises Institute for Public Policy Research, 1970), p. 11.

57. Iliya F. Harik, "Mobilization Policy and Political Change in Rural Egypt," in Richard Antoun and Iliya Harik, eds., *Rural Politics and Social Change in the Middle East* (Bloomington: Indiana University Press, 1972), p. 288.

58. Irma Adelman and Cynthia Taft Morris, *Economic Growth and Social Equity in Developing Countries* (Stanford: Stanford University Press, 1973).

59. Robert Mabro, *The Egyptian Economy* (Oxford, Eng.: Clarendon Press, 1974), pp. 218–27.

60. Mahmoud Abdel-Fadhil, *Development, Income Distribution, and Social Change in Rural Egypt* (Cambridge: Cambridge University Press, 1975), p. 28.

61. Ibid., p. 54.

62. Malcolm Kerr, "Egypt," in James S. Coleman, ed., *Education and Political Development* (Princeton: Princeton University Press, 1965), pp. 169–94.

63. Mabro, *The Egyptian Economy*, p. 156.

64. Kerr, "Egypt," p. 190.

65. James Iwan, "From Social Welfare to Local Government," *Middle East Journal* 22 (Summer 1968): 265–77.

66. Mabro, *The Egyptian Economy*, p. 110.

67. Ibid., p. 226.

68. Malcolm Kerr, "The United Arab Republic: The Domestic, Political, and Economic Background of Foreign Policy," in Paul Y. Hammond and Sidney S. Alexander, eds., *Political Dynamics in the Middle East* (New York: American Elsevier, 1972).

69. Iliya Harik, *The Political Mobilization of Peasants: A Study of an Egyptian Community,* Studies in Development 8 (Bloomington: Indiana University Press, 1974).

70. Ibid., p. 56.

71. Abdel-Fadhil, *Development, Income Distribution, and Social Change*, p. 122.

72. Harik, *The Political Mobilization of Peasants*, p. 60.

73. Ibid.

74. Mabro, *The Egyptian Economy*, pp. 222–24.

75. Harik, *The Political Mobilization of Peasants*, p. 171.

76. Ibid., p. 259.

77. James Heaphey, "The Organization of Egypt: The Inadequacies of a Non-Political Model for Nation-Building," *World Politics* 18, no. 1 (January 1966): 190.

Chapter 7

1. Peter Merkl, *Modern Comparative Politics* (Hinsdale, Ill.: Dryden; Holt, Rinehart and Winston, 1977), p. 88.

2. Sidney Tarrow, *Between Center and Periphery: Grassroots Politicians in Italy and France* (New Haven: Yale University Press, 1977).

3. Chae-Jin Lee, "Urban Political Competition in a Developing Nation: The Case of Korea," *Comparative Political Studies* 4, no. 1 (April 1971): 107–16.

4. Herbert H. Werlin, *Governing an African City: A Study of Nairobi* (New York: Africana, 1974).

5. Tarrow, *Between Center and Periphery,* pp. 235, 252.

6. Mark Kesselman and Donald Rosenthal, *Local Power and Comparative Politics,* Comparative Politics Series 5 (Beverly Hills: Sage, 1974), p. 39.

7. Richard R. Fagen and William S. Tuohy, *Politics and Privilege in a Mexican City* (Stanford: Stanford University Press, 1972), p. 171.

Index

A

Adbdul-Hamid II, sultan, 16
Agricultural politics, 19–20, 68–72, 82–83, 97–99, 115, 122–23
  Egypt, 180–81, 183–86
  France, 49, 136–38
  India, 66–72
  Iran, 139–44
  Mexico, 23–28
  Tanzania, 91, 97–99
Algeria
  Ben Bella, Ahmed, 117
  and China, 113
  and economic development, 113
Alliance for National Renewal (Brazil), 5
Allinson, Gary, 60
Amphictyonic League, 15
Arab socialism. *See* Egypt
Arab Socialist Union. *See* Egypt
Ataturk, Mustafa Kamal, president of Turkey, 35–36, 39, 43, 44, 191–92
Austria
  redistributive policies, 159

B

Badgley, John, 13, 85
Banfield, Edward, 124, 173
Banks in local politics, 3, 8, 110, 117, 120, 144, 180, 188
Ben Bella, Ahmed, 117

Bienen, Henry, 125
Brass, Paul, 71
Brazil
  Alliance for National Renewal, 5
  local elections, 5
  political participation, 6
Britain
  colonial policies, 11, 53, 66, 73
  education policy, 157
  elites, 21
  Greater London Council, xi, 158
  housing, 157–58
  Labour and Conservative parties, 157–158
  local councils, 22, 158
  local government structure, 21
  National Housing Act, 158
  participation in local politics, 6
British Labour government, xi
Bureaucracy, 11
  alliances with industry, 116–18, 121, 162. *See also* Local politics, industrial elites in
  control over local government, 40, 63–64, 73, 88, 105, 124, 127, 141, 194
  efficiency versus political control, 81, 86–87
  Egypt, 88, 177, 178–80, 188–89
  France, 3, 87, 127–36, 195
  India, 73
    interventionist government, 114, 117, 145, 151
  Iran, 141, 145–46

Local Politics and Nation-States *was edited by Lloyd W. Garrison. Copy editor: Paulette Wamego; typography: Shelly Lowenkopf; composition: McAdams Type, Santa Barbara, Calif.; proofing for the publisher: Jean Holzinger and Liz McNamara; cover art: Dick Palmer; printed and bound at the Crawfordsville, Ind. manufacturing division of R.R. Donnelley and Sons.*